Fallout from the Population Explosion

An ICUS Book

Science and Values series

Humankind has pursued truth about the extended, material world in recent centuries through strict scientific methods. Using the knowledge gained through these methods, man has achieved a remarkable degree of mastery over the world around him. Yet all this material progress holds limited promise for solving the deep and widespread societal problems which trouble humanity today. To ease this malaise, there is a need for a clear, universal value-system to guide mankind in personal life, in sociopolitical relations, economic relations and in the application of the power made available through science in the service of mankind.

Books in the Science and Values series seek to create an academic environment in which value considerations can be brought into scientific discourse and application. In particular, books in this series offer different perspectives regarding the dilemma of a "value-free" scientific approach while the world faces global-level environmental and societal crises. It is hoped that this series will help bring the value perspective into the application of man's knowledge.

Books within this series represent an attempt to direct scholarly discourse toward the essential interface of Science and Values precisely because this interface is so important yet so difficult to clarify. Each book differs in its relation to the overarching theme and none is expected to be able to consider all of the aspects elaborated in this statement. Nonetheless, in their cumulative impact the Science and Values books should make significant contributions toward harmonizing these two disparate domains.

Fallout from the Population Explosion

Edited by Claude A. Villee, Jr.

HB
883.5
·F34
1985
West

An ICUS Book

Paragon House Publishers
New York

Published in the United States by
PARAGON HOUSE PUBLISHERS
2 Hammarskjold Plaza
New York, New York 10017

Copyright 1985 by Paragon House Publishers.

All rights reserved. No part of this book
may be reproduced, in any form, without
permission unless by a reviewer who
wishes to quote brief passages.

An International Conference on the
Unity of the Sciences Book.

Library of Congress Cataloging in Publication Data
Main entry under title:

Fallout From The Population Explosion.

   "An ICUS book."
   Bibliography
   Includes index.
   1.   Population policy—Addresses, essays, lectures.
2.   Population—Addresses, essays, lectures.   I. Villee,
Claude Alvin, 1917–
HB883.5.F34   1985   304.6   85-12179
ISBN 0-89226-028-9

Contents

Introduction:
Population Policies: Past, Present and Future
Claude A. Villee, Jr. ix

Part I
World Population Trends 1

  1. Ethical Dimensions of International Population Trends
     George J. Stolnitz 3

  2. World Population Trends in the Second Half of the
     Twentieth Century
     Samuel Baum 9

  3. Japan as a Typical Miniature of World Population Growth
     Toshio Kuroda 27

  4. Ethical Dimensions of World Population Trends
     Richard L. Rubenstein 41
     Commentary
     Joel Kurtzman 49

Part II
Introduction:
Health Systems and Population Control
     Edward O. Pratt 55

  5. Health Services and Development: Population Issues
     C. O. Akerle 59

  6. Health Systems and Population Control
     Gervin P. Samarawickrama 71

Part III
Consequences of World Population Growth. 83

  7. Consequences of World Population Growth on Natural
     Resources and Environment
     Claude A. Villee, Jr. 85

8. Consequences of World Population Growth: Labor, Migration and International Trade
    Paul Demeny 95

Part IV
Financial and Societal Disincentives for Population Growth 105

9. China's "One-Child Family" Program
    Claude A. Villee, Jr. 107

Part V
The Future of Technology and Societies 125

10. Biomedical Sciences and Social Patterns in the Twenty-First Century
    Claude A. Villee, Jr. 127

11. A Perspective of Populations in Transition
    Edward O. Pratt 137

12. World Population Problem: Its Impact on the Family and Community
    Gervin P. Samarawickrama 151
    Commentary
    Stewart E. Fraser 167

Part VI
Human Population of the Future: The Food-Supply Crisis 173

13. Feeding the World's Increasing Population
    Kenneth Mellanby 175

14. National Policies for Population Control
    Gervin P. Samarawickrama 185

15. Resources Versus Population
    B. Connor Johnson 197

16. Changing National Policies of Population Size
    Stewart E. Fraser 203

17. Interactions Between Food Supply and Human Populations
    Gerald Stanhill. 209

18. Full Utilization of Food Resources
    P. V. Sukhatme. 213

19. Total Management of Health Care for the Aged
    Kikuo Fujiwara. 217

20. Geriatric Care in Western Countries
    Zedena Harant. 227

21. Learning and Aging
    Giselher Guttmann 235

22. Health Care Systems and the Elderly
    Roberta Spohn 241

Conclusion:
Human Populations: Yesterday, Today and Tomorrow
    Claude A. Villee, Jr. 245
Contributors. 251
Sources 253
Index 255

Introduction:

Population Policies: Past, Present and Future

Claude A. Villee, Jr.

A ttempts by governments to control the size of their populations are not a new practice. Ever since the beginning of political
philosophy, politicians have considered population problems and
their effects on the welfare of the state. Among the earliest
political philosophers were Plato and his pupil, Aristotle. By
Socratic reasoning they incorporated concepts of populations
into their political treatises—Plato's *Laws* and Aristotle's *Politics*.

Plato based his theories of population size on property and
wealth. He held that extreme wealth corrupted the soul of human
beings through luxury, whereas poverty drove humans to shame-
lessness. From this he concluded that for lawabiding souls there
must be a near equality of wealth among all the citizens of the
state and a near quality in the ownership of land. To Plato the
word "landowner" was essentially synonymous with citizen. His
considerations of population, therefore, were all in reference to
the number of landowning males present under the system of
government. It followed, of course, that the proper number of
citizens in a state is determined by the amount of land available.
In addition to the consideration about the ownership of land, the
population must be large enough to defend the city and state and
to aid its neighbors against injustice. Plato decided that there
should be 5,040 landholders in his theoretical city because this
number is divisible by fifty-nine other numbers, and simple
divisions are useful in drawing up contracts and associations.

Because civil order rests upon the nearly equal ownership of property by 5,040 citizens, Plato concluded that the number of hearths that he established must never be altered—must never become greater or smaller. To maintain this arrangement throughout the whole city, and throughout time, each allotment holder must always leave behind only one heir to his household from among his male children. Thus, each of the 5,040 allotments of property must always be willed undivided to the landowner's favorite son, who then becomes a landowner and citizen. Any of his other sons may be distributed to those citizens who lack a son. The daughters are to be married to the landowning sons of other families. Plato was confident that a city would be able to maintain a stable population of 5,040 citizens. He contended that there are many devices to keep the population size constant, including ways of preventing birth in those who conceive too many offspring and ways of encouraging a greater number of births, such as public honors and dishonors, when the state is underpopulated. Should there be an overpopulation problem, those who end up without a property allotment should be sent away from the city to some new area which then becomes a colony of the state. Conversely, the government may admit new citizens from the ranks of resident aliens and tradesmen if underpopulation results from war or a plague.

In contrast, Aristotle believed that overpopulation will be a problem whether or not colonization is employed. Aristotle suggested that governments should limit the size of the population and prevent reproduction rather than limit the amount of property. He stated that if no restriction is imposed on the rate of reproduction, poverty is the inevitable result, and poverty will lead to civil dissention and wrongdoing. This prediction has certainly been verified many times since then! The regulation of land ownership should be considered only when property has become very scarce, and then it should be accompanied by efforts to control the size of the population.

In his discussion of the proper size of a city-state Aristotle did not think quantitatively. He regarded the best state as that which best performed its natural functions; that is, the protection of its citizens' virtues. Thus a state must be large enough in area, with a large enough population, to be self-sufficient, and yet small enough to have law and order under a constitution. Aristotle felt it was difficult for a very large populous state to secure a general habit of obedience to law. States must have a population limit less than the point at which citizens can no longer recognize and know the character of every other citizen so as to ensure order, but it also must be large enough to be self-sufficient. In Aristotle's view, if a state were too large or too small it would forfeit its nature and could no longer be called a state.

Since Aristotle realized that overpopulation will tend to corrupt his beautiful state, he believed laws must be promulgated to limit the size of the population. Aristotle did not approve of infanticide to control population, but he found it appropriate for children born deformed to be killed. If a birth to a family would exceed the legal fixed limit for each family, then the woman should have a miscarriage induced before sense and life have begun in the embryo. Thus Aristotle explicitly recommended forced abortions to control population. However, like a true politician he sidestepped the dilemma of abortion by stating that whether it is right or wrong to induce a miscarriage will depend on whether sense and life are still to come or have already begun in the embryo.

The political philosophers of the Roman Age and Middle Ages were not as advanced as the Greeks, and ideas of population and population control had not advanced. The Roman emperor Augustus (31 B.C.–14 A.D.) believed that there had been a severe drop in the human fertility rate from the Republican Era, and adopted pronatalist policies. In 18 b.c. the *lex Iulia* prohibited marriages between the highest classes and freedwomen who had been slaves, but encouraged marriages among all other classes. It made illegal any attempt by parents to deter the marriage of their children and parental refusal to give a dowry at the marriage. This law made divorce more difficult to obtain by requiring a couple to have seven witnesses in order to obtain a valid divorce. Under another provision of the *lex Iulia*, unmarried people, and those who were married but were childless, and all widows and widowers who had not remarried within a specified time of the death of their spouses were prohibited from receiving legacies and inheritances except from very close relatives. Such people were also prohibited from attending the public games. Inheritances were very important to ancient Romans. It was a common practice, especially among childless people, to leave substantial bequests to friends. This law deprived childless and unmarried people of an important source of income and also deprived them of their entertainment. In contrast, those who married and had a certain number of children were rewarded. Men who had fathered three or more children were granted more rapid advancement in their public careers. Under this law the decision as to who should ascend to the magistracy went not to the man who was older or more experienced, but to the man who had the greater number of children. Those Romans with three or more children were exempted from the burden of serving as guardian for a ward. Freedmen who had two or more children were not bound to their former masters, and husbands and wives were permitted to receive as many tenths of an estate as there were children in the family.

This law was not only unpopular, it was unsuccessful. The complaint was made that it was unfair of Augustus to penalize those men who were unfortunate enough to have a sterile marriage. Augustus then commissioned two consuls, Papius and Poppaeus, to draft a new law in which the penalties for childlessness were decreased. However, it increased the rewards for large families and allowed widowers and widows a three year grace period in which to find a mate. It is ironic that both Papius and Poppaeus, the consuls who drew up this law, were childless and unmarried. These laws were unsuccessful in producing any noticeable increase in the birth rate, but they did increase the number of estates that were lapsing to the public treasury because none of the people named in the will were qualified to inherit it. There was also an increase in the number of professional informers who received a portion of an estate settlement when they successfully prosecuted those who had attempted to evade the law by being betrothed to a girl too young to consumate the marriage, by fictitious weddings, or by marrying and divorcing several women in rapid succession.

At about this time an official measure called "the right of three children" was set up. This enabled the person upon whom it was bestowed to enjoy all the privileges of those who had three children, and to avoid the penalties inflicted on the childless. Probably the original intent of the exemption was to reward those who had fulfilled their service to the state in other ways, but it became a political favor granted almost indiscriminately. The historian, Pliny, and the biographer, Suetonius, received this dispensation from the Emperor Traian. This right of three children was granted automatically to the Vestal Virgins and to soldiers.

The number of dispensations given made the law impractical and unsuccessful, but despite its failure it remained on the books until 320 A.D., when it was revoked by the Emperor Constantine. Perhaps the growing influence of Christianity, with its setting a high value on celibacy, led to the revocation of this law.

Other emperors tried other means to increase fertility. Augustus, who had a small treasury, was limited to those measures which required no public expenditures, but Trajan was able to draw on the larger treasury of his time to fund the program termed *alimenta*. This program, which consisted of the dispensing of free grain or money to families with children, was an ancient forerunner of the present-day Aid to Families with Dependent Children. The intent of the *alimenta*, however, was not really to relieve poverty, but to increase the size of the population. The *alimenta* may have made life a bit easier for the children who were already born, but it is not clear whether it actually encouraged the birth of more children.

From the kinds of laws that Augustus and Trajan promulgated, it seems clear that they believed there was a need to raise the Roman birth rate. However, the question of whether there really was a decline in the population of Rome and, if there was a decline, whether it was large enough to threaten the existence of Rome or the Roman Empire remains unanswered. It is exceedingly difficult to determine the total size of the Roman population, just as today it is difficult to count those who live in the so-called informal segment of society. In dealing with the Roman census it is not clear who was included in the total. Women were probably counted after 69 B.C. but probably were not counted before that time. Whether children, slaves, and foreigners were counted is not clear. It is even more difficult to determine the extent of the area which was included in a given census district. We cannot be sure how much of the rural area was included along with the urban area itself. For these and other reasons, the figures we have of the population of Rome and of the Roman Empire are really only conjectures. Estimates of the population of the Roman Empire range from fifty to one hundred million, and the city of Rome at the end of the first century B.C. is usually estimated as having about one million people, with a population density of about 650 per hectare.

The population of Rome was certainly large enough so that there was no danger of collapse of the empire due to a small population. However, it was perceived by the government that the rate of growth was too slow. This was due to the very high death rate not only in infancy and childhood, but in adult years as well. By looking at grave inscriptions it has been concluded that a baby born in the city of Rome had a life expectancy of about twenty-five years whereas one born in Spain or Germany could expect to live forty years if male, and thirty-five if female. The decreased life expectancy of women was due to the heavy mortality rate during the reproductive years. Because of the greater population density there was a higher mortality rate in urban Rome than in the more rural parts of the empire, with a death rate of about forty-five per one-thousand.

Emperor Augustus' perception that the population was increasing too slowly might have been based on what appears to have been a tendency for the upper class males not to marry or, if married, to have few or no children. A number of Roman historians refer to the deliberate effort of people to restrict family size in order to preserve the standard of living of the parents. There were three methods employed by people in addition to celibacy to control the rate of population increase. These were contraceptives, abortion, and infanticide. It seems clear that the Romans must have been using some kind of birth control to keep the birth rate fairly low. It is possible that some Romans used coitus interruptus, even though it is not a very effective method. Other Romans used pessaries made of wool and soaked in olive oil and honey which would at least partially block the opening of the cervix of the uterus. Vinegar and brine were also recommended as possible contraceptives, and these would function as spermicides. Among other suggestions for contraceptives were wearing the liver of a cat in a tube on the left foot during intercourse, or wearing part of the womb of a lioness in an ivory tube. When these contraceptive measures failed, abortion was available and legal. It was performed by various means and appears to have been quite common. Those who objected to abortion objected not so much because they thought it was murder, but rather because of a general mistrust of drugs and medicines. When the abortion failed, or if the desired boy baby turned out to be a girl baby, Romans resorted to infanticide, usually by exposure. The infant might survive and be taken in by the finder and reared as a slave, so that exposure resulted not in a decline in population, but rather in a shift of individuals from one social class to another. It appears that the desire of Augustus and Trajan for a larger population of Romans was based on a need to inspire confidence at home and fear and respect abroad—that is, the size of the population was a source of power for the state.

It is of interest to note that in Mussolini's Italy and in Hitler's Germany there were programs similar to that of Augustus to encourage increased birth rates. Higher wages were paid to fathers with children, and the more children a worker had the greater was his salary. Special taxes were imposed on bachelors and childless couples. Preference was given in competition for government service posts, for housing, and even for jobs in private industry to those individuals who had children. In the 1950s the Soviet Union made an effort to increase its birth rate. Women with a dozen children were given a prize of five-thousand rubles for each of five years and were honored as Heroes of the Soviet Union, receiving a personal greeting from Josef Stalin.

Relatively little thought was given to population size or to attempts to control population size during Middle Ages, and as late as 1651 Thomas Hobbes subscribed to ideas similar to those of Plato and Aristotle regarding citizens and property versus poverty and social unrest. He advocated sending the impoverished members of society off to some colony, but in contrast to the time of Plato and Aristotle, when Hobbes was alive the territory of the earth could no longer be viewed as infinite, and one could conceive that mankind would eventually reach a limit on the size of the world population. Hobbes rather cynically foretold that the last remedy of all is "war, which provides for every man either by victory or by death."

In the latter part of the seventeenth century political philosophers seemed to be more concerned with the possible decline in the human population rather than in overpopulation. This probably came about due to the rise of mercantilism, where a bustling population appeared to be both a cause and an effect of a healthy national economy. In 1674 Leyser advocated polygamy because he felt it would increase the population, but this controversial thesis was much debated during the succeeding century. Baron Montesquieu felt that all land was underpopulated and believed that a growing population is a reflection of a nation's internal health. The nation's lands become better cultivated when the population increases. This leads to increased trade, which raises more revenues for the state and provides the communication with other nations that brings about the mutual advancement of all mankind. To increase the rate of population Montesquieu advocated that the religious laws commanding vows of celibacy and establishing monasteries should be abolished, because they made too many men sexually unproductive. Montesquieu advocated the easing of the requirements for a divorce. When divorce is not possible, marriage becomes unendurable, the couple separates, and the man turns to prostitutes so that the couple becomes unproductive. Montesquieu rejected the practice of polygamy which he believed decreased the rate of population increase. Polygamy he viewed as detrimental to the aim of increasing the number of offspring, because one man monopolizes so many women and renders them useless for the propagation of the species. A man will be worn out long before he can satisfy a whole seraglio of women, and hence it was common to see a man have a large seraglio and yet a very small number of children—or none at all if he should happen to be sterile. In addition, a seraglio required a substantial number of slave girls as attendants, and these almost always grew old in a state of virginity. Montesquieu argued further that the practice of having a seraglio led to homosexuality.

Thus, population control has been a political concern for several millennia. Plato and Aristotle wanted to ensure a good life for their cities and their citizens. Civil order, and thus virtue, in their view was based upon property and wealth. Thus, Plato and Aristotle believed that poverty led to vice, and therefore the ideal population was one in which all of the citizens could live comfortably without poverty. In the seventeenth century the perceived fear of underpopulation led Montesquieu to advocate political guidelines which would foster the propagation of the species. The way to avoid poverty, reasoned Montesquieu, was to build a bustling mercantilistic economy. That view held for several centuries, but now population concerns have come full circle, and worldwide overpopulation is a major political problem. Overpopulation is seen not only as a threat to the good life, but as a threat to all life.

Part I

World Population Trends

1.

Ethical Dimensions of International Population Trends

George J. Stolnitz

Indiana University
Bloomington, Indiana, U.S.A.

Our twin topics here are the empirical and ethical dimensions of yesterday's, today's, and tomorrow's international population trends. Either dimension, it is safe to say, is primarily conditioned by a truly remarkable factual backdrop: Since the end of World War II, or roughly 1945–50, we have been experiencing a most unique period of population changes, indeed changes of watershed significance when compared to all previous demographic history. I will focus my comments on several of the key historic contrasts in this enormously broad field.

More demographic and development experience has accumulated over the past few decades than in all earlier history. This assertion, though startling, can be readily supported from any of a host of relevant standards for judging: numbers of people involved; numbers of nations; numbers of new nations; preoccupation with economic growth as an overriding objective from national or social viewpoints; extent and speed of breakaway from centuries-old or even millennia-long modes of economic intercourse and social lifestyles; leapfrogging rates of acceleration of main economic magnitudes; communications revolutions by the score; unprecedented nature of key recent and prospective demographic patterns; and much more.

In considering the demographic aspects, involving at conservative count some half dozen sweeping revolutions in recent international demographic patterns, we must distinguish two groups of nations. One consists of the so-called "developed countries (DCs)," or basically the United States and Canada in North America, very nearly all of Europe, Australia and New Zealand in Oceania, plus Japan and a very few other areas. The second group consists of the "less developed countries (LDCs)," or Africa and practically all of Latin America and Asia.

Taking up first the DCs, we find that an era of mortality trends which have lasted for some two hundred years is rapidly nearing an end, and that future prospects marking a revolutionary break with the past lie just ahead. Briefly stated, mortality rates of persons under fifty have declined to the point where they are close to vanishing practically throughout the DC parts of the world; these are the very rates which have been the effective cause of increasing length of life throughout the DC regions in modern times. Remarkably, these major and reliably documented facts continue to elude public and even expert attention. If today's DC mortality rates under age fifty were to drop suddenly all the way to zero, life expectancy would rise by only a very few years (below three or four, depending on the country) for females, and by little more (below about five years) for males. These are minor fractions of DC increases in longevity in the course of the past one hundred or even fifty years. Although there is still some room for perceptible declines in infant mortality, the leeways are no more than moderate even here and there is almost no room for further declines in death rates at the childhood, young-adult, and middle-adult spans of life.

It follows that future mortality declines large enough to have major long-run effects on life expectancy in the DCs would have to be concentrated in the post-midlife ages. This would be a pattern which has never been encountered.

A central implication of such declines, if they were to occur, is that mortality effects on national age composition and average age would differ markedly from past effects. Previously, mortality declines in all of today's low-mortality, industrialized countries

4

tended to increase the fraction of population under fifteen, and to decrease somewhat the fraction fifteen to sixty-five, while having limited effects typically on the fraction over sixty-five. Declining mortality meant that more people survived to the upper ages of life, of course, but it also meant that many more survived the perilous years shortly after birth to about age fifteen. The net result, surprising as it may seem, was that average age of population tended to fall, not rise.

These effects would be altered radically if truly major advances in longevity were to take place in the future. Since these would have to come from mortality declines at the upper ages, the effect could well be to raise both the absolute and proportionate sizes of population aged fifty-plus or sixty-plus by quantum orders of magnitude, when compared to the effects of previous mortality trends.

A related prospect, and another historic first, is that future mortality declines in the world's developed regions can play at most a minor role in raising their rates of natural increase (birth rates minus death rates). Since this point is easily and often misunderstood, let me be clear that the point being emphasized is the role of mortality, not the size of natural increase. Although history records long periods in which small or even negative natural increase must have been predominant modes of change over large parts of the globe, it has never been the case until now that declining mortality could have minor or minimal influence at best on any region's long-run pace of growth. If we assume as improbable, given peace, the appearance of large mortality up-trends or even fluctuations in the DCs, the decisive determinant of their population growth rates is bound to be fertility. (International migration could be significant for a number of smaller areas, such as Ireland, but is sure to be a secondary factor for the DCs as a whole and for most individual DC populations.)

With respect to DC fertility, as with mortality, the shift in prospects has been vast and unprecedented, as national rates of childbearing have declined to near-replacement or below-replacement orders of magnitude almost everywhere. In not a few cases among the forty to forty-five nations involved, current shortfalls below replacement are ten percent or considerably more. Available indications point strongly to the forecast (disputed, it is true, by some demographers) that the forces making for low or even lower fertility will predominate over those making for large or sustained upswings from current levels. Though one often needs to add qualifications for individual cases and circumstances, it now seems likely that average DC fertility will not often or long rise above replacement at any time in the foreseeable future, extending well into the next century.

If these anticipations hold up, it would follow that reproduction in a large part of the world is for the first time in demographic history not only reaching near zero or even negative levels of replacement, but is doing so in a way which cannot be significantly affected by declines in mortality.

Turning to a third demographic revolution brings us to the remarkable recent increases of life expectancy among the three-fourths or so of the world's population in the LDCs. The increases registered here in the postwar period have had few if any antecedents anywhere, as dozens of impoverished populations have managed to compress generations or even centuries of analogous DC changes within a decade or two. Suddenly for these dozens, their time-tested linkages between poverty on the one hand, and longevity on the other, have become profoundly severed. Nor are significant signs of long-run recidivism found anywhere under peacetime conditions. Although the risk cannot be ruled out that the prewar poverty-mortality linkages will reassert themselves, such dangers have remained only latent. Efforts by LDC governments to achieve relief from high mortality—when associated with political stability and implemented by disease-control technologies available even to low-income societies—have become sufficient to assure decisive breakaways from traditional rates and causes of death.

A fourth event of surely revolutionary proportions involves fertility in the underdeveloped regions. There are rapidly gathering signs that substantial to enormous downtrends of fertility have been taking place during the past quarter-century in some forty to fifty LDCs, involving no less than forty to fifty percent of the Third World's total population. With the still unclear case of India included, the numbers involved would rise to nearly seventy percent.

This is not to say that fertility has necessarily become low wherever the declines have been large; typically, it has not. LDC fertility levels are still on average something like two to three times the levels found in most developed nations. Clearly, at least in my own opinion, the levels encountered today in very nearly all

LDCs continue to be far too high, from the viewpoints of their own social well-being and individual welfare standards.

Fifth, it is well to consider that the LDCs as a group will account for over ninety percent of total world population growth during any future period we can foresee. Nothing approximating this order of magnitude had been documented over several centuries at least before the end of World War II. Assuredly, the emergence of many more giant-sized nations in the Third World than now exist will have major repercussions on global, regional, and national politics and policies.

Urban trends are a sixth set of demographic processes which are bound to have enduring and transformational signficance on the world scene. In the LDCs since about 1950, record rates of urban population growth have been such as to imply a doubling of urban numbers in less than two decades. Meanwhile in the DCs, urbanization has suddenly reached near-saturation levels almost everywhere, whether through upsurges in urban numbers proper or through the spread of urban life styles into non-urban areas.

Seventh, I would cite the phenomenal spread of population policies and demographic programming over large parts of the globe, again a first in human affairs. I refer here not only to family planning, but to governmental policies affecting urban-rural distribution and internal migration, to new forms of health control, and to the growing integration of population planning or policies with overall development strategies.

I could easily go on in similar vein, for example, by considering the post–1950 emergence of new patterns of international migration, but I will refer to only a few of the ethical aspects of these problems. It should be evident that our ethical judgments concerning population trends in all parts of the globe are sure to confront new forms and new degrees of challenge, in many ways as unprecedented as the population trends themselves. The questions pile on each other. In the DCs, should freedom of individual choice in deciding on family size be retained in the face of below-replacement fertility? What, if anything, should DC governments do if their populations begin diminishing at rapid rates, as could happen on a broad scale not many decades from now? Do governments have an obligation to preserve the "national identity" of their societies by hindering family planning, fostering "patriotic childbearing," and "reeducating" their young, or should a higher national purpose prevail?

With respect to DC-LDC relations, why should the DCs extend major-scale development aid to the LDCs when their own poverty problems are far from being solved? Is such aid bound to be an "operation rathole" if LDC population growth continues to be rapid? What ethical rationale should guide aid intended to enhance death-control systems in the LDCs if such systems are believed to entail increasing economic misery among the living? In the LDCs, how democratic, stringent, or compulsory should social action be which is directed to reducing fertility? How permissive or encouraged should abortion be?

In both DCs and LDCs, should health policies favor the young population at the expense of the old? Who should decide what information and methods the individual should have access to when making birth control decisions? Should this be the state, religious bodies, the individual, or "free market" decision-makers?

These are only a few of the deeply difficult issues and dilemmas we find quickly raised by the extraordinary demographic events of our time. How they will be answered will go far to determine the world we will live in tomorrow and the day after. For the answers will affect not only population as such, but the very fabric of society from which demographic processes are spawned and which such processes themselves spawn in major ways.

2.

World Population Trends in the Second Half of the Twentieth Century

Samuel Baum

U.S. Bureau of the Census
Washington, D.C., U.S.A.

The second half of the twentieth century has already proven to be one of the most dramatic in the history of world population growth. For the first time in recent human experience, the world population growth rate has stopped rising and started to decline. Recent assessments of world population trends by both the U.S. Bureau of the Census and the United Nations agree that the inflection point in the world growth rate occurred during the 1960s. Earlier assessments and projections, e.g., the 1973 U.N. assessment, did not expect the turning point to be reached until about 1980. Thus, the unprecedented acceleration of the world population growth that has already increased the globe's population by about 167 percent during this century appears to have finally passed the turning point. This earlier than expected peaking of the world's growth rate will probably have only limited impact on the size of world population at the end of this century, but can have a very substantial impact on world population growth during the twenty-first century.

This paper will attempt to explain how demographic trends

have brought about this downturn in the world's population growth rate, and what we may expect to happen during the remainder of this century. In particular, it will concentrate on estimated and projected trends for the period 1950 to 2000, as shown by recent analyses and projections of world population growth prepared at the U.S. Bureau of the Census (1978 and 1979). These analyses are essentially in agreement with similar analyses conducted by other national and international agencies, such as the United Nations, World Bank, and University of Chicago.

1950 to 1977

Table 1 shows the broad dimensions of world population growth. The estimates shown for 1950 to 1977 are based on annual estimates prepared for each of the two hundred separate countries and territories of the world. The assessment of population growth trends presented in our publication, *World Population 1977*, based on the most recent data available in 1977, points to declining growth rates on the world level, reflected in rates for the more developed and less developed regions as a whole and for most subregions. The major conclusion we draw from the estimates for the individual countries and from the aggregated time series for subregions and regions is that after many years of slowly and then rapidly accelerating growth rates, throughout the world a perceptible decline in population growth rates has begun to emerge, with the persistent exception of Africa. In some countries and regions, the decrease is substantial, in others incipient; but in general, the decline is no longer questionable.

Our finding of a downward trend in the world's population growth rate confirmed our finding in a similar report two years earlier *(World Population: 1975)*. However, at that earlier time, the pattern was not quite as pervasive among regions and subregions, and we were uneasy about the large impact of the estimates we had accepted for the People's Republic of China. As can be seen in Table 1, with or without China, the trend in population rates for the world, less developed regions, Asia, and less developed regions of Asia is slightly downward.

At the first level of analysis, what has brought about this downturn in growth rates is, of course, a faster decline in birth rates than in death rates. We are all probably well aware of the

Table 1

World Population and Average Annual Rates of Growth, By Continent and Development Category 1950 to 1977
Midyear population (thousands)

Region	1977	1975	1970	1965	1960	1955	1950
WORLD	4,257,655	4,100,271	3,721,518	3,371,239	3,057,737	2,769,606	2,525,852
More developed	1,154,439	1,137,410	1,087,279	1,036,567	975,288	913,389	855,150
Less developed	3,103,216	2,962,861	2,634,239	2,334,672	2,082,449	1,856,217	1,670,702
AFRICA[1]	430,757	407,368	356,384	313,369	277,011	247,032	222,039
ASIA	2,486,045	2,382,246	2,132,872	1,902,520	1,710,322	1,533,925	1,386,861
More developed	159,870	155,561	143,256	133,187	124,306	115,944	106,305
Less developed	2,326,175	2,226,685	1,989,616	1,769,333	1,586,016	1,417,981	1,280,556
LATIN AMERICA[1]	341,599	324,341	284,295	248,501	216,389	188,539	165,764
NORTHERN AMERICA[2]	240,258	236,409	226,308	214,075	198,661	181,740	166,075
EUROPE AND SOVIET UNION[2]	737,096	728,566	702,217	675,129	639,540	604,249	572,577
OCEANIA	21,900	21,341	19,442	17,645	15,814	14,121	12,536
More developed	17,215	16,874	15,498	14,176	12,781	11,456	10,193
Less developed	4,685	4,467	3,944	3,469	3,033	2,665	2,343
Excluding the People's Republic of China:							
WORLD	3,275,124	3,157,234	2,874,938	2,617,222	2,374,662	2,159,386	1,978,488
Less developed	2,120,685	2,019,824	1,787,659	1,580,655	1,399,374	1,245,997	1,123,338
ASIA	1,503,514	1,439,209	1,286,292	1,148,503	1,027,247	923,705	839,497
Less developed	1,343,644	1,283,648	1,143,036	1,015,316	902,941	807,761	733,192

Average annual rate of growth (percent)

	1975–77	1970–75	1965–70	1960–65	1955–60	1950–55
WORLD	1.9	1.9	2.0	2.0	2.0	1.8
More developed	0.7	0.9	1.0	1.2	1.3	1.3
Less developed	2.3	2.4	2.4	2.3	2.3	2.1
AFRICA[1]	2.8	2.7	2.6	2.5	2.3	2.1
ASIA	2.1	2.2	2.3	2.1	2.2	2.0
More developed	1.4	1.6	1.5	1.4	1.4	1.7
Less developed	2.2	2.3	2.3	2.2	2.2	2.0
LATIN AMERICA[1]	2.6	2.6	2.7	2.8	2.8	2.6
NORTHERN AMERICA[1]	0.8	0.9	1.1	1.5	1.8	1.8
EUROPE AND SOVIET UNION[2]	0.6	0.7	0.8	1.1	1.1	1.1
OCEANIA	1.3	1.9	1.9	2.2	2.3	2.4
More developed	1.0	1.7	1.8	2.1	2.2	2.3
Less developed	2.4	2.5	2.6	2.7	2.6	2.6
Excluding the People's Republic of China:						
WORLD	1.8	1.9	1.9	1.9	1.9	1.7
Less developed	2.4	2.4	2.5	2.4	2.3	2.1
ASIA	2.2	2.2	2.3	2.2	2.1	1.9
Less developed	2.3	2.3	2.4	2.3	2.2	1.9
Less developed						
More developed						

Source: U.S. Bureau of the Census. 1978. *World Population 1977—Recent Demographic Estimates for the Countries and Regions of the World.* Washington, D.C.

11

significant declines in birth rates of the more developed countries (MDCs) following the post Second World War baby boom. These declines are well documented by reliable and up-to-date vital registration systems. The equally, if not even more, significant declines in birth rates of many large less developed countries (LDCs) has been more difficult to detect because of the still very unsatisfactory situation concerning the availability of demographic data in most LDCs. However, analyses of population census and sample survey data provide convincing evidence that "since 1965 there have been substantial declines in the crude birth rates of many countries in the developing world, particularly the largest countries" (Mauldin, 1978). For example, recent detailed reports by the U.S. Bureau of the Census on the demographic situation in selected developing countries show declines in the birth rate for many of the developing countries thus far covered by these reports (Table 2).

However, what is sometimes overlooked is that birth rates had declined somewhat in the LDCs as a whole prior to 1965. Growth rates increased rather than decreased during the 1950s and early 1960s because death rates in these regions were dropping more rapidly, as can be seen in Table 3. What has occurred during the period since about 1965 is that the decline in the LDCs birth rate has accelerated. In some large countries with previously declining birth rates, the decline became more rapid; in other large countries, previously constant or perhaps even rising birth rates started their downward course. Chronologically at least, these accelerated fertility declines since 1965 are associated with the adoption and implementation of national family planning programs in many of the developing countries.

Birth rate declines in the developed countries have also contributed to the reduction in the world's population growth rate. A number of European countries have already reached zero population growth and most developed countries have already dropped below replacement fertility levels, even though they still have a positive natural increase. Should present trends continue, most developed countries would exhibit zero or even negative rates of natural increase by the end of this century or shortly thereafter.

A second factor contributing to the downturn in world population growth rates has been an apparent slowdown in mortality decline in recent years. Data to support this conclusion are more limited, but scattered data from various regions suggest that the

Table 2

Birth Rate Trends in Selected Developing Countries

Country and year	Birth rate (per 1,000 population)	Country and year	Birth rate (per 1,000 population)
Costa Rica		Ghana	
1950	45	1960	50
1963	45	1970	48
1970	33	Sri Lanka	
1974	39	1953	44
Guatemala		1963	35
1950	48	1971	30
1964	44	1974	28
1970	40	China—Taiwan	
1973	42	1956	44
Panama		1966	32
1960	42	1970	28
1970	37	1975	23
1975	31	1976	26
1976	33	Thailand	
Jamaica		1960	43
1960	42	1970	39
1965	40	India	
1970	33	1951–61	42–45
1976	29	1961–71	40–43
Honduras		1971	39
1961	49	1975	37
1971–72	49	Republic of Korea	
1974	48	1960	45
Chile		1966	33
1950	34	1970	32
1955	36	1975	26
1960	36	Indonesia	
1965	35	1961	46
1970	27	1971	42
1975	24	1975	36–38
Mexico		Nepal	
1950	46	1971	43
1960	46	1975	45
1970	43	Pakistan	
Colombia		1961	46
1964	46	1972	45
1973	34		
1975	33		
1978	31		

Source: U.S. Bureau of the Census. *Country Demographic Profiles.*

Table 3

Crude Birth and Death Rates, Less Developed Regions: 1950 to 1975

Period	Birth Rate (per 1,000 pop.)	Death Rate (per 1,000 pop.)
1950–55	41.8	22.2
1955–60	41.6	19.3
1960–65	40.0	16.8
1965–70	37.7	14.8
1970–75	35.5	13.2

Source: United Nations. 1979. Department of International Economic and Social Affairs. *World Population Trends and Prospects by Country, 1950–2000: Summary Report of the 1978 Assessment.* New York. p. 52.

rapid declines in mortality common to perhaps most LDCs after the Second World War have not been continuing, even though many of these LDCs still have high and medium mortality levels.

In regard to infant and child mortality, a major contributor to the overall level of mortality, the United Nations (1979a) noted:

A feature of infant mortality rates that is common to all developing areas where it can be measured properly is an apparent divergence among national levels. Generally, rates appeared to have dropped faster in already low mortality areas than in high mortality countries. This assertion applies equally well to childhood mortality rates.

As a result of the significant declines in birth rates since 1965, and the apparent slowdown in mortality progress, most of the world's population lives in countries which experienced declines in growth rates during the period since 1965. Figure A compares growth rates for the world's fifty largest countries in 1966 and 1976. (Ninety percent of the world's population lives in these fifty countries). In twenty-four of these countries, containing about three-quarters of their combined population, the population growth rate declined during the ten-year period. Every continent is represented among the countries where declines occurred. Such declines took place not only in developed countries, where growth rates were generally already low a decade ago, but also in many of the less developed countries.

Especially notable are estimated declines in annual growth rates during the last decade in Sri Lanka, the Philippines, Thailand, the Republic of Korea, Columbia, South Africa, Turkey, and China (Taiwan). Annual growth rates in these countries ranged from 2.3 to 3.0 percent in 1966; all but three were below 2.3 percent by 1976.

Decreasing rates of world population growth, however, should not be confused with declining absolute increments in the population. Although the world growth rate was estimated to be lower in 1976–77 than in 1966–67, the larger base population during the more recent period resulted in a population increase between July 1976 and July 1977 of about 80 million persons, as opposed to 68 million during the comparable period 10 years earlier.

Distribution of World Population and Population Growth

Whereas the growth rate of the LDCs was only about fifty percent greater than that of the MDCs at mid-century, by 1975 the LDCs population was growing about three times as rapidly as the MDCs. Because of the increasing gap in growth rates, a disproportionately large share of the population growth that the world experienced in the third quarter of this century occurred in the LDCs. Thus, by 1977 the MDCs share of world population had declined to 27.1 percent as compared to 33.9 percent in 1950. It should be noted, however, that the current distribution of the world's population into MDCs and LDCs is similar to the proportions prevailing in 1800, before the rapid growth of population in the MDCs.

To the Twenty-First Century

Recently a number of organizations have prepared projections of the world's population to the year 2000 (Table 4). What is most striking about these projections is not their differing results on the size of the world's population expected in the year 2000, but rather their general agreement on some key points such as the minimum world population projected for the end of the century, the large differentials in LDC and MDC growth rates, expected changes in age structure, and expected regional distribution of the world's population.

Before discussing the results of these projections, it may be well to adopt a note of caution. Since all population projections involve

Figure A

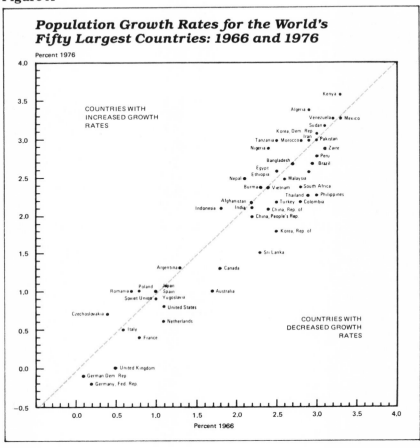

a considerable amount of guesswork about the course of future events, there is a very large amount of uncertainty built into the results.

The three projection series prepared by the U.S. Bureau of the Census (1979)—high, medium, and low—are provided as a way of acknowledging the uncertainty which is necessarily involved in population projections. The high and low series are not meant to define the range of possibility, but rather to set reasonable limits within which population growth and its component elements are expected to fall. Our medium series projections are illustrative of a path of population growth based on assumptions about the future course of fertility which lies between those of the high and low series. In our judgment, the medium series is the "most likely," but the tendency for users to look at and use only the medium series places more "certainty" on these numbers than the researchers who produced them believe is warranted. Indeed, the fact that projections such as those shown in Table 4 are published may serve to promote public policies and actions which will greatly affect the trends of fertility and mortality during the remainder of this century.

The following sections summarize the results of the U.S. Bureau of the Census world projections.

Population Size, Vital Rates, and Growth

The medium projection of the world's population for the year 2000 prepared by the Census Bureau envisions 6,350 million persons inhabiting the earth at that date (Table 5). This represents a fifty-five percent increase in twenty-five years over the medium estimates (4,090 million) of the world's population in 1975 and a 150 percent increase since 1950.

In the medium series projection, the world population would increase by fifty-five percent—the more developed regions about seventeen percent, the less developed regions by almost seventy percent—during 1975 to 2000.[1] This significant population growth differential is obviously related to quite different expected levels and trends in vital rates. By the year 2000, birth rates in the less developed regions are expected to remain almost twice as high as those in the more developed regions. However, projections in all three series anticipate lower crude death rates in the LDCs than in the MDCs, not because mortality will be lower in the LDCs, but because of the relatively young age structure of their populations.

The rate of natural increase for the world in 1975 is estimated to have ranged from 1.7 percent to 1.9 percent in the low and high series, respectively. For the same year, the rate of natural increase for the more developed regions (0.7 percent) was only about one-third the rate in the less developed regions (2.1 percent). For the year 2000, the world's rate of natural increase has been projected to vary from 1.3 to 2.0 percent.

The cumulative effect of a growing population can be highlight-

17

Table 4

Alternative Estimates and Projections of Populations for the World, More Developed Regions, and Less Developed Regions: 1975–2000.

(Numbers in millions)

Source	World		More developed regions		Less developed regions	
	1975	2000	1975	2000	1975	2000
U.S. Bureau of the Census:						
High series	4,134	6,797	1,131	1,377	3,003	5,419
Medium series	4,090	6,350	1,131	1,323	2,959	5,027
Low series	4,043	5,921	1,131	1,274	2,912	4,647
World Bank	4,033	6,054	1,134	1,346	2,899	4,707
United Nations:						
High series	4,033	6,508	1,093	1,319	2,940	5,189
Medium series	4,033	6,199	1,093	1,272	2,940	4,926
Low series	4,033	5,855	1,093	1,229	2,940	4,626
Community and Family Study Center:						
High series	4,017	5,975	1,133	1,320	2,884	4,655
Medium series	4,017	5,883	1,133	1,314	2,884	4,569
Low series	4,017	5,756	1,133	1,302	2,884	4,456

Sources: U.S. Bureau of the Census. 1979. *Illustrative Projections of World Populations to the 21st Century.* Current Population Reports Special Studies. Series P-23, No. 79. Washington, D.C.
World Bank, Population and Human Resources Division, Development Economics Department. 1978. *Stationary Population* by K.C. Zachariah and My Thi Vu. pp. 6–11.
United Nations. 1979. *World Population Trends and Prospects by Country, 1950–2000: Summary Report of the 1978 Assessment.* ST/ESA/SER.R/33. pp. 15, 17, and 88.
University of Chicago, Community and Family Study Center. 1978. *Projected Population of the World, Regions and Nations for the Year 2000.*

Table 5

Total Population, Birth Rate, Death Rate, and Rate of Natural Increase For the World, More Developed Regions, and Less Developed Regions, 1975 and 2000: High, Medium, and Low Series Projections

(For definitions of regions, see page 1. For meaning of symbols, see text.)

Subject and projection series	World				More developed regions				Less developed regions			
	Year		Change, 1975–2000		Year		Change, 1975–2000		Year		Change, 1975–2000	
	1975	2000	Absolute	Percent[1]	1975	2000	Absolute	Percent[1]	1975	2000	Absolute	Percent[1]
Total population (millions)												
High series	4,134	6,797	2,663	64	1,131	1,377	246	22	3,003	5,419	2,416	80
Medium series	4,090	6,350	2,260	55	1,131	1,323	192	17	2,959	5,027	2,068	70
Low series	4,043	5,921	1,878	46	1,131	1,274	143	13	2,912	4,647	1,735	60
Birth rate (per 1,000 pop.)												
High series	32.0	29.4	−2.6	−8	16.1	17.4	1.3	8	38.0	32.4	−5.6	−15
Medium series	30.4	25.6	−4.8	−16	16.1	15.2	−0.9	−6	35.9	28.4	−7.5	−21
Low series	28.8	21.9	−6.9	−24	16.1	13.0	−3.1	−16	33.7	24.3	−9.4	−28
Death rate (per 1,000 pop.)												
High series	12.9	9.4	−3.5	−27	9.6	10.1	0.5	5	14.1	9.2	−4.9	−35
Medium series	12.3	9.1	−3.2	−26	9.6	10.4	0.8	8	13.4	8.7	−4.7	−35
Low series	11.9	8.9	−3.0	−25	9.6	10.7	1.1	11	12.8	8.4	−4.4	−34
Rate of natural increase [%]												
High series	1.9	2.0	0.1	(x)	0.7	0.7	—	(x)	2.4	2.3	−0.1	(x)
Medium series	1.8	1.7	−0.1	(x)	0.7	0.5	−0.2	(x)	2.2	2.0	−0.2	(x)
Low series	1.7	1.3	−0.4	(x)	0.7	0.2	−0.4	(x)	2.1	1.6	−0.5	(x)

[1] *Percentages are calculated on the basis of unrounded figures.*

Source: U.S. Bureau of the Census. 1979. *Illustrative Projections of World Populations to the 21st Century.* Current Population Reports Special Studies. Series P-23. No. 79. Washington. D.C.

ed by contrasting the population growth projected for the last quarter of the twentieth century with the growth that is estimated to have occurred in the preceding quarter century. In the medium series projection, 2,261 million persons would be added to the world's population from 1975 to the year 2000. This figure contrasts with the estimated growth from 1950 to 1975 of 1,557 million. In fact, the low series projection, which has twenty-one percent more persons being added in the 1975–2000 period than in the 1950–75 period, shows an average annual growth rate (1.5 percent) which is about twenty-one percent lower than the corresponding rate for 1950 to 1975.

The population dynamics of high growth rates are drawn even more sharply in the less developed regions. With approximately the same average annual growth rates estimated for 1950 to 1975, and projected in the high series for 1975 to 2000, almost twice as many persons are to be added to the populations of the less developed regions in the latter period as in the former period. Regardless of the series, ninety percent or more of the number of persons added to the world's population in the final quarter of this century is projected to be added to the population of the less developed regions (Figure B). This contrasts with a corresponding figure of eighty-two percent for the 1950–75 period.

Regional Distribution of the World's Population in the Year 2000

The census bureau medium series projection for the year 2000 envisions substantial changes in the regional distribution of the world's population. In the year 2000, regardless of series, the number of persons living in the more developed regions of the world is expected to account for about twenty to twenty-two percent of the world population; the remainder, almost four-fifths, will be living in what are classified as the less developed regions. The percent distributions estimated for 1975 and projected for 2000 are as follows:

Although comparatively little change is projected for Asia and Oceania, Africa and Latin America are expected to post substantial gains in percentage of world population, whereas the more developed major regions are expected to experience corresponding losses. In fact, the medium series projection calls for the number of persons living in Africa in the year 2000 to equal or

Figure B

Twenty-Five Years of World Population Growth:
Medium Series

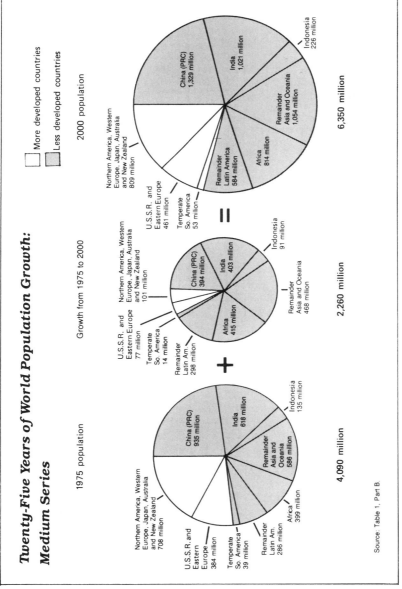

1975 population

Growth from 1975 to 2000

2000 population

More developed countries

Less developed countries

1975 population

Northern America, Western
Europe, Japan, Australia
and New Zealand
708 million

U.S.S.R. and
Eastern
Europe
384 million

Temperate
So. America
39 million

Remainder
Latin Am.
286 million

Africa
399 million

Indonesia
135 million

Remainder
Asia and
Oceania
586 million

India
618 million

China (PRC)
935 million

4,090 million

+

Growth from 1975 to 2000

Northern America, Western
Europe, Japan, Australia
and New Zealand
101 million

U.S.S.R. and
Eastern Europe
77 million

Temperate
So. America
14 million

Remainder
Latin Am.
298 million

Africa
415 million

Remainder
Asia and Oceania
468 million

Indonesia
91 million

India
403 million

China (PRC)
394 million

2,260 million

=

2000 population

Northern America, Western
Europe, Japan, Australia
and New Zealand
809 million

U.S.S.R. and
Eastern Europe
461 million

Temperate
So. America
53 million

Remainder
Latin America
584 million

Africa
814 million

Remainder
Asia and Oceania
1,054 million

Indonesia
226 million

India
1,021 million

China (PRC)
1,329 million

6,350 million

Source: Table 1, Part B.

21

Major region	Estimated 1975	Projected (Medium Series) 2000
Africa	9.8	12.8
Asia and Oceania	55.6	57.2
Latin America	7.9	10.0
Soviet Union and Eastern Europe	9.4	7.3
North America, Western Europe, Japan, Australia, New Zealand	17.3	12.7
	100.0	100.0

Source: U.S. Bureau of the Census. 1979. *Illustrative Projections of World Populations to the 21st Century.* Current Population Reports Special Studies. Series P-23, No. 79. Washington, D.C.

exceed those living in the combined area of North America, Western Europe, Japan, Australia, and New Zealand.

Population Age Structure in 1975 and 2000

The net result of the differences in fertility and mortality between the more and less developed regions would have an impact on the age structures. While one-quarter of all population growth in the less developed countries is projected to occur in the zero to four years age group, in the more developed regions only one-twelfth will go to such ages. In contrast, while only six percent of the population growth in the LDCs will be added to persons sixty-five years old and over, MDCs will add one-quarter of their total population growth to these older ages.

Although the age structure would become older in both MDCs and LDCs, the LDCs would still have a significantly younger population. For example, the median age of both LDC and MDC populations will increase by about four years during the last quarter of the century. However at the end of the century, the median age in the LDCs would still be almost twelve years younger than in the MDCs (23.2 and 34.9 years respectively) (See Figure C).

Alternative Projections

Population projections depend not only on the best estimates of base-date population, but also on educated "guesses" about the

Figure C *Population by Age and Sex (1975 and 2000)*

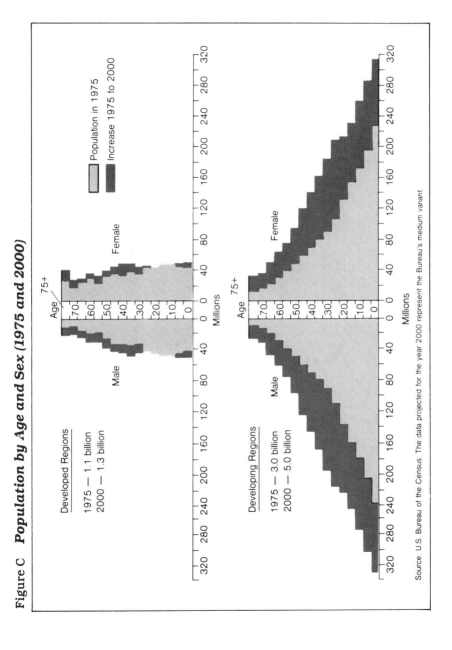

Source: U.S. Bureau of the Census. The data projected for the year 2000 represent the Bureau's medium variant

future course of population growth. Global population projections to the year 2000 have recently been made by several organizations besides the U.S. Bureau of the Census; among these are the World Bank, the United Nations, and the Community and Family Study Center (CFSC) of the University of Chicago. Although these organizations assume a future path of mortality similar to that assumed by the Census Bureau, significant differences among the agencies regarding the size and rapidity of change in levels of fertility produce a considerable range in projected population for the year 2000. The results of different base-year population estimates and projection assumptions employed by these various organizations are shown in Table 4.

Estimates of the 1975 population for the world and for both the more and less developed regions show very little variation among the four agencies. The range of the estimated population for the world in 1975 is from 4.0 to 4.1 billion in the medium series, with the University of Chicago (CFSC) and the Census Bureau having the lowest and highest estimates, respectively.

By the year 2000, the end of the projection period, the range of differences in the medium series is almost half a billion people, from 5.9 billion projected by the CFSC to 6.4 billion projected by the Census Bureau, with the World Bank and the United Nations projecting 6.1 and 6.2 billion, respectively. The differences projected for the more developed regions are very small; the major differences are found in the less developed regions. The Census Bureau projects a population of 5.0 billion for the less developed regions, while the CFSC projects a population of 4.6 billion.

It is interesting to note that in their low series projections of the world's population in the year 2000, the range of difference among the U.S. Bureau of the Census, the United Nations, and the University of Chicago is only 165 million persons, or less than three percent of the total world population.

Demographers have become considerably more optimistic about the prospect for rapid fertility decline in the LDCs (see Freedman). Nevertheless, there are a number of serious social consequences of rapid population growth in the LDCs which remain of great concern to the governments of these countries as well as to the world community.[2] For example, as a heritage of past and current high fertility in LDCs, the population of working age in these countries will grow rapidly till the end of the century. Excluding China, the fifteen to sixty-four year age group is expected to double between 1975 and the year 2000, an annual average rate of 2.9 percent. While the number of youths entering the working ages is soaring, job-creating developments proceed too slowly. Likewise, the flow of migrants from rural areas into crowded cities is a matter of concern for many LDCs.

> It has been estimated that while developing countries' populations are doubling about every 25-30 years, their cities are doubling every 10-15 years and their urban slums or shantytowns every 5-7 years.[3]

To sum up, recent and prospective world population trends during the remainder of this century give cause for both optimism and pessimism about humankind's ability to solve some of its most serious problems. Although population trends during the remainder of this century are to a large extent predetermined by past trends, what precise course is followed will have tremendous impact on the human condition in the twenty-first and following centuries.

Notes

1. In order to simplify the problem of making population projections for individual countries and regions, the assumption was made that there will be no migration from one country to another between 1975 and the year 2000. Although this assumption certainly introduces an element of error into any population projection, it seems likely that net migration will be the least important factor influencing population growth for the large territorial aggregation discussed in this paper.

2. These aspects of the population and development relationships are clearly and concisely discussed in "World Population: Silent Explosion." Department of State *Bulletin*, Fall 1978, prepared by Marshall Green and Robert A. Fearey.

3. "World Population: Silent Explosion," p. 17.

References

Freedman, Ronald. 1979. "Theories of Fertility Decline: A Reappraisal," in Phillip M. Hauser (editor). *World Population and Development.* Syracuse University Press. pp. 63-69.

Mauldin, Parker. 1978. "Patterns of Fertility Decline in Developing Countries." *Studies in Family Planning.* vol. 9, No. 4.

United Nations. 1979a. *Report on Monitoring of Population Trends.* Population Commission, Twentieth Session. (E/CN.9/XX/CRP.1), January 24, 1979.

United Nations. 1979b. Department of International Economic and Social Affairs. *World Population Trends and Prospects by Country, 1950-2000: Summary Report of the 1978 Assessment.* New York.

U.S. Bureau of the Census. 1978. *World Population 1977—Recent Demographic Estimates for the Countries and Regions of the World.* Washington, D.C.

U.S. Bureau of the Census. 1979. *Illustrative Projections of World Populations to the 21st Century.* Current Population Reports Special Studies. Series P-23, No. 79. Washington, D.C.

U.S. Bureau of the Census. 1977 to 1979. *Country Demographic Profiles.* [Various countries]. Washington, D.C.

3.

Japan as a Typical Miniature of World Population Growth

Toshio Kuroda

Nihon University
Tokyo, Japan

Introduction

At least up to the 1960s, the prospects of world population growth were very pessimistic. Most experts in the field expected the rate to exceed two percent. Annual rate of population increase in the world was around two percent, and a doubling of population in less than thirty-five years is really worthy of being called an explosion. Since it is not possible that mankind could continue to increase infinitely because of finite resources and the space of the earth, which is the only inhabitable planet for human beings, it is only natural that the United Nations, individual countries, and many experts of different disciplines have come to be seriously concerned with demographic problems. A great deal of effort had been directed towards fertility control in order to reduce population increase and to achieve quick modernization and the raising of people's living standard.

Tremendous efforts to reduce excessively high fertility made in the majority of developing countries, particularly during the 1960s, have begun to reveal some successful results. Taking into account these results, the United Nations made revised population projections two times, in 1973 and 1978, following their 1968 World Population Projection. This world population in the year 2000 was as much as 6,494 million, according to the 1968 projection, but was smaller in two later successive projections;

namely, 6,253 and 6,196 million respectively. In ten years the projected population in the year 2000 was estimated to be about 300 million less. Such a reduction is due to decreasing rates of population increase, resulting from declining trends of fertility in both more developed and developing countries in which a further declining trend of already low fertility appeared to emerge. Several developing countries that had been characterized by remarkably high fertility have come to show quick reduction in fertility. They are mainly small countries like Malaysia, Singapore, Sri Lanka, Puerto Rico, Barbados, Hong Kong, Taiwan, and so on.

However, even in large countries where very high fertility still prevails, such as India, Indonesia, Thailand, and so on, evidence of declining fertility, though slow but certain, is recognizable. In spite of an unexpected decline in fertility in many developing countries, attention should be paid to the fact that the size of population in developing regions is enormous, more than seventy percent of the world population, and also the population momentum inherent in the young populations characterizing developing populations. Population momentum implies that even after so-called replacement-level fertility (net reproduction rate equal to 1.0) is achieved, the population of countries with a currently young age distribution (very common in developing countries) will continue to grow for another fifty to sixty years, at which time it may be from fifty to one hundred percent larger than when replacement level fertility was reached.

It is, of course, desirable to see that the world population is expected to slow down in the future, but we should be seriously concerned with effects of the population momentum in considering the consequences of world population growth.

Japan is a small island-country with a large population and relatively few natural resources. The population density per square kilometer is over 300 persons, but the density per square kilometer of arable land exceeds 2,000 inhabitants, highest in the world. Various conditions of survival for the Japanese population are seriously limited, not only in spatial size for living, but also in the capacity to provide necessary foods, raw materials, and natural resources. In this sense, Japan may be an excellent case to demonstrate the intricate relationship between population change and development, and also could be a suitable condensed example of demonstrating the typical consequences of world population growth in the future. Emphasis will be mainly on population trends after World War II, and social and economic issues in relation to demographic change explicitly expected to emerge in the years ahead, up to the end of the century.

Demographic Transition

A brief discussion of demographic transition in Japan may be useful to engender understanding of the specific nature of population change in the foreseeable future, and also its drastic effects on social and economic development.

The view that the modernization process is associated with changing vital rates is widely supported. At the initial stage of modernization, only mortality begins to decline steadily, leaving fertility unchanged with some time lag. However, fertility also comes to show a declining trend as modernization accelerates. Natural increase eventually comes to be stable at a low level through a different combination of birth and death rates corresponding to economic advancement and social progress. This kind of demographic process has been called the "demographic transition," and has been documented by several scholars on the basis of experiences of Western countries. It is not easy to determine the exact starting point of demographic transition. However, it may be advisable to adopt the beginning of fertility decline as an initial step of the demographic transition.

A sign of demographic transition began to appear around the period 1910–1920 in Japan. Table I indicates that death rates continued to decline slowly from 1920 to 1943, with exceptionally high death rates during the period 1920–1924, due to Spanish influenza.

On the other hand, it is clearly recognized that fertility continued to decline regularly and steadily since the early 1920s. It may be reasonably concluded that demographic transition in Japan started around 1920. However, it was interrupted by World War II through extraordinary low birth and high death rates in the three years, centering on the year of termination of the war, 1945. A drastic decline in fertility and mortality was accomplished in only ten years or so after the war. The birth rate dropped from thirty-four per thousand population in 1947 to seventeen in 1957, and the death rate went down from fourteen in 1947 to seven in 1958. Both were exactly halved in this short time. Thus, the last stage of demographic transition, namely low birth and death rates similar to those in developed countries, was achieved very quickly in Japan.

Fertility Decline

Fertility transition is a more crucial factor in demographic change than mortality transition. This is because behavioral

Table 1

Vital rates in Japan

Year or period	Birth rate	Death rate	Natural increase rate
1920–24	35.0	23.0	12.0
1925–29	34.0	19.8	14.3
1930–34	31.8	18.1	13.6
1935–39	29.3	17.4	11.9
1940–43	30.7	16.3	14.4
1944*	29.2	17.4	11.8
1945*	23.2	29.2	−6.0
1946*	25.3	17.6	7.7
1947	34.3	14.6	19.7
1948	33.5	11.9	21.6
1949	33.0	11.6	21.4
1950	28.3	10.9	17.3
1955	19.5	7.8	11.7
1960	17.3	7.6	9.7
1965	18.7	7.2	11.5
1966	13.8	6.8	7.0
1967	19.4	6.8	12.7
1968	18.6	6.8	11.8
1969	18.5	6.8	11.7
1970	18.8	6.9	11.8
1971	19.2	6.6	12.6
1972	19.3	6.5	12.8
1973	19.4	6.6	12.8
1974	18.6	6.5	12.1
1975	17.1	6.3	10.8
1976	16.3	6.3	10.0
1977	15.5	6.1	9.4
1978**	14.9	6.1	8.8

Source: Vital Statistics, Ministry of Health and Welfare.
Remarks: Annual average for each period, from 1920 to 1943.
*Denotes estimated figures from the United Nations Demographic Yearbook.
**Denotes provisional figures.

change toward childbearing strongly depends on individual choice, but there is no choice at all for mortality reduction. It does not mean that mortality transition is not significant in demographic transition, for the argument that reduction in mortality is a prerequisite for a decline in fertility is frequently made. However, it is true that mortality reduction is favored by all people, but fertility reduction is not necessarily unanimously accepted by all. In this sense, changes in the level of national fertility could be the more explicit sign of demographic transition.

The postwar change in fertility in Japan may be divided into four periods: the baby boom of 1947–1949, followed by a rapid decline in fertility, 1950–1957, then a period with a constant level, and lastly a disturbance due to the "fire-horse" years 1965–1967, followed by a slow increase in the birth rate.

What is important from the standpoint of demographic transition are the reasons why the fertility decline was so rapid. Before we can answer this question, we must examine fertility decline in more detail.

The baby boom ended in only three years. The number of births sharply decreased after 1950 in spite of an increase in the population of females of reproductive age. The number of births was 2.34 million in 1950, but fell to 1.72 in 1957. Eliminating the effect of change of age-sex population, the standardized birth rate also showed the same tendency, declining from 25.47 in 1950 to 14.69 in 1957. Such a drastic decline in fertility has never been experienced before by an advanced country. Even the German fertility decline after World War I, which was considered most drastic, was slower than that of Japan after World War II.

The real per capita national income in the years immediately after the war was nearly half the prewar level. In 1955, when living standards had barely returned to their prewar level, the fertility trend and also motivation, and measures for fertility limitation underwent remarkable changes successively.

It may be easily understood that economic motivation was a dominant reason for fertility regulation in a period when people were in extreme poverty due to the war. Public opinion surveys on family planning, conducted by the Mainichi Shimbun every two years since 1950, clearly indicate that the most important motive for limiting the number of births was "economic difficulty" in the early period 1950–57. According to the official statistics of induced abortions permitted by the Eugenic Protection Law enacted

31

in 1948, their number increased rapidly, reaching 1.17 million in 1955. In view of the remarkable increase of induced abortions, the government started a family planning campaign designed to protect maternal health.

The standard of living in Japan rose quickly due to the high economic growth between 1958 and 1964. At the same time, the crude birth rate stabilized at a low level of seventeen to eighteen percent. At this time there were remarkable changes in motivation and measures of fertility limitation. The Mainichi surveys mentioned above, conducted after 1960, suggested that the dominant motive shifted from economic difficulty to better education of children by limiting their number. In addition, methods of contraception had been disseminated to a great extent during this period. The practicing rate in 1955 was only 33.6 percent, but rose to 55.5 percent in 1965. It was noticeable that the differential rate of currently practicing contraception between urban and rural areas almost disappeared.

The rapid spread of family planning practices naturally resulted in decreasing the number of induced abortions. The reported number of induced abortions continued to decline after peaking in 1955, decreasing to 0.67 million in 1975.

The current practicing rate of contraception stood at 60.5 percent in 1975, which was the highest ever in Japan. If 21.0 percent who have practiced before but do not practice now are included, the rate exceeds 80.0 percent. It should be noted that the reason for practicing contraception changed from economic to educational in the 1960s, with "maternal health" becoming the biggest reason in the 1970s.

The fourth stage of fertility change is characterized by a slightly rising trend after three years of disturbance due to so-called "fire-horse" year, 1966, which is very specific for Japanese people. Many couples made efforts to avoid childbearing in that specific year due to a superstition that female babies born in this year are destined to unhappy lives. That is the reason why unusually more babies were born in 1965 and 1967. However, the annual average rate and number of births for three years are very similar to those of previous years. Slightly higher birth rate after disturbances due to "fire-horse" year can be explained by the tremendously increased young population who were born in the baby boom period and had reached marriageable age.

Fertility behavior in terms of overall reproduction rates does not

show any significant change since the demographic transition
was completed around 1957. Table 2 gives an historical summary
of the various reproduction rates. With the exception of a "fire-
horse" year, a net reproduction rate of one has been maintained
in this last stage.

Special attention should be paid to the newly emerging trend of
fertility. After peaking in 1973, the birth rate started suddenly to
decline from 19.4 per thousand population to a lower level every
year, and reached 14.9 in 1978, which is shown in Table 1. The
total fertility also has been in continuous decline from 2.16 in
1971 to 1.79 in 1978. Both gross and net reproduction rates have
come to be less than unity, even declining to 0.87 and 0.86 in
1978 respectively. Such a drastic declining trend in fertility is
quite significant, particularly because it not only accelerates
the aging process of the population, but also causes severe
change of age composition of the young population in the near
future.

Mortality Reduction

Another component of demographic transition is mortality. The
reduction in mortality in postwar Japan has been remarkable.
The crude death rate was 14.7 per thousand population in 1947,
but sharply declined to 7.4 in 1958, just halved in about ten years
and has continued to decline, reaching 6.1 in 1977 and 1978.
The decrease in the infant mortality rate represents a dramatic
improvement of mortality in Japan. This rate finally reached 8.4
(per thousand live births), lowest in the world next to that of
Sweden.

The average expectation of life, a most refined indicator of
mortality, has been greatly prolonged in the post-war period. They
were only 50.1 years for males and 54.0 years for females immediately after the end of the war. After twenty years or so they reached
67.7 for males and 72.9 for females in 1965. According to the
1978 abridged life-table, average longevity at birth attained 73.0
years for males and 78.3 years for females, which are among the
longest in the world.

It should be noted that a dominant factor in the aging of the
population has been the fertility decline, which has been documented by several scholars, and not the mortality decline. However, it seems to be apparent that mortality decline has begun to

Table 2

Reproduction rates of female population in Japan

Year	Total fertility rate	Gross reproduction rate	Net reproduction rate
1925	5.11	2.51	1.56
1930	4.71	2.30	1.52
1937	4.36	2.13	1.49
1940	4.11	2.01	1.44
1947	4.54	2.21	1.72
1950	3.65	1.77	1.51
1955	2.37	1.15	1.06
1960	2.00	0.98	0.92
1965	2.14	1.04	1.01
1966	1.58	0.76	0.74
1967	2.23	1.08	1.05
1968	2.13	1.03	1.00
1969	2.13	1.03	1.00
1970	2.14	1.03	1.00
1971	2.16	1.04	1.02
1972	2.14	1.04	1.01
1973	2.14	1.04	1.01
1974	2.05	0.99	0.97
1975	1.91	0.93	0.91
1976	1.85	0.90	0.88
1977	1.80	0.87	0.86
1978*	1.79	0.87	0.86

Source: Computed by the Institute of Population Problems, Ministry of Health and Welfare.
Remarks: Base population used for calculating various rates before 1940 includes foreigners living in Japan.
*Denotes provisional figures.

exert effect on the aging process by the remarkable improvement in mortality among aged people. For example, the average expectation of life at sixty-five years old for males was extended by 19.5 percent, by 20.2 percent at seventy years old, and by 20.8 percent at seventy-five years old, in the period from 1960 to 1976 (according to life-tables calculated for each year) in Japan. The mortality rate for the male population aged fifty-five to fifty-nine declined by 36.6 percent between the period 1949–1953 and 1969–1973, in Japan. The corresponding rates were much less in the United States of America. (7.6 percent), France (14.4 percent), and Sweden (8.5 percent), and even an increase of mortality among this age group was found in the Netherlands, Norway, and

Denmark. (Population Bulletin of the United Nations, No. 11, 1978, p.19, Table b).

Newly emerging declining trends in fertility, coupled with mortality decline among old people, tend to accelerate the aging process in Japan, to which serious attention should be paid, from the standpoint of necessary adjustments of social and economic policies to cope with more serious effects of aging of the population.

Drastic Change of Population and its Serious Consequences

The reason why some space was devoted to explain the demographic transition in Japan is that the more drastic the change of population, the more serious are the effects on society and the economy. Actually, the Japanese experience in the field of population was unique and drastic, never before experienced in the history of the present developed countries.

However, the population change in the three decades after World War II was favorable for rapid economic growth with the exception of a few years of extreme difficulties due to food shortage, unemployment, housing problems, and so on. The abundant supply of the young labor force, who were badly needed for rapidly expanding industries, was brought about by the enormous numbers of the baby boom population born in 1947, 1948, and 1949, reaching working age after fifteen years when rapid industrialization was at its initial stage. Population change, namely, fertility transition, was a very timely factor for economic development by accident.

There was a remarkably low dependency ratio caused by an unusual decline in fertility and slow aging process, with a consequent expansion of the productive age population aged sixty-five and over. The dependency ratio was around seventy for a long time but began to decline after 1950 mainly due to quick reduction of fertility. Finally, it reached 44.9 in 1970, which is the lowest ever experienced in the world. It should be noted that the dependency ratios in many European countries are generally around sixty. The lowest one in developed countries is perhaps forty-seven in Hungary in 1973. Rapid decline, even to the lowest level in the world, in dependency ratio in Japan, could be a powerful factor to facilitate and accelerate economic growth.

There are many factors enabling rapid economic growth which are pointed out by economists. In general, they overlook population factors. However, on the other hand, these population factors cannot be favorable for economic and social development infinitely. It should be recognized that they may turn out to be unfavorable for national development and social welfare.

Future Population Projection

Taking into account the unexpected declining trend of fertility which began to emerge around 1973, a new population projection by our study group was made public in October 1978. A few points which seem to be remarkably significant from the standpoint of social and economic consequences are mentioned.

First, about 15 million additional population is the expected increase by the end of this century, according to the median variant of our projection. After reaching 128 million in 2006, the Japanese population should start to decrease gradually. Maximum population will be about 129 million by high variant in 2007, 127 million by low variant in 2005. Thus, our projection implies that total population of Japan will not exceed 130 million. However, it means that total population will increase by at least 16 million before early next century from about 12 million in 1975. The magnitude of population increase in the near future should be so great in view of extremely high density, very much limited arable land without margin of expansion, inadequate shelter, and extremely scarce natural resources necessary to maintain industrial activities providing employment opportunities to the increasing population. Not only raw materials, but also essential materials of foods, with the exception of rice, have to be imported. Self-supporting capacity of food in Japan is lowest in the world. Arable land was nineteen percent of the total area in 1970, but reduced to fifteen percent in 1975, due to increasing conversion of land under cultivation to housing, factories, road construction, and so on, resulting from the necessity of providing basic needs of the increasing population. As noted earlier, rapid decline in fertility, even sufficiently lower than replacement level, is a major factor in reducing the population increase rate, only 0.88 percent in 1978. Our projection made an assumption that the total fertility rate will continue to decline from 1.80 in 1977 to 1.65 in 2025 in case of medium variant. Special attention should be given by policy planners to the fact that even under such a low fertility our population is expected to increase by the considerable size mentioned above.

Summary results of our future population projections are shown in Table 3, showing three variants and a supplementary one for reference.

Rapid Change of Age Composition

In addition to the population increase in the future, serious attention should be paid to another important aspect of population change. That is the drastic change of age composition of the population in Japan. It is well-known that aging of the population in Japan will be rapid, compared with experiences in Western advanced countries. The proportion of population aged sixty-five years old and over had been around five percent for a long time. However, it started to rise since about 1955, and reached eight percent in 1975. According to our projection, this old population will be about fifteen percent by the end of this century, and even more than twenty percent in 2015. It will take only forty-five years

Table 3

Future Population Projection for Japan
—1975 to 2025, Unit thousand—

Year	High variant	Medium variant	Low variant	Supplementary
1975	111,940	111,940	111,940	111,940
1980	116,852	116,838	116,823	116,852
1985	120,220	120,131	120,039	120,247
1990	122,773	122,549	122,328	122,875
1995	125,262	124,832	124,399	125,498
2000	127,830	127,104	126,383	128,264
2005	129,466	128,383	127,298	130,140
2010	129,390	127,894	126,402	130,340
2015	217,944	125,955	123,955	129,229
2020	125,923	123,345	120,802	127,643
2025	123,903	120,586	117,337	126,161

Source: Made by a study group, Nihon University in 1978.
Remarks: High variant assumes constant level of total fertility at 1.80 in 1977, medium variant declining to 1.65 in 2025, and low variant declining to 1.50 in 2025. Supplementary assumes returning to 1.91 in 2025 after maintaining 1.80 up to 1980.

for the population of elders to attain a fifteen percent level starting from five percent, but it was more than one century in France and Great Britain and around ninety years in Germany. Rapidity of the aging process of the population in Japan compares with experiences of Western countries and suggests severe consequences in societal and economic fields, never experienced in advanced countries.

Special attention should be paid to the fact that as a result of rapid aging, the population of middle and high age groups among the productive age population will increase remarkably. Such a unique aging of population in Japan may be called "dual structure" of aging. For example, in contrast to the remarkable increase of population aged 35-49 and 50-64, the population aged 20-34 will decrease during the period, 1975-1990. The rates of increase of middle and older working-age groups are nineteen percent and fifty-three percent respectively for the period. The rate of decrease of the young working-age group is fourteen percent for the same period. Such an imbalanced change of working-age population in the future will necessitate drastic measures in order to adjust to rapidly changing age composition, not only among the private sector, but also the public sector. Rapid aging of the labor-force population is inevitable. Industrial organization and economic structure must be geared to the changing labor-force situation.

Child population is also expected to change drastically. The population aged zero through fourteen will decrease from 27 million in 1975 to 21.8 million in 1995 due to rapidly declining fertility. Primary school-age population will be expected to make a reduction of 4.4 million in only fifteen years from 1980 to 1995. It will raise serious educational problems, including training programs of teaching staff, educational facilities and materials and so on.

Furthermore, it is very important to recognize that such a drastic change of age composition of the population creates new problems of industrial adaptation as a result of a change of consumption and life pattern characterized by age and sex.

The age profile of the population is a basic framework of society. If it changes drastically, social and economic change is unavoidable. The only alternative left for the society is to adjust ourselves appropriately to newly emerging age profiles which we have never had before. For that purpose, foresight and innovative ways of thinking are necessary. In relation to this area of the problem, we must be aware above all things that priority should be accorded to the social and economic considerations of population change.

4.

Ethical Dimensions of World Population Trends

Richard L. Rubenstein

The Florida State University
Tallahassee, Florida, U.S.A.

Let me begin by sharing with you one of the reasons why a theologian has agreed to participate in a book that is primarily concerned with issues of demography and population. I began my scholarly work with an inquiry into the theological significance of the death camps of World War II. I asked questions such as: "What is the meaning of the death camps in the light of the Judeo-Christian tradition?" I found, however, that any attempt to understand the phenomenon of genocide in traditional ethical or theological categories proved to be inadequate. As a result, I was drawn increasingly to sociology, political theory and European history in order properly to understand what took place during World War II. Among the conclusions I arrived at was that the death camps of World War II were an example of the bureaucratic elimination of a surplus population. It is that conclusion that has brought me to today's topic, namely, the ethical dimensions of population trends. I would point out that when I use the term surplus population, I do not refer to people who have no conceivable usefulness, but to people who, for whatever reasons, be they political, sociological, economic, or other, no longer have a viable place in their native community and whom the decision-makers in their community decide to eliminate by one means or another. As you know, there have been a number of such target populations in our century. Moreover, it is my conviction that there may very well be more such target populations in the foreseeable future.

In any discussion of the ethical dimensions in population trends a number of variables ought to be considered. One is, of course, population itself. Another variable is obviously the availability of resources and technology to support the population. Yet another, and this I take to be the crucial variable, is the symmetry, or lack of it, between the labor supply and the number of available job slots. Where the relation between labor supply and available job slots is asymmetrical, a condition that is most likely to occur when there are more people seeking work than jobs, there will be danger of a social crisis. Any discussion of population which does not consider the relationship between the labor supply and the available jobs, but simply considers the raw data of population increase or population decrease, oversimplifies the problem. Yet another important variable is the question of class stratification and distribution. For example, a middle-class population that has reason to fear downward social mobility because the symmetry between available jobs and population has been disturbed, is likely to be politically dangerous. In his book on German emigration to the United States in the nineteenth century, Mack Walker points out that the Germans who emigrated to the United States were predominantly lower middle class people who had some resources and were not prepared to accept the consequences of the downward social mobility that the industrial revolution and the rationalization of agriculture was bringing upon them. Had they remained in Germany without hope of improvement, they might have been a source of social instability.

Yet another important population variable is the question of whether escape hatches are available to countries with surplus people. I am convinced that one of the crucial differences between the future that awaits us and the past we have recently left behind is that the monumental safety valve available to our forefathers, namely, a relatively unpopulated New World, is no longer available to us. One of the hypotheses I set forth in my book, The Cunning of History (Harper & Row: 1975), is that the closing of the American frontier was an important element in creating the problem in Europe of what to do with its surplus population. As long as emigration to the New World was feasible, it was always possible to encourage an unwanted population to emigrate. In the 1930s that option was no longer available.

There is one other element that is relevant to any discussion of ethical considerations: the distinction between public and private morality. Unfortunately the distinction is all too frequently ignored. It is, for example, possible for a man to be faithful to his wife, a good and trustful neighbor, an honorable communicant in his church, and, at the same time, to be completely amoral and value-neutral in the way he initiates or implements public policy. Actually, because of the internally compulsive nature of modern economic and political structures, decision-makers are often compelled to make amoral decisions affecting large numbers of people in spite of the fact that in their private lives, they are very concerned with moral principles. As a theologian, I might observe that clergymen very frequently fail to make the distinction between private and public morality. They do not see that when they exhort public decision-makers to moral decisions, they are in fact using the frame of reference of private and personal morality, which is appropriate to the small community but not to the large community.

Yet another concept that is important in any discussion of ethics and population is the term rationality. Before offering a definition of rationality, I want to remind you that the rational is not necessarily identical with the humane. In Herman Melville's *Moby Dick* there is a point at which Captain Ahab says that all his means are rational; only his end, the pursuit of the great white whale, is insane. When I characterize certain odious political actions as rational, I do not do so in order to give offense to our sense of morality. For example, I have argued that the elimination of Jews from Germany was entirely rational, given the priorities of the Germans at the time. That does not mean that the German action was other than obscene. Unfortunately, in the future there may be other entirely rational actions involving large-scale demographic violence. The actions may be "rational" yet totally inhumane.

I would also like to suggest that in considering the question of ethics and population, at least two very different approaches are possible. One approach involved cataloging the various political and social dilemmas related to the continuing growth of population, and then examining the religious and ethical resources with which such dilemmas could be resolved. At the most fundamental level, this involves the question of the religious and ethical criteria by which we can decide who shall live and who shall die. The relevant issues include birth control, death control, abortion, and even international *triage*; that is, the question of whether to support a nation in a period in which it cannot sustain its own population. When such issues are discussed in terms of exhortations to act in accordance with values presumed to be sacred within the Judeo-Christian tradition, it is my conviction that we get nowhere. People who urge us so to act are seldom decision-makers. This is certainly true of both clergymen and academics. In times of radical distress decision-makers are seldom able to act in accordance with these presumed values. In such periods, decision-makers are more likely to decide on the basis of the other approach, that of value-neutral calculating rationality; that is, the attainment of a precisely defined end by use of those means which are estimated to be the most economical. This is, of course, a rationality of means rather than ends.

Let me offer you four examples of how the radical destabilization of a population has already led policy-makers to employ a rationality of means in our century. In the examples that I offer, the decision-makers sought to eliminate a target population which they regarded as politically, economically, ethnically, or religiously not part of their fundamental community. Because of this, the policy-makers did not regard themselves as bound by customary moral norms in dealing with the target population.

The first example is the World War I massacre of the Armenians. Without going into detail, it is important to recognize that the massacre did not take place until rationally-trained Turks, educated in western Europe, took over the government. As long as the older, corrupt regime of Sultan Abdul Hamid remained in power, there was some killing and hatred, but not the kind of controlled, systematic elimination of a population in which every aspect of the operation was handled in the most efficient manner possible. The massacre of the Armenians was a very modern operation.

A second example to which we can point is, of course, the destruction of the European Jews. I'm going to pass over that because I have dealt with it at length elsewhere. Instead, I want to turn to the third example, genocide in Cambodia, and quote a few crucial sentences from the October 31, 1979 hearings before the

Judiciary Committee of the Senate of the United States, on the subject of what was currently taking place in Vietnam and Cambodia. In the discussion, Senator Edward Kennedy asked the following question:

> I have just one final question and then my time is up, and that is, what possible political gain is there for the Vietnamese or the Soviet Union, or for the puppet regime in letting these hundreds of thousands of children starve? What possible political advantage does this ensure to their benefit?

I would add that before Senator Kennedy asked this question it was established that all attempts to bring food into Cambodia were frustrated by the communist authorities. They used every conceivable evasion to prevent food from entering Cambodia. For example, the most effective way to bring in food was by means of a truck bridge from Thailand. This was permitted by the Vietnamese. However, they stipulated that their Cambodian puppets also had to agree. Predictably, the Cambodians first stalled and then finally refused. Commenting on this in the Senate hearings, which were *in camera*, Senator Danforth of Missouri stated,

> I think, Mr. Chairman, that the answer is clear that . . . in fact there is an essential advantage for them (i.e., the communists) to gain, and this is it . . . What the Vietnamese have in mind is the total domination of Indochina, and that is going to be a long-term objective of theirs. Cambodia is a very fertile agricultural area, inhabited by the Khmer people, who are ethnically different from the Vietnamese. The Vietnamese want that very fertile agricultural area. They want complete domination, and genocide is part of their policy to accomplish it.

I would like to emphasize that Senator Danforth was not speaking before the public. He is a man of great integrity. He had no interest in being sensational. He was not trying to score political points. I must confess that I have been a student of genocide for too long to be surprised at this new example of inhumanity. Unfortunately, it would seem that, if a nation is militarily strong, but lacks the resources, either of food or of productive land, to support its population, it may take them from a weaker neighbor, as did Vietnam in Cambodia. Moreover, if such a nation finds in its territory an unwanted population, it may decide to eliminate the population, using the most rational means to do it.

I do not think it was accidental that the elimination of the Jews was called the "Final Solution" by the Germans. On the contrary, murder is always the most economical way to solve the problem of eliminating an unwanted group. If we link this with the question of the availability of food and other scarce resources, we see that decision-makers with the power to define and enforce social goals may be tempted simply to eliminate groups that could deny them the resources they want. The target group could be either a minority group within one's own community or a conquered population. Lest we think that what happened in Cambodia was an aberration, let us also consider the problem of the "boat people." In this case the problem of the class distribution and stratification of the population is important. In Vietnam, as most all of you know, the middle and professional classes were largely Chinese. They have been called the Jews of Southeast Asia. Like the Jews, they were essentially a literate, lower middle class, artisan and professional group, involved primarily in commercial and professional endeavors.

The communist Vietnam government sought to change the social structure so as to eliminate the middle class. This was the class that Lenin said had to be eliminated under socialism. Now although Lenin insisted that the bourgeoisie must be eliminated, he did not specify how the bourgeoisie was to be eliminated. In the case of Vietnam, class difference aggravated ethnic distinction, so that whatever intuitive moral sense might have impeded the policy-makers' intentions *vis a vis* the target group was entirely absent. There was, however, an important difference between the Vietnamese treatment of the Khmer people and the treatment of the ethnic Chinese. In the case of the Chinese, expulsion was the preferred method of population elimination; in the case of the Khmers, it was outright murder. Nevertheless, about half of the ethnic Chinese found their Auschwitz in the South China seas, as indeed the Vietnamese government knew they would.

I would like to conclude by asking a question about moral values: Could it be that the decline and the total disappearance of any moral code from large scale decision-making in the matter of the state-sponsored strategies of population-elimination that we have discussed is not an accident, but is itself intrinsic to the transformations of the modern period that have resulted in a worldwide shift from subsistence agricultural economies to highly rational technological manufacturing economies? Put differently, could it be that genocide is an intrinsic hazard of the modernization process? The transformation of society to which I refer is the same transformation as that identified by Emile Durkheim from mechanical to organic solidarity. Karl Polanyi called it the "great transformation" involving the shift from a traditional economy to the self-regulating market economy of modern times.

It has been observed that when population density is high, an individual is in close contact with many persons. High population density thus leads to a higher proportion of social contacts that are likely to be superficial or secondary relations. As such, they are likely to be functionally specific and affectively neutral. By contrast, in societies in which a high proportion of the contacts are low density, most people will be bound to each other by some form of kinship, thereby facilitating some common moral bond between them. Where relationships become secondary and functionally specific, not only are they likely to be affectively neutral, but there is a heightened possibility that they will be rationalized contractual relationships. In essence, this means the relationships will be calculable in money terms. Money then becomes the way in which one measures all things, regardless of whether they are good or evil, right or wrong. This in itself fosters the total dissolution of any possible public moral framework. In a time of crisis, this would mean that decision-makers might be bound by no moral or ethical standard as they attempt to solve the population crisis. Crises might be solved by power and violence devoid of all moral content. He who has the power to define social reality is likely to do so on his own terms. He who is without power to define social reality will be at the mercy of those who possess it.

I must tell you that I am a theologian who has pondered these issues for many years. I wish I could have come to less grim conclusions, but I am not optimistic about the direction in which things are going. For those of you who are sociologists, I would like to add that the thinker who has helped me the most in understanding modern civilization was Max Weber. He was not very optimistic about our civilization. He characterized the future as an "iron cage." He saw no way out. As of today, neither do I.

Nevertheless, we cannot rest content with this pessimistic note. If the argument of this essay has merit, it should be apparent that the cost of continuing to separate morality from public policy could be much too high to be tolerated.

Commentary

Joel Kurtzman

United Nations Institute for Training and Research
New York, New York, U.S.A.

The current relationship between population, technology, and the theological and sociocultural surround offers us prospects which are not optimistic for the future. In the area of development, which is the area in which I work, the statistical anthropologists such as Murdock and others have noted that there is an increasing tendency toward violence, dehumanization, and persecution as the size of population increases, and as those populations become more technologically oriented and more structurally complex. There is, for example, an ascending scale of violence as we move from hunters and gatherers to horticulturalists, where we develop the institution of slavery, to agriculturalists, where we have hierarchical class societies, organized warfare, and fixed roles, in addition to slavery, and to industrial society with a level of violence that is unprecedented, capable of destroying the entire world and engaging a far higher percentage of the world's human and technical resources than ever before.

The vision of a world ascending toward a better, more humane and harmonious state through technological innovations, in light of some of the empirical evidence about how larger populations organize themselves, is simply not true. Greater population aggregates produce greater violence.

In the area of development, where industrial cultures are in the business of exporting technologies, rationalized methods of accounting and managerial expertise, we are creating, to use Dr. Rubenstein's phrase, vast numbers of "redundant populations." If you take the example of Peru, which was the modern miracle of South America, you see that the exportation of advanced technology and managerial expertise has caused the displacement of millions of people from the farms, through the use of modern agricultural machines, and created vast slums in Lima that now approach two million people. This is happening in other areas of the world where we have technology transfer that looks at the problems of underdeveloped countries simply from an economic perspective. The situation exists such that when we export a technology it is also accompanied by a perspective such as cost benefit analysis, or another bureaucratic form where people are seen only in terms of their economic value to industrial society. There is also an attendant psychological and social restructuring that accompanies the introduction of a technology into a country and affects both perceptual and organization skills as well as normative values, and often reduces human beings to the level of expendable objects.

With the increase in the transfer of technology, rational processes, and social and managerial organization techniques, we see the case whereby the population as a whole declares itself, because of its technology and via its methods of accounting, as an economic value to be factored into its overall planning and managing so that people are transformed solely into economic entities.

This is the problem we face in development which fits within the context delineated by Dr. Rubenstein. It is difficult to see where the way out is, especially as our use of rationalization techniques grows and the accounting and cost benefit mentality spreads. It reminds me that in traditional cultures it appears to be a universal that, unlike objects, living beings are not usually counted. Traditional people rebel against separating an animal from the herd or an individual from the tribe and, from the rationalistic, economic perspective. The Celts, for example, considered it a very grave offense to count cattle. Traditional Jews would count people by saying, "not one, not two, not three," and so on, to avoid transforming people into things which are expendable, instead of parts of an integrated whole.

In our society, with its strictly rationalized, economic perspective, we have made the decision to build DC-10s, or Three Mile

Island nuclear reactors, for example, without enough regard for life, not consciously, but because our level of development has its organizational imperatives which require us to regard people as little different from objects. The bureaucratic mentality has few other means at its disposal. This, I think, is the essential feature of what Dr. Rubenstein is presenting, and I think it is a very disturbing picture, and unfortunately a very true picture of our current world.

Part II

Health Systems and Population Control

Health Systems and Population Control

Edward O. Pratt

The World Bank Washington D.C., U.S.A./Sierra Leone

Introduction

Population control emphatically does not advocate the cataclysmic postulates of Malthus. The intent, purpose, and execution of population control recognize and respect the basic principles of human rights of every individual. Workers in the field of population control are aware of the misconception, doubt, and mistrust which exist with regard to population programs and because of this, do exercise themselves in preserving the recognition of ethical considerations consistent with the human rights principle, *vis-a-vis* the dignity of the human being.

The perspectives of population control include some of the determinants which predicate the development of health systems as a contributory mechanism towards the achievement of defined social, demographic, and economic goals.

Predominantly, the theme is set within the context of the developing countries. Forgive me if my attention is focused on the developing milieu—for our purposes, that is where the action is. However, relaxed issues in the developed world spectrum should be brought up or presented and considered experientially or otherwise.

Population control presents a multifaceted scenario with a host of program areas involving:

1. family planning

2. fertility control

3. behavioral or social and cultural perspectives

4. application of demography in the scope of national planning

5. utilization of political mechanisms based on socio-economic factors to control, for example, migration

6. improvement of the status of women

7. designing solutions for problems involving youth, such as delinquency, unmarried mothers, destitute children or orphans . . .

8. resolving the problems caused by the by-products of urbanization and the ecological metamorphosis of the rural environment

9. seeking solutions for the low socio-economic plight of the poor

10. exploring models to resolve such issues as housing, schooling, food production . . . and so on

However, one or two or so of these programs indexed may be associated with health delivery systems—family planning, fertility control . . .

Health systems are developed through various modules, with specific application to developing countries in the context of population control for such principle services as:

1. maternal and child health

2. nutrition

3. general medical care for episodic illnesses and other general medical conditions

4. preventive and promotive care including communicable disease control, environmental sanitation, the production of safe, potable water . . . and so on

The predominant health theme is the application of a basic health service for all levels of the community system ensuring coverage particularly for the unserved and underserved (poor) communities in the outreach areas.

Within the health scenario itself, as relating to the developing countries, there are myriad problems and multiplicity of factors which compound the problems of unrestrained population growth.

A whole lot of correlations are developed between maternal and infant mortality *and* fertility rates; between customs, taboos, religious ethics, *and* reproductive habits . . . and so on. Thus we may see total fertility rates, crude birth and death rates (among other variables) as significantly affecting the demographic status of a country.

While improving the health status through applied medical technology, towards better quality living and increased longevity of all age/sex-specific groups, a concurrent population strategy would ensure a built-in control mechanism to check the inevitable outcome; that is, of increased population growth rate.

Again, while appreciating the role medical and health personnel can undoubtedly play in the planning, development, and management of health systems, yet within the context of population control programming it will be fallacious to assume that they only reserve the competence to design and effectively implement that aspect of the population-related program.

5.

Health Services and Development: Population Issues

C.O. Akerele

World Health Organization
Dar es Salaam, Tanzania/Seychelles

Introduction

This paper reviews some aspects of development and its relationship to the provision of social services in the developing countries. The disadvantages of an uncontrolled population growth on services, especially the delivery of a comprehensive health service system that is accessible and acceptable to a large proportion of the Tanzanian population, are discussed. Although there is no explicit population policy, *per se*, some of the steps being taken by Tanzania in the provision of child spacing facilities, through their Maternal and Child Health (MCH) program, as an integral part of the national health services are also outlined.

Background

During the past decade or so, there has been considerable attention given to the subject of population control and its relationship to overall developmental processes of the emerging or the so-called Third World countries in general, and development in Africa in particular. Africa's political leaders and academics have consistently argued against any overt population control policies and programs. And many of their governments have paid little attention to population variables in their planning process- es, their rationale being that they believe that the continent is still relatively underpopulated. Previous colonial and imperial perfor- mance, together with the present activities of minority regimes, in Africa, have done nothing to dispel the prevailing suspicion that an overt family planning program is part of a grand genocidal design.

Man shares the ability to reproduce with the most primitive of beings, yet he has a unique responsibility to rear his offspring in a manner that promotes his total physical and mental well- being. Some elements in Tanzania's socio-economic developmen- tal experience will be described here. The implementation of its family planning program is effected through the integ- ration of activities into a well-conceived and properly executed Maternal and Child Health (MCH) program, this being part of a comprehensive national health services delivery sys- tem.

The popularity of any population control policy and program within a given situation will depend to a large extent on the degree of prevailing socio-economic development. Ultimately, the population control program will be a varying mix of overt fertility and subtle infertility control activities; subject, of course, to the particular needs of a given country.

The desired product of any acceptable family planning program should be the generation of activities that will initiate, promote, facilitate, and be considered part of an overall national develop- ment commitment. These activities will of necessity take many forms. They will, however, be conditioned mainly by factors such as the level of development of the national health infrastructure, the urgency that is needed to correct a given developmental situation, and the political will of the nation to take such firm, corrective steps. In addition, family planning services could be emphasized through the combined efforts of different develop- mental sectors, or through those of a single developmental sector such as health. In either case, government should provide the necessary leadership in terms of a well thought out policy and material support.

Although external support is relatively easy to obtain for family planning activities, such support should only be complementary

to national initiative and efforts. The rapid turnover of policy
makers in most developing countries dictates that any adopted
national policy should have the greatest acceptance possible, in
order to ensure some degree of continuity in future program
implementation.

Development, Health Services and Population

Health services should in any country be a major contributor to
the socio-economic developmental processes. Unfortunately, this
important developmental sector has often displayed an ineffective
leadership in many countries, especially those of the developing
world. However, the inequality in the health services that origi-
nated from colonial situations in these countries is now being
recognized as one of the major challenges which is in need of
corrective measures, if the expected fruits of political independence are to be realized for the people. During the past few years,
advancements in modern communication techniques have
brought the advantages of progressive technology within the
range of the majority of the world's population. These advantages,
however, continue to remain the exclusive prerogative of only a
privileged few in both developed and developing countries. The
gap between the rich and the poor, between and within national
boundaries, is not growing narrower, but is steadily widening.
The discrepancy within the health sector is even more glaring.
Concerned about the present deteriorating global health situation, the Executive Board of the World Health Organization, in an
organizational study in 1973, noted its concern as follows:

> The board is of the opinion that in many countries the health
> services are not keeping pace with the changing population either
> in quantity or in quality. It is likely that they are getting worse.
> . . . There appears to be widespread dissatisfaction of population
> about their health services for varying reasons. Such dissatisfac-
> tion occurs in the developed as well as in the Third World. The
> causes can be summarized as a failure to meet the expectations of
> the populations; an inability of the health services to deliver a level
> of national coverage adequate to meet the stated demands and the
> changing needs of different societies; . . . rapidly rising cost with-
> out a visible and meaningful improvement in services; and a feeling
> of helplessness on the part of the consumer, who feels (rightly or
> wrongly) that the health services and the personnel within them

> are progressing along an uncontrollable path of their own which may be satisfying to the health professionals but which is not what is most wanted by the consumer.[1]

Although the ability of the health services to provide appropriate leadership in socio-economic development has become more precarious today, the situations in some African countries are not as hopeless as the board has so vividly portrayed. There is a growing number of countries that have taken appropriate actions to provide basic health services to the majority of their population, thus giving health the desired priority within their overall developmental framework.

Although adequate and appropriate tools are being developed for the control and ultimate eradication of most communicable diseases, it would appear that only significant improvement in the socio-economic conditions, including the quality of life, will lead to the disappearance of some of the world's major communicable diseases. However, the recent declaration of the global eradication of smallpox[2] is a glowing testimony to the possibilities that exist for concerted action. Regrettably, in some instances, progress in the field of health has not always been matched by parallel progress in other sectors. For example, the recent dramatic reduction of global perinatal and infant mortality has almost brought us into a head-on collision course with the Malthusian nightmare through the reckless growth rate of our population, which has now reached an all-time high of approximately three percent; and this in comparison with our relatively less enthusiastic rate of food production.

While it would be preferable to leave the subject of population explosion and its gloomy consequences to the prophets of doom, it is becoming evident that this unhealthy trend that is constraining to development needs to be interrupted immediately if a major calamity is to be averted. This implies an intelligent choice from among the following limited, almost non-viable options: mass starvation; political chaos or population control through decreased birth rate.[3]

An uncontrolled population growth has, *inter alia*, an unfavorable influence on the design and implementation of any social services system, including the development of a holistic national health services system; especially one that is built on the principles of justice, equality, and people's participation.[4] It should however be remembered that the social and demographic characteristics of Africa are unique to that continent. Pockets of high fertility co-exist with areas of low fertility.[5] Therefore any population program design would have to be specific to a country for it to respond positively to the prevailing fertility pattern.

Tanzanian Approach

Although considerable lip-service has been paid in the past to the noble notion of provision of basic health services to their populations, few governments have found effective means of implementing their programs. One of the few governments in Africa that has been bold enough to embark on innovative approaches is the government of the United Republic of Tanzania. Tanzania's departure from traditional developmental approaches, including health, together with her continuing exploration of new concepts, have facilitated a unique experiment in development that is now paying a healthy dividend. The impact of these developmental efforts in terms of reduction of mortality as well as increased life expectancy will be more or less precisely known after the analysis of the recent population census results. However, the health status of the population as a whole could be said to have improved greatly over the last decade.[6]

These socio-economic experiences, especially those in the health sector, are of necessity conditioned by two major constraints; namely, paucity of available resources, and the magnitude of the problems to be addressed following political independence.

Geography and Administrative Features

The United Republic of Tanzania consists of the mainland, the islands of Zanzibar and Pemba. A union state was agreed upon in 1964. Tanzania has a land mass of 939,767 square kilometers and is located on the east coast of Africa, south of the equator. The climate is largely tropical but there are temperate areas in the mountainous northern parts of the country, including the snow-capped Kilimanjaro mountain.

The indigenous inhabitants of Tanzania are mainly Bantu. Small Arab, Asian, and European communities are also found in urban and semi-urban centers. Considerable inter-marriage has taken place over the years amongst the different communities. Kiswahili is understood everywhere and is the official language of the government. A majority of the population is either Moslem or Christian. As a result of deliberate National Policy of Villagization (Ujamaa), only approximately five percent of the population live in towns. Government considers the intensive movement of scattered population into organized registered villages (ujamaa) as an essential step in the implementation of the National Rural Development Policy. A certain degree of subtle social-engineering measures were sometimes applied during such movements in the past, by some over-enthusiastic party workers. The rest of the population are found in the more fertile agricultural areas. It is estimated that over half of the population is concentrated on only one-sixth of the total land area.

Tanzania is divided in twenty-five administrative regions with twenty regions on the mainland and five on Zanzibar and Pemba. Each region is headed by a regional commissioner who is also the party's Chama Cha Mapinduzi (CCM)—regional representative. He is responsible for the coordination of the party's and other developmental activities in the respective regions. The next administrative levels are the 86 districts under district development directors. Below this, there are 1735 administrative wards under divisional secretaries. Registered villages represent the smallest administrative units. The villages are made up of cells of ten houses, each with a ten-cell leader who reports to the village chairman. There is a good degree of decentralization of administrative authority. This unique politico-social structure has provided natural entry-points for the extension of social services, including health, to the periphery. For example, the ten-cell leadership system has been used for the distribution of prophylactic chloroquine to vulnerable age groups as part of the national malaria control program.

Health Services and the Population: Policies and Programs

The country's main policy in the provision of social services, especially health services, is dictated by the broad guidelines that were articulated in the Arusha Declaration of 1967, which is the ideological basis for the transformation of a new Tanzania society. The broad objective of the health policy was to rapidly extend services to the outlying areas in order to meet with the essential, basic health needs of a greater proportion of the population. The strategy was to provide a country-wide system of established health institutions consisting of a chain of village health posts, dispensaries, rural health centers, district and regional hospitals, with consultant and teaching hospitals, as the apex of a well-graded referral system. The health service was to complement, support, and promote the National Villagization Program (Ujamaa villages). These health care facilities were to provide health care to individuals, families, and entire communities, and were to include a broad spectrum of preventive and curative activities.

Under this policy, due emphasis was to be given to the preventive, including environmental health, in preference to the traditional, sophisticated, hospital care, and in keeping with local realities. Traditional healers whose services the communities continue to use and depend on were duly recognized as primary health care workers. Government was to assume major responsibility for the operational cost of existing facilities and the establishment of new ones, in order to provide free medical care to all. The system was to rely to a large extent on the use of inexpensive and modestly trained multipurpose health workers who will be sensitive to the needs and aspirations of the community and who will be complementary to the staffing needs of the expanding national health service and other developmental activities that have bearing on health.

There are four major providers of health care services in Tanzania, namely: (i) Government, whose services constitute up to sixty percent of the total; (ii) Voluntary agencies which are primarily religious organizations; (iii) Industrial firms and companies that provide occupational health services; (iv) The private sector, whose practitioners provide both allopathic and traditional medical services to parts of the population. In essence, government has as its ultimate goal the provision of a rationalized, comprehensive health care system; one that will be responsive to needs and the cultural lifestyle of its population in terms of available resources, including appropriate manpower and technology.

The government of the United Republic of Tanzania has not taken any rigid position on population-related issues, neither has it endorsed any overt population control program. The vast expanse of uninhabited land mass seems to justify government's stance. However, government has demonstrated its support for responsible family life by limiting the tax deductible children's allowance to a maximum of four. The national census held in August 1978 showed Tanzania to have a population of 18.052 million. Table 1 shows some salient national vital rates.

In addition to the high infant mortality rate of 152 per thousand, it is estimated that an additional ninety per thousand children die before the age of five. This means that approximately twenty-five percent of the population die before the age of five. Morbidity figures are not readily available but it is estimated to be rather high. Major causes of infant death are mainly preventable diseases such as: malnutrition, of one kind or the other, measles, pneumonia, gastro-enteritis, tuberculosis, neonatal tetanus, malaria, and anaemias.

The maternal mortality rates for institutional deliveries is 2.7 per thousand. Maternal mortality is mainly associated with short pregnancy intervals and malnutrition resulting in contracted pelvis and obstructed labour.

Tanzanians as a whole tend to marry at a relatively early age. However, Moslems marry at an even earlier age. (Before the U.N. recommended minimum of fifteen years.) The government's commitment to eradicate illiteracy and its policy of universal primary education for all seem to have imposed a constricting influence on the practice of early marriage within the past few years.

The indigenous ethnic groups in Tanzania knew about and practiced child spacing. These practices were religiously observed in the past by many. The ancient initiation ceremonies that boys and girls undergo before being accepted as members of the clan, were in fact instructional situations, where behavioral codes, including family life, were taught to the adolescent in the society. During the rapid transition from the more traditional way of life to the so-called "modern society," old ways were often discarded without something of value replacing them. Even breast feeding has now become unfashionable, whereas the same trend is being reversed in the developed countries.

Family life topics covered during initiation ceremonies dealt with, amongst others, instructions on marriage; how to cope with pregnancy; child-birth, and responsible parenthood (including child spacing practices). These instructions and practices were usually reinforced all through child-bearing years. Elders

Table 1

Important National Variables[7]

Crude Birth Rate	46.0 per 1000
Cude Death Rate	17.7 per 1000
Rate of Growth	2.8 percent
Infant Mortality Rate	152.0 per 1000
Life Expectancy at Birth	47.0 years
Total Fertility	6.2
G.N.P. Per Inhabitant	U.S. $183.00
No. of Health Care Establishments[8]	2,732
No. of Nurses Including Auxiliaries[9]	10,338

take over the role of teachers. The transition into "modern ways" has to some degree conditioned attitudes towards child birth and child rearing practices adversely, especially in towns.

According to the national demographic survey carried out in 1973 by BRALUP[10] the under fourteen population constituted 47.4 percent of the total population, giving rise to a very high dependency ratio. The same survey showed that the child bearing population equally constituted a high proportion (20.3 percent), thus making the size of the vulnerable group of the population very large with consequential increased demand on the nation's social services, including health.

Tanzanian leadership has realized that the impact of the present population growth is incompatible with the attainment of the socio-economic targets that have been set by the party and the government. Therefore, at one time or the other they have made public statements expressing their concern over this issue. Addressing the TANU[11] bi-annual conference of May 28, 1969, His Excellency Mwalimu Julius K. Nyerere conferred the much needed political will on the subject by declaring:

Giving birth is something in which mankind and animals are equals, but rearing the young, and especially educating them for many years, is something which is the unique gift and the responsibility of men. It is for this reason that it is important for human beings to put emphasis on caring for children rather than thinking only about the number of children and the ability to give birth. For it often happens that man's ability to give birth is greater than his ability to bring up children in a proper manner.

The main concern was for an improved quality of life for the entire family, especially the health of mothers and children. Although family planning activities were being carried out as far back as 1959 by the Family Planning Association of Tanzania (UMATI), an affiliate of International Planned Parenthood Federation (IPPF), it was not until 1974 that the Ministry of Health demonstrated a co-ordinated response to the president's plea by making child spacing and infertility facilities available and free of charge in all health institutions. Child spacing and infertility facilities were to be integrated into the Maternal and Child Health (MCH) program which was a part of the comprehensive national health services. Activities were to be implemented through the network of health post, health centers, and hospitals. Again the service was to rely mainly on moderately trained (eighteen months) MCH aides.

The objective of the MCH program is the detection, prevention, and treatment of conditions associated with child-birth and child-rearing. Activities include: ante-natal, natal, and post-natal services to pregnant mothers; increased surveillance of children with malnutrition through education of the masses on ways and benefits of utilizing local nutritive foods; maintenance of a high vaccination status in vulnerable age groups with effective anti-bodies against diptheria, polio, tetanus, measles, pertusis, small-pox, and tuberculosis; chloroquine distribution to vulnerable age groups for prophylactic chemo-suppression of malaria; health education on personal hygiene and environmental sanitation; child spacing practices, including the provision of contraceptives; and detection and treatment of common ailments and the referral of complicated cases to the appropriate level of the health services system. It should be noted that the MCH service was estimated to be providing services to approximately sixty percent of the eligible population in June 1979. UMATI was to continue to run a demonstration clinic in Dar es Salaam with the responsibility of providing information, education, and communication; training of MCH aides, and the provision of contraceptives. The MCH program has substantial financial and material inputs from government and non-governmental, bi-lateral and multilateral agencies.

In the implementation of their MCH program, Tanzania authorities are conscious of the presence of pockets of high incidence of infertility and low fertility, especially among minority ethnic groups. To this end a research effort is planned by the department of obstetrics and gynecology of the Muhimbili Medical Centre in collaboration with WHO to determine the distribution and possible causes of infertility within the country.

Conclusion

A brief review of the implication of an uncontrolled population growth on development (especially the developmental processes of the so-called Third World) was undertaken. Some elements of Tanzania's developmental experiences were described. The implicit concern of government for an improved quality of life that is compatible with the socio-economic developmental goals that were enshrined in the Arusha Declaration of 1967 was the rapid expansion of social services, including health to the rural areas. The Maternal and Child Health (MCH) program which was part of a comprehensive health services system provided an appropriate entry-point for the implementation of a family planning (child spacing) service to the community.

Tanzania took a bold jump forward when its leaders decided to depart from the rigidity of traditional developmental approaches that often promote stagnation in many of the developing countries. The practicability of Tanzania's approach described was conditioned by paucity of available resources. The elements that were described are not exhaustive by any chance. However, they could form a basis for replication in other settings if some of the ideas are successfully adapted to local situations. The ramifications surrounding population control activities and their relationship to the developmental processes of the emerging nations are sufficiently ominous and imminent enough to warrant the active participation and meaningful involvement of the academic community in the search for absolute value.

Notes

1. WHO official Record No. 206 Geneva 1973 p. 103.
2. WHO Weekly Epidemiological Record No. 43 Geneva 26 October 1979.
3. McNamara, Robert S., 1969 Address to the University of Notre Dame, Published by IBRD Washington.
4. Akerele, O. & Litsios S. "Development of a National Health Policy; Zimbabwe" unpublished paper.
5. Adadevah B. Kwaku, "Sub–Fertility and Infertility in Africa" The Caxton Press (West Africa) Limited Ibadan 1974.

6. Akerele, O., Dhalla A., Qhobela Q., "Country Health Profile—United Republic of Tanzania" WHO/government working document. Dar es Salaam 1979.

7. Source—Interpolated from the National Demographic Survey 1973 by BRALUP (Bureau of Resource Assessment & Land Use Planning) and from the Ministry of Health Statistic Unit. Rates from 1978 census not yet available.

8. Includes all hospitals, health centres, dispensaries, and health posts (1929 Inventory of Health Services).

9. These include medical assistants, midwives, nurses, and nursing aides. Figures for physicians have been deliberately omitted to emphasize government health manpower policy.

10. Bureau of Resource Assessment & Land Use Planning.

11. Tanganyika African National Union.

6.
Health Systems and Population Control

Gervin P. Samarawickrama

University of Sri Lanka
Peradeniya, Sri Lanka

Introduction

The population of the world is now 4,321 million. It increased by more than 1,000 million between 1950 and 1970; the increase between 1930 and 1950 was only 400 million. The rest of the population growth has increased steadily to the unprecedented current level of nearly two percent per year, which leads to a doubling of the total population within apporximately thirty-five years. The previous doubling took about fifty years; the doubling before that 110 years.[1]

The principal determinant of future population growth, the birth rate, had shown a small but steady decline in developed countries since the 1930s, and in the developing countries since about 1960.[2] The birth rate distribution is highly bimodal, falling into two distinct groups. Countries with a per capita Gross National Product (GNP) below $600 have an average birth rate of 39.2, and in countries with a per capita GNP above $600 the birth rate is half this average.[2]

The main reasons for this difference in birth rate are the relatively early age at marriage and the near universality of marriage in most developing countries. The average age at marriage of females in the Asian developing countries range from sixteen to twenty-three years. In Europe, the age of marriage is between twenty-five and twenty-nine years, and about ten to twenty percent of European women remained unmarried throughout their reproductive years. In developing countries, the corresponding proportion of unmarried women has been less than four percent.[3,4,5]

The present fertility rates in developing countries have a potential for future population growth that is explosive. While fertility rates have remained relatively stable or have declined only slowly since 1950, an unprecedented decline in mortality rates has taken place in all developing countries until the current average death rate of the world is about thirteen per 1000 population; nine in developed and fourteen in developing countries.[1] Infant mortality rates indicate that substantial mortality differences still exist between developing countries, where they are estimated to be around 140 per thousand live births, and developed countries where they are about twenty-seven.

What are the Problems?

Many of the ills of our present-day society are attributed to the rapid growth, the size, and distribution of our populations. It is difficult to disentangle the effects of population growth from the many other influences on economic growth. Population growth has made many problems harder to solve, and contributes significantly to inequality. It has made social targets, such as universal literacy or full employment, much harder to attain, and slowed down improvements in health and nutritional standards. It diminishes an individual's chances for education, and, in the competition for entry into the educational system, children from poorer backgrounds do relatively badly. When opportunities for productive employment are limited, again the poor will suffer. In many countries, population growth has started to push against the limits to cultivable land, leading to small holdings and perpetuating rural poverty and malnutrition. Those who leave rural areas for the cities increasingly find urban underemployment and wholly inadequate shelter and other amenities.

With overcrowding comes increased physical and mental illness, more crime and delinquency, and a loss of the personal identification with a neighborhood. Population increase not only creates an ugly environment but also a real and potential health hazard for ourselves and future generations. These include the problems of air, water, and soil pollution; the extensive use of pesticides; the widespread use of food additives; and the growing use and abuse of drugs. All these are in addition to the most pressing problems of housing, education, and provision of health services. New problems emerge as old ones come under control, costs rise rapidly, and adequate solutions seem to be in short supply. There are many dimensions to the problem, but basic to all of them is the inadequate investment in the resources such as manpower, facilities, organization, and research essential to the task.

Manpower shortages are evident, as shown by the doctor/patient ratio in many developing countries, e.g., in Asia three doctors per 10,000 population, compared with about fifteen to twenty per 10,000 in developed countries. Equally serious problems exist in nursing, dentistry, and in some of the allied health professions.[6] Maldistribution creates even more serious problems for many, especially for those living in rural areas. In addition to the investments needed to overcome the manpower shortages and the major changes required in the organization and delivery of health services, we must have new health policies responsive to the changing character and distribution of the population and the problems it faces.

The crisis in the delivery of health care has many manifestations. The number of women of child-bearing age (fifteen to forty-four years) is expected to rise rapidly in the next few years, an upsurge of population growth. At present, millions of women of child-bearing age receive seriously inadequate health care. The two most sensitive indicators of health care—maternal and infant mortality—indicate that the poor, the minorities, and those in the rural areas do not receive adequate care. A special problem is posed for unmarried mothers. There has been a striking increase in the number of illegitimate births during the last two decades.[7] One factor for this rapid rise may have been the advance of medical science which has produced effective chemotherapeutic and antibiotic drugs against venereal disease. There has been a sharp drop in sterility due to venereal disease during this same period. Many other factors undoubtedly contribute. One of the most important appears to be immigration of the rural poor to the cities.

There are a number of health problems directly related to

childbearing, and these are accentuated for unmarried mothers because of their inadequate health care. The problems faced by the illegitimate child are often traceable to the inadequate prenatal and maternity care provided to the mother. Unmarried pregnant women are more likely to deliver their babies outside a hospital and without medical supervision. Other health problems directly related to child bearing include the relationship among the number of pregnancies, the spreading of pregnancies, age of the parents, and a variety of socio-economic factors that influence the outcome of a pregnancy. A woman is much less likely to carry an infant to full term after her fifth pregnancy. Fetal mortality for the fifth order births is almost twice that for second order births, and it rises to three times the rate with sixth order and above.[8] Both infant mortality and mental retardation rates are higher than average for fourth and subsequent live births. Spacing of pregnancies is also important. It is found that the neonatal death rate of infants born one year or less apart is five times that for those births where the interval is two or three years.[9,10] Prematurity and immaturity have also been found more frequently where pregnancies are closely spaced. According to Siegel[11] increase in family size is associated with:

    i. increased fetal, neonatal, and postnatal mortality rates.
    ii. higher prematurity rates.
    iii. less adequate prenatal care and more limited educational aspiration for their children.
    iv. increasing incidence of infectious diseases in parents and children.
    v. poorer growth—both height and weight—among preschool and school children.
    vi. lower IQ scores among children.
    vii. increased prevalence of selected diseases among parents.

Role of Health Systems

The subject has frequently been confused by the failure to differentiate family planning and population control, and the failure to define conception control, fertility control, and population control. Family planning has focused on conception control, utilizing medical (oral contraceptives, IUCD) and non-medical (condom, rhythm method) means. The purpose is to prevent conception. Strictly speaking, these methods must be used to plan a family. There are thousands of married couples who are unable to produce children due to subfertility or infertility. Family planning methods help many of them to have children. Fertility control is the prevention of births, using contraceptive methods as well as abortion. Such measures are more suitable for mothers with heart disease and for those with several children. Population control is quite another matter and is dependent on the balance between fertility and mortality.

The role of personal health services in our present population problems and their potential role in the solutions has long been a matter of dispute. There is, however, little question that adequate health services are now an essential element in the services required to enhance the quality of life for the individual citizen.

Integration of family planning, fertility, and population control programs into health services has many administrative and technical advantages and also brings about many important educational implications. Various types of personnel may be available, such as physicians, nurses, midwives, health educators, and social workers. Their services may be used to extend coverage and to provide broader services to reach more individuals, families and community groups. It should be possible in many instances to provide the community as a whole with more comprehensive care at a lower cost. The use of existing resources and personnel can help also to prevent duplication and to avoid fragmentation of programs, and can hence serve to promote efficiency.

Where Maternal and Child Health (MCH) administrators are not given, or do not accept, responsibility for family planning, other administrators are likely to assume leadership and use the resources in this field. There is then a danger that family planning and other MCH services will not be developed in a complementary and balanced manner. It must be recognized that in both developed and developing countries some personnel are already leaving key positions in MCH for family planning work, not infrequently because higher salaries are available. A related problem is the diversion of funds from public health services and MCH into family planning, thus weakening the basic health services. At the same time, the close contact that MCH services have with mothers provides a good opportunity for family planning and population control work that is sometimes missed. Permanent services for maternal and child health, within the context of broader health services, are able to provide the continuity and follow-up that are desirable for family planning and population control efforts. Perhaps even more important, a long standing relationship of health workers with families and community groups is desirable for overcoming indifference and even apathy to family planning and population control programs.

Many methods included in these programs in some areas are too difficult or unpleasant for regular use by individuals who are not highly interested in or concerned about planning their families. In addition the major and minor side effects of many methods discourage regular use. Inadequate provision of easily accessible health services of good quality for follow-up of these conditions has served as a deterrent to increased participation by the people concerned, particularly in the rural areas where eighty percent of the population is found in developing countries.

The establishment of the concept that family planning is potentially a part of any health service to families will help to clear up some misunderstandings and to remove some discrepancies between the definition of family planning, fertility control, and population control and their purposes. In some countries, these activities began without the benefit of government health services. However, experience accumulating shows that health and medical personnel are required for the follow-up of side effects of certain methods and for continued health supervision. The voluntary agencies, especially those whose major concern is family planning, constitute important providers of services. Often the activities they initiate and promote are subsequently taken over by the official agencies. Since it is medical and health personnel who have the most knowledge of the health aspects of family planning and population control and are the most competent to deal with them, it is reasonable to conclude that these should be activities within the health services. The attitudes and advice of physicians to their patients can have a strong influence on what families do. Private physicians constitute another important element of health services in many countries. Their favorable attitude to family planning and their assistance in counseling their patients are essential to the full success of family planning and population control programs.

Integration makes it possible to provide care for girls and

women of child-bearing age at several stages during antenatal, natal, and post-partum periods, or when counseling parents and other family members on child care needs, such as nutrition and immunizations. It also provides opportunities for the continuing contacts and supervision that are necessary for successful family planning care. Many cultural beliefs, values, and traditional practices are antithetical to family planning and population control practices. In a society where a wife may be returned to her family if she does not bear several children, couples are not likely to adopt measures to space or limit their children.

Likewise, in a society where marriage occurs at an early age and the birth of a child within a reasonable period after marriage determines the suitability of the wife, or where demands to produce male offspring are paramount, measures to delay the birth of the first child or to adopt measures for child spacing or limiting before one or more male children are born are not readily accepted and practiced. The subject is surrounded also by various emotional overtones. In almost all societies, sex, pregnancy, and reproduction are associated with certain taboos. Males may discuss certain aspects with males, and females with females, but there are certain subjects in almost all cultures that cannot be discussed in mixed groups or even at all. Individuals who are influenced by these taboos may not feel free to discuss family planning with their spouse or their children. They are likely to be more reticent to discuss the subject with a health worker who is a stranger, particularly one of the opposite sex.

Regardless of the primary objective of family planning and population control, its final success depends on people, the decisions they make, and the actions they take. This dependence on people is not limited to the members of families concerned or those of reproductive age. It applies to politicians, religious and community leaders, educators and governmental authorities as well as to all health workers, public and private. In this ultimate dependence on decisions and actions of individuals, essential also in the solution of some other health problems such as nutrition, smoking and drug addition; family planning and population control differ considerably from health problems that depend for their solution mainly on a change in the environment, e.g., treatment of water supplies. A major factor in the effectiveness of population control programs is the extent to which decision-makers such as politicians support the activities, and acceptable services are made readily accessible to consumers. However, the most important factor of all is the extent to which individuals and couples become convinced of the desirability and health benefits of family planning, and voluntarily decide to take those actions that will help them to achieve their respective family goals for the betterment of their living conditions.

To achieve more effective results and to facilitate continuing family planning and population control activities within the context of health services, particularly of maternal and child health services, there is a vital need to strengthen the manpower resources, facilities, budgetary means, supplies, equipment, and administrative infrastructure of health services, including peripheral health services. Factors such as availability, suitability, and quality of services have a most important effect on people's confidence in staff and their services.

Health Education in Population Control Programs

As mentioned earlier, integration of the population control programs into general health services has important educational implications, and is best carried out by trained personnel. Health education in family planning and population control is concerned with the way people think and live and with the decisions and actions they take voluntarily to achieve the health and well-being of the family group, and thus to contribute effectively to the social development of their community, their country, and the wider world community. The objectives of such a program are:

(a) To develop within a community a social environment and attitude wherein population control is an accepted and advocated practice among leaders and opinion-moulders, in short to legitimize the practice.

One of the important educational tasks is to locate and inform the relevant local opinion-leaders who can influence the consideration and adoption of various actions.

(b) To help people comprehend the health and other values of family planning and population control and the ways in which these help to satisfy their needs and wants as a family. People would be well informed about the ways in which the planning or control of a family can help them to achieve their own goals.

(c) To make people understand that the continued observance

of family planning, population control, and associated health problems is necessary if they are to achieve the benefits they desire for their families.

This implies giving people a thorough understanding of what family health services are available, easily accessible, and within their means, and how to use various methods for family planning and other health and related measures. The information should be so complete and understandable that it will prevent subsequent doubts that might facilitate the spread of rumors by persons ill-informed or opposed to population control.

(d) To ensure that the overall plan includes provision of psychological support for those who adopt various practices that are essential for better health, including measures for child spacing and prevention of unwanted pregnancies. Sympathetic support and reassurance from health workers is an important educational stimulus for continued practice.

(e) To ensure that all family health services and contacts with staff are satisfying to the individuals. This implies providing services at a time and place convenient to the users, and in a manner that preserves human dignity. It also involves coordination of all the resources upon which people depend for their information and services, so that people have a consistently favorable experience.

Coordination of Effort

It is essential to coordinate the educational and informational efforts of a variety of national and international agencies contributing to countries' programs concerned with health and related aspects of population dynamics, family planning, and human reproduction. There are voluntary agencies in several countries making a major contribution to the overall national objective, either in coordination with or independent of official agencies. In many countries, international agencies, groups from bilateral assistance organizations, and foundations are assisting in a variety of ways. It is vitally important that educational efforts of all groups and agencies be planned jointly and carried out, so far as practicable, in a coordinated manner. For example, little benefit is derived from an information program conducted by one agency when the timing of the information is not geared to the scheduling of services by another agency.

Coordination and cooperation in educational activities require planning, whereby each agency agrees to assume responsibility for those activities it can do best with the resources at its disposal. The focus must be on the task to be done, rather than on the coordinating mechanism such as a council or committee. Too often a mechanism is developed before there is agreement on a problem and the way it should be solved, and the council or committee devotes an excessive amount of time to details of organizational structure and status. In such cases, attempts at joint program efforts are ineffective.

The objectives of health education in health aspects of family planning can be more readily attained if the health education service collaborates in the use of communication media with other agencies and organizations that are already in contact with the people through various educational activities, e.g.:

(a) Ministries of education and other agencies responsible for the education of young people and adults, e.g., literacy projects, agricultural extension services, voluntary associations, and trade unions.

(b) Ministries of information and individual media organizations, e.g., radio and television broadcasting companies, film companies, audio-visual teaching centers, and the press.

(c) Departments of schools of medicine, nursing and midwifery and environmental health, postgraduate schools of public health, and other education and training institutions for professional and auxiliary health workers.

(d) Academic departments of education, sociology, and mass communication that can contribute to the preparation of health personnel in the theory and practice of communications and education.

Notes

1. Population Reference Bureau (1979) World population data sheet. Washington D.C.
2. Population Reference Bureau (1979) World population data sheet. Washington D.C.
3. Hajnal J. (1953) "Age at marriage and proportion of marrying." In "Population Studies" Vol. 7.
4. Hajnal J. (1965) "European marriage pattern in perspective" In "Population in History" Eds. D.V. Glass and D.C.E. Eversley. Chicago Aldine Publishing Company.

5. Bogue D.J. (1969) *Principles of Demography*. John Wiley & Sons. New York City.

6. Population Reference Bureau (1979), *Children in the World*, IYC publication of the Population Reference Bureau. Washington D.C.

7. Clague A.C. and Ventura S.J. (1968) "Trends in illegitimacy" National Centre for Health Statistics. Series 21, Number 15. Washington D.C. Dept. of Health, Education and Welfare.

8. Dept. of Health, Education and Welfare (1968) "Report of the special study group on the delivery of family planning services" Washington D.C.

9. Lee P.R. (1971) "Health services and an optimum level of population" In "Is there an optimum level of population?" Ed. F. Singer. A Population Council Book, McGraw and Hill Book.

10. World Health Organization (1971) W.H.O. Technical Report Series 483.

11. Siegel E. (1969) "The biological effects of family planning. A Preventive Pediatrics: The potentials of family planning." J. Med. Educ. 44;74-80.

12. World Health Organization (1969) W.H.O. Technical Report Series No. 428.

Part III

Consequences of World Population Growth

7.

Consequences of World Population Growth on Natural Resources and Environment

Claude A. Villee, Jr.

Harvard University Medical School
Boston, Massachusetts, U.S.A.

The vast increase in the human population is due to a marked decline in mortality rates resulting from improved public health practices, without a corresponding decrease in birth rates. Whether we limit our perspective to the effects of high fertility on individuals and families or to the aggregate effects of high fertility on nations, the world community, the world's natural resources, and our environment, it is clear that improved regulation of fertility and a reduction in fertility rates must be urgent objectives in both industrial and developing nations. Millions of individuals are unable to regulate pregnancy adequately to determine whether they will bear children and when their children will be born. This has contributed to the current unprecedented rate of growth of the world population that is retarding economic development in many nations. The high fertility rate is also a major factor associated with the increased incidence of such adverse outcomes of pregnancy as prematurity, infant mortality, mental retardation, congenital defects, maternal mortality and morbidity, the unwanted child, and child abuse. The causes of our inability to regulate pregnancy range from our ignorance of many aspects of the basic biological processes of reproduction to the grinding poverty and malnutrition that affect many of the people in this world.

Last year throughout the world approximately 375 million humans were conceived. Of these, perhaps 175 million terminated in spontaneous miscarriages and stillbirths, about 60 million were terminated by induced abortion and the remainder, about 140 million, resulted in live births. Some forty to sixty million of these births were neither planned nor wanted by the parents at the time of conception. As we become more aware of the problem of child abuse, we realize that a major cause of child abuse is the parents' reaction to a child that was not wanted in the first place. Of the 140 million babies born, 25 million were born prematurely, and many of these are unlikely to survive or to grow normally. About fifteen million died before the end of their first year and an additional twenty million are expected to die before age fifteen. At least seven million had chromosomal abnormalities, hereditary biochemical disorders, or major congenital defects, resulting in handicaps that are either untreatable or require intensive and sophisticated health resources. Some four to five million were seriously retarded, and most of these will remain retarded as long as they live. An unknown but large number of infants were malnourished either pre- or post-natally, increasing the risk of retardation and chronic debilitating illness. Some 220,000 women died before the gestational period was completed or during parturition. An unknown but large number of women suffered from malnutrition, anemia, infection or chronic illness, and about thirty million experienced serious illness or complications of pregnancy and delivery.

A major medical concern at the present time is the large and increasing number of pregnancies among teenage women. Nearly twenty percent of all the children born in this country were born to women under the age of twenty. One in every three abortions in the United States is a teenager. Early parenthood has marked negative effects on the life and career plans of both parents, but especially on the female. Consider the impact of pregnancy on the prospects of an unmarried American adolescent at age sixteen. She is faced with the difficult choice of terminating the pregnancy or carrying it to term. If she chooses the latter, she faces, in addition to increased health risks because of her age, consequences such as dropping out of school and not completing her education. She will bear an out-of-wedlock child or rush into a precipitous, perhaps unwanted, marriage. Either course severely limits her chances to obtain employment and establish a career. Teenage marriages have a greater than fifty percent probability of ending in divorce.

Bearing children at too young or too old an age, or too close together, or having too many children are all factors contributing to adverse outcomes of pregnancy, increasing maternal mortality and morbidity, fetal malformations, and congenital defects. Unplanned and unwanted pregnancies are particularly prevalent among women less than twenty or more than forty years old. The risks of adverse health outcomes are greatest and the socioeconomic consequences are most acute when the woman is less than eighteen or more than thirty-five years old. If it were possible to avoid all unwanted births in the United States, there would be fewer babies born with chromosome defects such as Downs Syndrome; there would be reduced perinatal mortality and greatly reduced maternal mortality.

The total population of the world is growing at present at an annual rate of about two percent, a rate without precedent in history. From the appearance of the human species on earth up until early historical times, the rate of increase averaged nearly zero, perhaps plus 0.002 percent per annum. By the middle of the 1700s the average annual rate of growth had increased to about 0.3 percent. The rate has accelerated since then and reached one percent in the 1950s and doubled to two percent in the 1970s.

Birth rates obviously are far from uniform among and within nations. They are higher in developing nations than in industrial countries, and within each country they are typically higher among the poorest and least educated segments of the population. In developing countries, which include more than two-thirds of the world's population, annual growth rates average 2.5 percent and reach as high as 3.4 percent. These are extraordinarily high by any kind of historical standard and greatly exceed the rates of growth in Europe during the nineteenth and twentieth centuries. This unprecedented rapid growth of population is related to problems of national development, food supply, depletion of natural resources, and degradation of the environment.

The term "development" includes all of the complex transformations of the entire social order as a traditional agrarian society is transformed into an industrialized society. Every national and social system is committed to policies and programs that will reduce mortality levels, and thus the only way of reducing growth rates involves the reduction of fertility. A decline in fertility increases the rate of development of a nation by reducing the burden of child dependency which, in the short run, permits a higher level of productive investment and makes less difficult the provision of employment opportunities. In the long run, reducing fertility restrains the over-all levels of growth in population size and density, and reduces the increased social demands that these carry with them.

The severe shortages of food in many parts of the world have led to widespread malnutrition and famine. Changes in climate and economic and political factors play a role in this, but a major cause is the increase in the size of the population. This has led to increased cultivation of less fertile land and more intensive cultivation of present farm land. These require major inputs of capital, energy, fertilizer, and technology. The balance between food supply and demand has become more delicate, so that some minor fluctuation in climate or productivity can trigger a complex reaction of price change and supply. A major question is how the world will be able to feed a doubled population by the year 2010.

A striking model of the biological catastrophe and accompanying environmental disaster that results from overpopulation was provided by the Kaibab deer. In 1907 a group of some 4,000 deer lived on the isolated Kaibab Plateau on the north side of the Grand Canyon of the Colorado River, along with a considerable population of mountain lions, wolves, and other predators. In 1907 a concerted effort was made to protect the deer by killing off these predators. Although there was no increase in birth rate the decreased mortality rate increased the deer population tremendously. By 1925 some 100,000 deer lived on the plateau, far too many for the supply of vegetation. The deer ate everything in reach—grass, tree seedlings, shrubs, and branches of the trees, and there was intense damage to the vegetation and denuding of the soil. The vegetation was insufficient to support the deer population and in the next two winters vast numbers of deer starved to death. The deer population fell to less than 10,000, and there were irreversible changes in the vegetation.

The intensive cultivation of soil needed to feed our ever-increasing population has taken its toll of the land available for farming. Wind and water have caused soil erosion through all geological ages, but unwise farming and forestry practices have greatly increased the rate of erosion in many parts of the globe. The destructive exploitation of farm lands by planting a single crop, such as corn or cotton, year after year has damaged certain areas and resulted in erosion and depletion of soil nutrients. The great increase in agricultural production termed "The Green Revolution" has been accomplished with the use of fertilizers, irrigation, pest control, and genetic selection of specific strains of high-yield crop plants, such as wheat and rice. This industrialization of agriculture requires the input of large amounts of energy. Doubling the crop yield, for example, is achieved only by a ten-fold increase in the use of fertilizers, pesticides, and fuel economy. As a result, industrialized agriculture is a major user of energy and a major producer of air and water pollution.

The productivity of the Western Atlantic off the coast of North America is two and one-half to three and one-half tons of organic carbon produced per year per acre of surface. The productivity of an average forest is about one ton per acre, and most cultivated land fixes only about three-quarters of a ton of organic carbon per acre. Only the very rich and intensively cultivated corn fields of Ohio produce as much as four tons of organic carbon per acre. Despite the high productivity of the ocean, our actual harvest from the ocean in terms of the mass of fish caught per acre of surface is very low. Only the rich fishing grounds of the North Sea produce as much as fifteen pounds of fish per acre. The ecological reasons are very clear—the fish are secondary or tertiary consumers and are on the top of a vast pyramid of producers. Many organisms, in addition to the edible fish and crustacea harvested from the sea, compete for the food energy fixed by the algae. The annual harvest of marine fish over the entire globe was eighteen million tons in 1938. This reached seventy million tons in 1970, but, because of overfishing, has been declining rapidly since then. Almost eighty percent of the fish harvest comes from the North Atlantic, the Northern and Western Pacific, and off the West Coast of Peru and Ecuador in South America. About half of this harvest is used as human food, the remainder is used as food for pets, poultry, and livestock.

Because it was assumed that the supply of mineral resources

would last for centuries to come and that there was no way of conserving them, little attention has been paid to this aspect of conservation. However, neither of these assumptions is correct. The relationship between the resources available and their utilization is expressed by the demographic quotient "Q," with the total resources available in the numerator and the population density times the per capita consumption in the denominator. The quality of life decreases as the quotient "Q" goes down, and it is decreasing rapidly at present. Even if the total resources available could be kept constant by recycling, the value of "Q" would continue to decrease as the population density increases and as the per capita consumption increases. The utilization of natural resources in the United States is increasing at about ten percent per year. The demands of iron, copper, lead, tin, and even aluminum are such that the country is no longer self-sufficient, either in mineral resources or in the fossil fuels needed to extract the new mineral resources. We are all greatly concerned at the moment over the exhaustion of energy sources, such as oil or natural gas, but the depletion of our mineral resources should be of equal concern. In our utilization of natural resources, we have typically used first those resources which are least expensive and most easily obtained. As these become exhausted, we must turn to alternative sources which usually require much more capital investment and much greater input of energy.

The earth's supplies of natural gas and petroleum will be depleted in a relatively few decades, and our supply of coal will last for a few more centuries. There are at present no feasible means of generating substantial amounts of electricity either by solar power or by wind power, and, ultimately, whether we like it or not, we will have to rely on nuclear power.

The limiting factor in the utilization of industrial energy will probably be pollution rather than supply. The ultimate cause of pollution is people, and, as the number of people increases, there is a corresponding increase in the amount of pollution. The number of people has increased, the amount of energy used by each person per year has increased, and total energy consumption has increased at a very high rate. This is reflected in the air pollutants from the exhaust stacks of industrial plants and electric generating plants burning fossil fuel, and from the exhaust gases of automobiles transporting people to and from their work and play.

The National Academy of Sciences defined pollution as "an undesirable change in the physical, chemical, or biological characteristics of our air, land, and water that may or will harmfully affect human life or that of desirable species, and that may harmfully affect our raw material resources." Pollutants are residues of the things we make, use, and throw away. Pollution increases not only because, as people multiply, the space available to each person becomes smaller, but also because the demands per person are continually increasing so that each throws away more year by year. As the earth becomes more crowded, there is no longer an "away." One person's trash basket is another person's living space.

From an ecological viewpoint we can recognize two types of pollution—that involving biodegradable pollutants and that involving nondegradable pollutants. Biodegradable pollutants, such as domestic sewage, can be decomposed rapidly by natural processes or by a carefully engineered sewage treatment plant. Problems arise when the input of degradable pollutants exceeds the environment's capacity to decompose or disperse them. Urban populations have grown much faster than their sewage treatment facilities. There are limits to the total amount of organic matter that can be decomposed in a given area and an over-all limit to the amount of carbon dioxide that can be released into the air. The nondegradable pollutants include metals, such as mercury, trace metals, iron, and aluminum together with a few organic chemicals, such as DDT, that are degraded only very slowly.

Although the pollution of the air over the entire world is serious enough, the most striking aspect of air pollution is the local concentration of pollutants that may occur over large cities such as Los Angeles, Mexico City, and Tokyo during a temperature inversion. The kinds of pollutants and their relative proportions vary from place to place, but they usually include carbon monoxide, oxides of nitrogen and sulfur, hydrocarbons, particulate matter, and lead. Certain combinations of pollutants may react in the environment to produce additional pollution. Certain components in automobile exhaust can combine in the presence of sunlight to produce the more toxic photochemical smog. One component of photochemical smog blocks a key reaction in photosynthesis and kills plants by inhibiting the production of food.

It is clear that, if we are to raise enough food crops to supply our burgeoning population, we must have some way of dealing with the insect pests that are competing for this same supply of food. Further, we must protect ourselves against the diseases transmitted by insects: malaria, yellow fever and dengue transmitted by mosquitoes; sleeping sickness transmitted by tsetse flies; plague transmitted by fleas; typhus transmitted by fleas, ticks or mites; and typhoid which is frequently transmitted by flies. We must continue, therefore, to use effective insecticides. When insecticides are used unwisely or overenthusiastically, two undesirable effects may appear. Strains of insects develop which are resistant to the pesticides, and toxic materials accumulate in the food chain. Chemical insecticides must be used only in appropriate areas and amounts, and with adequate controls. Some insects can be controlled by supplying hormonal factors, such as juvenile hormone which prevents the insect from completing its life cycle, or by using sex lures and other pheromones to confuse the reproductive efforts of the insects. For many insects, however, the only effective countermeasures are chemical insecticides. If all chemical pesticides were banned, the agricultural production of the United States would decrease by thirty percent or more. Food prices would soar, and there would be a distinct danger of starvation in this country. The developing nations of the world would probably suffer even more from disease and hunger than the developed nations if chemical insecticides were banned.

Most human beings now live in urban areas where there is not only greater air pollution, but the climate is modified by urbanization. The absorption of solar radiation by vertical surfaces and the production of heat by the many machines in a city cause the air temperature in a city to be one to three degrees higher and the humidity to be about six percent lower than in the surrounding countryside. Because of the particulates in the air, cloudiness will be ten percent greater, and there will be thirty to one hundred percent more fog with the higher value occurring during the winter months. Precipitation will be ten percent greater, and there will be fifteen percent less sunshine and ten to thirty percent less ultraviolet radiation in the city than in the countryside.

The average population density in the United States in 1970 was one person to every ten acres of ice-free land. The average population density of the world was at this same level. Even if the anticipated reduction in birth rate occurs, the population of the United States will double in the next thirty years, and there will be only five acres of land for every man, woman, and child. The production of a diet that includes meat, fruits, and vegetables requires at least one and one-half acres per person. Another acre is required to produce the paper, wood, and cotton needed by each person, and an additional half-acre is needed for the roads, railroads, airports, buildings, and other areas not involved in food production. Only about two acres per person remain for all of the many other uses that humans have for land. The key in determining the maximum human population density should be adequate and useable pollution-free living space and not simply how much land is needed to provide the food. E.P. Odum in his *Textbook of Ecology* said, "This earth can feed more warm bodies sustained as so many domestic animals in a polluted feedlot than it can support human beings who have a right to life in a pollution free environment, a reasonable chance for personal liberty, and a variety of options of the pursuit of happiness." He believes that at least one-third of all land should remain protected for use as national, state, or municipal parks, greenbelts, wild-life refuges, wilderness areas, and so on.

The human population is clearly in danger of multiplying beyond the ability of the earth to support it. The population explosion is not due to an increased birth rate, but to a decreased death rate which has resulted from improved public health measures, such as pure drinking water, pasteurized milk, and improved sewage disposal, together with improvements in medical practice and drugs, such as antibiotics. The rate of population increase is greater in some nations than in others and is generally greater in the less developed nations. Some nations, such as Taiwan, Singapore, and Greenland, have taken effective measures to decrease the rate of population increase. The productivity and carrying capacity of the earth for human beings can be maintained and perhaps increased somewhat, but eventually the human biomass must be brought into equilibrium with the space and food available. The continued explosive growth of the human population has forced us to consider the ultimate limitations of the earth, rather than simply local limitations. The planet earth is simply a big spaceship with finite limits to its productivity and to its ability to cope with pollutants. A key question in human ecology is whether we are in greater danger of running out of resources or being overcome by polluted air and water. It is becoming clear that technology alone cannot solve the problems of population and pollution. In addition, moral, economic, and legal constraints are required—ones which arise from full and complete public understanding that human beings and the environment are a unit. The technological advances to solve many aspects of the population and pollution problems have been made. What is urgently needed now is a general worldwide appreciation of the nature of the problem, and a willingness on the part of everyone to apply ecological principles for the benefit of all. This will require the use of principles and techniques from economics, law, politics, urban planning, and other areas of humanistic science to solve our ecological problems.

8.

Consequences of World Population Growth: Labor, Migration, and International Trade

Paul Demeny

Center for Policy Studies
The Population Council
New York, New York, U.S.A.

℉ uture population growth patterns, even if contemplated in the relatively short time perspective terminating at the end of the 1980s and only on the level of such massive geographic aggregates as the economically more developed and the less developed countries (to be referred to here, for the sake of brevity, as "North" and "South"), are uncertain. The cause of uncertainty, in part, is lack of precision in the estimates of the current levels and recent trends on which demographic projections must be built. More significantly, it is impossible to predict the most important component of future demographic change—fertility—with accuracy and assurance. An outline of the most salient population growth patterns that are likely to affect trends in the growth of the labor force, migration, and international trade in the 1980s may then be best attempted by focusing on the relatively fixed features of the demographic terrain that lies ahead.

Patterns of World Population Growth

Up to 1990, projections of the adult population—which, conveniently if somewhat arbitrarily, may be defined as the population of age fifteen and older—are exempt from the major potential errors that may affect predictions of the total population or of its most youthful component. In discussing the economic issues at hand, it will be therefore preferable to concentrate on expected trends of the adult population only. The need to keep our presentation of demographic facts within manageable limits imposes further selectivity—a focus on the demographic changes most salient for our discussion of the impact of demographic change on North-South differentials bearing on labor force trends, migration, and international trade. Examination of the coming demographic shifts with respect to widening North-South differences—a structural feature of prime importance within the world economy—as well as considerations of the flow of new entrants into adulthood as an influence on economic structure, clearly identifies a broad younger segment of the adult population —those age fifteen to twenty-nine—as of special salience.

Table 1 presents the estimated and projected populations aged fifteen to twenty-nine in 1960, 1975, and 1990 by regional groupings that divide each of the two broad categories of development status—North and South—into six country subgroups.

The table, which indicates both average annual rates of growth of the young adult population and absolute increases during the two successive fifteen-year periods bracketed by 1960 and 1990, supplies dramatic evidence that, with respect to regional differentials, the demographic dynamics of the post-1975 period will be anything but a replay with small variants of those experienced in the 1960s and early 1970s. Expansion of the young adult population during the period 1960 to 1975 was vigorous or exceptionally rapid, in both the North and the South, with Japan providing the sole exception among subregions, at least on the level of aggregation shown in the table. Northern America, Oceania, and Latin America showed the highest annual growth rates—in excess of three percent—but growth of the young adult population was nearly as rapid in the remainder of the South, and rapid or fairly rapid in the Union of Soviet Socialist Republics and in Eastern and Western Europe. During the entire period, growth in the South amounted to forty-five percent, and in the North to twenty-seven percent.

Between 1975 and 1990, this picture is certain to change radically. In Northern America, Eastern Europe, the Union of Soviet Socialist Republics, and Japan, projected growth not only ceases but turns into decline: in Eastern Europe the young adult population decreases by as much as .5 percent per year. Western Europe sees its former moderate growth halved, to below the .5 percent annual level. In contrast, with the exception of China, whose growth rate is also sharply cut, and of Latin America, whose growth rate decreases slightly, growth of the young adult population accelerates appreciably in each of the less developed country subgroups, reaching in all regions, except China, an average annual level of 2.8 to 3.1 percent. For many reasons concerning the economic impact of such changes, magnitudes of growth are of greater interest. Between 1975 and 1990, the total gain in the number of young adults in the North is projected as less than two million. In contrast, the expected gain in the South amounts to 334 million. As a result of these cumulative changes, the numerical differences between the number of young adults in the South and in the North will have changed from 312 million in 1960 to 824 million in 1990.

It is notable, furthermore, that much of the contrast will emerge in full force only in the 1980s. A breakdown of the absolute change for the three quinquennia of the period 1975-90 is presented for the six country subgroups of the North in Table 2. During the current quinquennium now drawing to its end, the earlier dynamics of the expansion of the young adult population was still continuing. In particular, in the Union of Soviet Socialist Republics and Northern America, growth of the 15-29 age group has been still substantial. By the early 1980s, however, gain turns into absolute numerical loss, and the trend will intensify in the latter half of the decade. For the North as a whole the 1975-80 gain of 10.7 million contrasts with the 1985-90 net change of -6.4 million. The table shows only aggregate figures for the South, since the variance of absolute changes over the three successive segments of the period is modest.

As to the dynamics of the entire adult population, by 1990 its global size is expected to exceed 3.4 billion, of which over 900 million will have been added in the preceding fifteen years. The corresponding growth of the adult population excluding those over age sixty—that is, roughly growth within the labor force ages—will amount to three-quarters of a billion persons. About

Table 1

Size, Average Annual Growth Rate, and Absolute Increase of the Young Adult Population (Ages 15–29) by World Regions, 1960–1990

REGION	Young Adult Population (millions)			Growth Rate (percent)		Absolute Increase (millions)	
	1960	1975	1990	1960–75	1975–90	1960–75	1975–90
Northern America	39.3	63.9	62.0	3.24	−0.20	24.6	−1.9
Western Europe	71.3	82.2	88.1	0.95	0.46	10.9	5.9
Eastern Europe	21.6	26.4	24.3	1.34	−0.55	4.8	−2.1
Soviet Union	52.1	65.3	64.9	1.51	−0.94	13.2	−0.4
Japan	26.0	27.7	27.1	0.42	−0.15	1.7	−0.6
Oceania	2.6	4.3	5.1	3.35	1.14	1.7	0.8
North	212.9	269.8	271.5	1.58	0.04	56.9	1.7
China	158.7	230.9	273.8	2.50	1.14	72.2	42.9
South East Asia	66.4	93.2	147.6	2.26	3.07	26.8	54.4
South Asia	151.6	212.8	328.3	2.26	2.89	61.2	115.5
West Asia/N. Africa	36.2	55.4	87.8	2.84	3.07	19.2	32.4
Sub-Saharan Africa	58.3	83.3	127.5	2.38	2.84	25.0	44.2
Latin America	54.0	85.8	130.7	3.09	2.81	31.8	44.9
South	525.3	761.4	1095.8	2.47	2.43	236.1	334.4
WORLD TOTAL	738.2	1031.3	1367.3	2.23	1.88	293.0	336.0

Source: Population Council Data Bank, based on United Nations Estimates

eighty-nine percent of this growth will accrue to the population of
the South.

Consequences of World Population Growth

The fifteen-year period 1960-75 witnessed an unprecedented
expansion of the world economy. Despite the major disturbances
of the early and mid-1970s, total output increased rapidly in both
major regions, but, in relative (but not in absolute) terms, faster
in the low-income South. Rapid population growth, however,
more than negated gains toward narrowing the vast North-South
relative income gap in per capita terms. Such an influence of
differential demographic rates is likely to be repeated and amplified during 1975-90, especially if a slowdown in aggregate economic expansion imparts greater numerical significance to the
effect of differential demographic growth. However, it would be
wrong to see the economic influence of the demographic growth
may exert on the speed and structure of economic expansion
itself. While demographic influence on that process is obviously
only one among many influences, in the coming years the pure
demographic impact on the relative development of North and
South is bound to be greater than at any time in recent history.
Additions to the adult population of labor force age during
1975-90 will amount to nearly 700 million persons in the South
but barely 80 million in the North. In the latter region, expansion
in the number of young adults virtually comes to a halt, while in
the South 1.1 billion persons are expected to be of age fifteen to
twenty-nine in 1990—a figure of some 330 million greater than in
1975. In and of themselves the estimates just quoted are indicators of major structural shifts taking place in the contemporary
world. Our concern here is with their influence on labor force
growth, international migration, and trade.

Differences in relative factor endowments that widen relative
differentials of labor productivity and per capita income between
North and South are likely to intensify in the 1980s. As to
endowments in nonreproducible resources, including land, this
is an almost automatic consequence of sharply differing rates of
natural increase of the adult population, since these rates imply
broadly similar contrasts in the rates of labor force growth. As to
capital-labor ratios, existing absolute North-South differentials
are likely to widen further. This is so mainly because, owing to

Table 2

Quinquennial Absolute Change of the Young Adult Population (Ages 15–29) By World Regions, 1975–1990 (millions)

REGION	1975–80	1980–85	Total 1985–90	1975–90
Northern America	3.7	−1.7	−3.9	−1.9
Western Europe	3.6	2.8	−0.5	5.9
Eastern Europe	−0.1	−1.2	−0.8	−2.1
Soviet Union	5.6	−2.3	−3.7	−0.4
Japan	−2.5	−0.3	2.2	−0.6
Oceania	0.3	0.2	0.3	0.8
North	10.7	−2.6	−6.4	1.7
South	112.9	104.8	116.7	334.4
WORLD TOTAL	123.5	102.2	110.3	336.1

Source: See Table 1.

the underlying differences in demographic growth, the costs of equipping increments to the labor force (including capital costs of training) will claim a much smaller portion of capital accumulation in the North, leaving by the same token a wider scope for increasing capital per head and permitting replacement of capital before full physical obsolescence. These circumstances will tend to hinder successful exploitation by the South of such advantages of relative economic backwardness as opportunities for rapid acquisition of new skills and adoption of already existing advanced technology. Furthermore, particularly in densely populated areas, such needs of the expanding population that cannot be advantageously met or safely assured through international trade may necessitate investments (e.g., in food and energy production, and in infrastructure) that are highly capital-intensive on the margin (e.g., in fertilizer production, dry-land irrigation, offshore oil exploration, and environmental sanitation schemes) and that would not have been necessary or could have been postponed, had population size been expanding more slowly.

The preceding comments, which imply sharpening relative North-South differentials in per capita income during the 1980s, assume that the North will successfully neutralize potentially deleterious effects of the appreciable deceleration of the growth of the adult population in general, and of the cessation of growth (and perhaps incipient decrease) of the young adult population in particular. Undoubtedly, the relatively vigorous postwar demographic growth in the North—amplified by the availability of not yet fully tapped labor reserves in agriculture in almost all countries, by the increasing labor force participation of women, and, in a number of instances, by the admittance of significant numbers of migrant labor—has had strongly positive effects on the growth of aggregate income. Demographic expansion both helped sustain aggregate demand and permitted flexible supply responses. However, economic policies capable of appropriately managing both of these factors are readily envisaged. Thus, while the demographic transformation the North is now experiencing will inevitably slow expansion of aggregate output, it should have the opposite effect on income per head. The transformation should also facilitate rather than retard the structural transition toward a postindustrial economy, ease problems of unemployment, and alleviate environmental and resource pressures, or at least check the costs of coping with them.

In contrast, rapid demographic growth will tend to perpetuate or at least retard elimination of the dualistic character of many of the national economies of the South. The often impressive gains registered by less developed countries during 1960-75, even in per capita terms, are often due mainly to the rapid expansion of the modern—typically urban-industrial—sector of the national economy, which looms large in its contribution to total income in national accounts but engages only a small fraction of the total national labor force. Continued rapid expansion of this sector (including its modern service sector component) by drawing away labor from the low-productivity sectors—notably from traditional agriculture and from marginal urban and rural service activities—and by mopping up outright unemployment would eventually do away with economic dualism, and create an integrated, modern, high-productivity and high-income economy. However, continued rapid replenishment of the traditional sectors through demographic growth, in addition to the sustained rapid natural increase of the population of labor force age within the modern sector itself, tends to make the process of economic modernization unduly difficult and protracted. Given the small relative size of the modern sector and its high capital-labor ratios, and an annual increase on the order of two and one half to three percent in the total population of labor force age, even a very rapid growth in the modern sector will not absorb more than a fraction of the annual additions to the number of potential job-seekers. A very large proportion of these additions, therefore, will have to be accommodated within either the rural areas or the low-productivity urban subsectors. Both solutions are painful and fraught with undesirable economic and social consequences.

Even in the absence of rapid population growth, the process of modernization imposes a heavy strain on the social fabric of transitional societies. In the political sphere, by concentrating disproportionate power in the hands of a small urban-industrial elite—a tendency reinforced by prevailing etatist ideologies and by the temptations of modern technologies of communication and social control—it creates exploitative relationships and generates intense class antagonisms. In the economic sphere, by decasualizing employer-employee relationships in industry, by undercutting the economic base of handicrafts, and by commercializing the agricultural sector, modernization tends to create open unemployment in urban areas and, in the countryside, an increasing underclass of marginal cultivators, landless laborers, and a rural lumpenproletariat. At the same time, it erodes the age-old informal networks of mutual obligation and support that have provided a measure of security to members of the traditional society. Historically, these familiar concomitants of early industrialization have proven both manageable and transient. However, if aggravated and amplified by the impact of exceptionally rapid population growth, such problems could become major and prolonged social ills. The resultant stresses that will be experienced by many countries of the South will reach unprecedented proportions in the coming decade. In the 1980s, rapid population growth will be a major factor contributing to polarizing the population into competing economic classes, to widening income inequalities, and to sharpening political conflicts.

As was shown in the first section of this paper, the major numerical shifts now taking place in the regional distribution of the world population in favor of the South will further accelerate in the 1980s. These shifts—OPEC, Taiwan, Singapore, and other success stories notwithstanding—will be paralleled by further widening of the overall material advantage of the world's Northern tier. In a world made small by modern means of transportation and communication, the resulting disparity is bound to introduce an increasingly powerful source of tension and antagonism between North and South. The means that are presently available to mitigate this tension seem plainly inferior.

In a 1980s perspective, to set store by the potentials of population policy intervention is not particularly helpful. A liberal international migration policy could be a significant equalizer of relative economic fortunes, for there is little doubt that open frontiers would generate major South to North population movements. Equally plainly, the North's tolerance of policy changes in that direction is narrowly circumscribed. Despite the significant increase of international migration flows, particularly of labor migration during the last two decades, these flows represent only a minor equalizing influence on relative North-South income levels. With respect to labor markets, North and South remain effectively de-linked.

In contrast, purposeful social intervention to affect future fertility trends is likely not only to have great potential importance, but also to command increasing agreement on both sides of the North-South divide. However, any major beneficial economic and welfare effects (in contrast to costs) can be expected from fertility policy only after a time lag of at least a decade and a half. The most important demographic process in the 1980s—growth of the population of labor-force age—is now beyond the reach of population policy intervention. It is a case, for better or worse, of chickens coming home to roost.

In population matters, then, the immediate task for the 1980s is to accommodate the inevitable growth while drawing lessons for wise long-term policy. This is primarily a task within the competence of national states. However, the success of national endeavors will be greatly affected by North-South arrangements for trade relations, for transfers of capital and technology, and to a much lesser degree, by policies regulating international labor migration.

As to North-South trade, the population shifts discussed above are less than auspicious. The North's sluggish demographic growth has a dampening effect on demand for important classes of potential Southern exports, at the very time when Southern competition for Northern markets is increasing. Conversely, the headlong demographic expansion in the South has contributed to making that region increasingly dependent on Northern exports

103

of a key commodity: foodgrains. Thus, other things being equal, the demographic factor tends to shift the terms of North-South trade against the South. Still, it is obvious that in all recent Southern success stories, exploitation of the potential gains from international trade has played a central role. Northern willingness to encourage and accept would-be imitators of such trade-oriented development policies, even if the imitator is a country in the 100-million rather than 10-million population class, could make a major contribution to successfully accommodating Southern population pressures.

As to capital and technology transfers, contemporary discussions accord disproportionate attention to various forms of government-to-government aid, even though the magnitude of such flows in real terms has never been very large, and, in recent years, has been declining. While aid has probably acquired an enduring legitimate function in international economic relations, its checkered past performance is too well known to inspire confidence as a major tool for lessening disparities of income and welfare, either internationally or within the recipient countries. Capital and technology transfers through the time-honored methods of international commerce are bound to remain far more important. Yet their magnitude in the contemporary world still falls far short of what would seem to be warranted, both on the basis of the extreme differences in factor proportions between labor-abundant South and capital-rich North, and on the basis of comparisons with the volume of capital flows that financed the industrialization of the United States, Canada, or Australia during the late nineteenth and early twentieth centuries. Devising new institutional arrangements that would foster greatly increased North-South capital transfers and assure their economically efficient and politically benign use should make the major international contribution during the 1980s in helping the South to cope with the consequences of man's past procreative miscalculations.

Part IV

Financial and Societal Disincentives for Population Growth

9.
China's "One-Child Family" Program

Claude A. Villee, Jr.

Harvard University Medical School
Boston, Massachusetts, U.S.A.

Worldwide attention has focused on the population policies of the People's Republic of China, that include the financial and societal disincentives that are termed China's "One Child" Program. China's present population policy has evolved over the past 35 years in response to the economic and political changes the country has undergone. At the close of the communist revolution in 1949, China's population was estimated to be about 450 million. The new government initially embraced the traditional Marxist view that overpopulation is not a problem for a socialist state since "overpopulation is the reaction to unequal distribution of wealth and the result of capitalist methods of production." The government assumed that China would undergo rapid economic development when China's semifeudalistic system was abolished and when foreign exploitation ceased. It was believed that human labor could be used to compensate for lack of capital equipment and advanced technology, so that when China's economy advanced to the status of an advanced industrial state the size of the population would be an asset rather than a liability. The national census of 1953 revealed that the population numbered 586 million, 136 million more than had been assumed, and the government recalculated the production of grain needed to feed a population of that size.

A statement was issued at the Seventh National Congress of the Communist Party (March, 1955) that gave limited support to birth control. A recognizable program of birth control began in 1956 and continued until 1958. Because of its major emphasis on the urban population, the program was ineffective. It relied on propaganda campaigns and included the distribution of free contraceptives. The stated incentives for birth control were simply those of self interest: too many children are unhealthy for the mother, early marriage slows one's advancement, and fewer children raise the family's living standard. These proved to be too weak in a traditionally pro-natal culture such as China's. The program suffered further from the poor quality of the contraceptive devices available, resentment over outside interference with their lives, fears of the public regarding the possible effects of contraceptives on health, and the lack of an effective family planning organization, especially in rural areas.

The "Great Leap Forward," introduced by Chairman Mao Tse-Tung in 1958, noticeably lacked any component for population planning, and the ineffective program instituted two years earlier withered and died. However, Mao himself was in favor of controlling population, for in 1957 he endorsed zero population growth as an absolute necessity for the advancement of China.

The Great Leap Forward proved to be an inefficient and disorganized crash economic program that resulted in decreased rather than increased industrial and agricultural production. Famines occurred in the land. During the early years of the Great Leap Forward, there was a resurgence of pronatalism and discussion of the possibility of future labor shortages. However, during the program there was an overall reduction in population growth which may have achieved zero population growth, caused by a rising death rate and falling birth rate, caused by the tremendous disruptions of Chinese life.

The new economic policy of 1967 included a family planning program that administratively resembled that of 1956-1958. It did, however, initiate a formal system to teach birth control methods and the ideology of population planning. It popularized the intrauterine device (IUD) and included an element of coercion into family planning. Despite these changes the program again was ineffective in rural areas.

The Socialist Education Movement, introduced in 1962, em-

108

phasized the direct involvement of the peasants into the design and implementation of family planning. It involved a variety of women's organizations to organize and carry out the family planning program, and provided increased opportunities for women to have jobs outside the home as an incentive for women to practice birth control. The health care network was reorganized as a channel for educating the populace in family planning and reemphasizing the need for political education, participation, and control. There was a favorable response to this plan, and in June 1965 Mao stated that the health services would in the future concentrate on the rural population and that the health services would serve as a means for teaching fertility control. This Socialist Education Movement was disrupted by the Cultural Revolution of 1967, and the manufacture and distribution of contraceptives broke down. The weakened level of party control permitted earlier marriages. The program was not abandoned entirely, however, and by 1969 the People's Republic of China was promoting oral contraceptives which had been developed during the second half of the 1960s. As the Cultural Revolution and the turmoil associated with it became a thing of the past, a reorganized system for the delivery of health care was established that included an educational program for family planning. This program was extended in 1971 with the introduction of the *wan, hsi, shao* campaign (later, longer, fewer) which called for delayed marriages, greater spacing between babies, and fewer babies in total. This campaign incorporated the best features of the various previous programs and aimed at both urban and rural populations. Along with a greatly expanded system for the distribution of contraceptives, it included some coercive measures. The program was effective in reducing the rate of natural increase from 2.3 percent in 1971 to 1.2 percent in 1978. Even with the success of this plan the population of China continued to increase, and in 1979 the government was shocked to find that the nation's population exceeded one billion. Moreover, population projections for the year 2000, even with the reduced growth rate, indicated that the population would exceed 1.28 billion. The implications of these figures for the future economic success of the regime led the party leadership to introduce the One Child Program in 1979. The program was outlined in a newspaper article written by Chen Muhhua, the vice-premier in charge of population planning and the woman with the highest position in the Chinese government.

The goals of the One Child Program are to reduce the rate of natural increase to 0.5 percent by 1985, and to achieve zero population growth by the year 2000. To achieve these goals the government has instituted a broad range of incentives and disincentives. Vice-Premier Chen states the first objective of the program is to "reduce and then eliminate altogether the phenomenon of multiparity." A multichild tax is imposed on those couples who have a third child except as a result of a multiple birth at the second confinement. Third children are ineligible for a variety of medical and other benefits. Eliminating multiparity would reduce the birth rate to about thirteen per thousand in 1986, and decrease the natural rate of increase to less than 0.7 percent. Promoting the practice of having only one child is the primary method by which the rate of natural increase can be brought down to zero, stated Vice-Premier Chen.

A complex system of incentives and penalties, which vary in different localities, was implemented to encourage the ideal of one child. Parents who make a pledge to have only one child receive an allowance for health care for five years that amounts to more than ten percent of their annual income. They are further given priority enrollment in nursery school for their child, exemption from school tuition, and priority in employment for the child. Childless couples are guaranteed health care and a pension equal to their combined working salaries when they retire. Mothers who are sterilized after their first child are entitled to join a special health care program for the child, because if it dies they will not be able to have another. "Only-Child Health Clinics" have been established where regular check-ups are given by qualified pediatricians, and parents do not have to wait weeks to have their children examined by a nurse. There are penalties imposed upon couples who have three or more children. At present, parents who have two children are not penalized, but those with three or more have to pay a special tax equal to ten percent of their income for the first fourteen years of that child's life.

The community plays a very active role in deciding whether a couple is to have a child. This is particularly true in the communes, where the entire community may vote on which couples are permitted to have a child that year. Prospective parents in some regions must secure a certificate to give birth without which they cannot receive prenatal care or have their babies delivered by registered midwives or doctors. Before she can apply for this certificate the woman must have the approval of her work unit, the local residents' committee, and the police. If the woman finds herself pregnant, and all the certificates for that district have been allotted, she must have an abortion. She has the alternative of getting the clandestine services of an unregistered midwife, but the resulting baby would be a nonperson, unable to be registered and without an identity card for enrolling in school and for finding employment.

One of the strongly held preferences of the Chinese is to have a male child, and this is proving to be a major obstacle to the realization of the One Child Program. To discourage couples from having another child if their first one is a girl, the government is attempting to establish a "new social system" that stresses that girls are as valuable as boys and that the birth of a daughter is no reason to attempt an illegal second pregnancy. The government is attempting to promote equal opportunities for women and to establish the principle of equal pay for equal work, regardless of sex. In some provinces the parents are promised that if they have a girl as an only child, she will be allowed to take over her father's job when he retires. These measures are intended to improve the financial worth of a girl baby to her parents, and her ability to care for them in their old age. The government is also encouraging young couples to live with the wife's parents if the parents have no son, and help support them in their old age. The legal marriage age has been raised to twenty-seven for males and twenty-five for females.

The expanding birth control programs are designed to minimize or eliminate the need for abortions. Contraceptives of all kinds are free and easily obtained. The impressive efforts of the Chinese government to control the rate of population growth are not without some cost to personal liberty and privacy. There are reports of mandatory birth control programs in some villages in which women seven, eight, or nine months pregnant have been forced to undergo abortions if they already have the prescribed number of children. There are also reports of high rates of female infanticide in certain provinces, especially in rural areas. At present the government does not provide old-age benefits to people in rural areas, and many couples want to be sure that their only child will be a male who will support them when they can no longer work. Daughters are typically taken into their husband's families, and hence are regarded as lost by their own parents.

Infanticide can be accomplished fairly easily, for most births take place in the home, and midwives and husbands cooperate in concealing the deaths. Babies need not be registered with the authorities until three days after birth; if they die before that time they are assumed to be stillborn. Complaisant officials, eager to show low birth rates in their jurisdictions, look the other way. Infanticide serves as a form of population control.

A number of special institutes for population research have been established since 1978, with teaching programs at both the postgraduate and undergraduate levels. A recent survey indicated that sixty-nine percent of Chinese women practiced birth control in 1981. In 1981, first births accounted for forty-seven percent of total births, a great improvement over 1970, when first births accounted for only twenty-one percent of total births. Third births numbered twenty-seven percent of total births in 1981. Although China's fertility rate has declined considerably over the past ten years, there is a tremendous potential for a renewed high-fertility rate because of the country's youthful age structure. Some eleven million couples enter the age of marriage and childbearing each year. To achieve its goal of a population of less than 1.2 billion in the year 2000 requires an annual increase in population of no more than ten million during each of the next sixteen years.

The effective administration of a One Child Program is obviously quite difficult and many problems have arisen. The key to this program is the established political structure in China which extends down to the individual and is the basis for strong peer pressure. In addition, there are substantial financial rewards to couples having only one child, and large financial penalties for those having more than one. The objective of reducing the country's birth rate is communicated to everyone in the population by intensive and persuasive media campaigns. Reproduction is monitored by a network of community and work place organizations called "danwei." Everyone in China belongs to a danwei. Workers belong to the danwei at their place of employment. Others are members of a danwei located at their school or in their neighborhood. Within a given danwei there are charts which keep track of each woman's menstrual cycle, the type of contraception the couple is using, and the presence or absence of the husband. Permission to have a child must be obtained at the couple's danwei.

In urban areas where housing is limited and most women are

members of the labor force, the birth rate has declined rapidly. However, in the rural areas where eighty percent of the one billion Chinese live, compliance with the birth control policy has not been complete. Peasants have always depended upon large families to increase their household income and to provide financial security for their old age. The various programs to elevate the status of women in China will go a long way in overcoming this problem.

However, other byproducts of the new one child policy have arisen. These include forced abortions and infanticide which, though officially forbidden, occur because of the one child policy. There are reports that in the spring of 1981 local authorities in a district of Kwangtung Province forced as many as 50,000 pregnant women to have abortions in order to meet the birth quota assigned by the central authorities. In recent years large numbers of female infants have been drowned, killed, or left to die. In addition, those women who have given birth to female infants have been maltreated. The number of female infants killed is large enough so that male infants are beginning to outnumber female infants by a sizeable margin because of the traditional preference for a male child. Because of the bonuses for parents who cooperate with the One Child Program, and penalties for those who do not, many families have been forced to resort to infanticide.

Initially the fifty-five minority groups that live in China were exempted from the stringent family planning program. Because of their exemption the number of minority individuals has been growing faster than the Han majority, with some of the minority groups having a growth rate as high as four percent. The government has exempted the minority nationalities to prevent the kind of ethnic friction that developed during the Cultural Revolution, when the Han majority in power suppressed the traditions and dress of the minorities in an attempt to assimilate them within the majority. The fact that the minorities were not subject to the one child policy annoyed the Han Chinese that wanted to have more than one child. However, the inclusion of the minorities is a delicate situation, for there is a suspicion among all minorities that prejudice and fear are the primary motives of the majority in pushing a policy that would minimize the growth of the minority population. Thus, the Chinese government must somehow persuade the minority to feel that the one child policy is within their own best interests also.

The agricultural sector of China today feeds nearly one-quarter of the world's human population on seven percent of the globe's cultivated land. The acreage in China sown to crops is seventy percent of that in the United States, but it must provide food for three to four times as many people. There have been some increases in the area under cultivation in China during the last few decades, but these increases have lagged far behind the increases in population, so that the cultivated area per capita has declined. In China a large number of people must be fed by the yield from a limited acreage, and hence Chinese agriculture must maximize the production of calories per acre. China must concentrate on the production of higher energy yielding grain, and some eighty percent of the total sown area is allocated to wheat and rice.

To achieve and maintain maximal agricultural productivity, the Chinese government in the last year or two has begun to offer incentives to raise productivity. This introduction of an earnings incentive has given each individual peasant some power in making decisions and perhaps in increasing his income. These economic reforms have led to an increase in agricultural output, and this will enable China to move along the road of development and increase the living standards of its population. However, these liberal economic policies in the countryside conflict with the control of population growth. It has become more difficult to implement the one child policy in the countryside because the economic interests of the peasants in not complying with the government have increased substantially. The expansion of private plots of land, and the policy of assigning quotas of output to individual peasants, have increased the enthusiasm and productivity of the peasants. This has made it advantageous for the peasant household to have a larger number of children to serve as laborers and increase the output of the family farm. Thus, China's new economic course will make it difficult to have a completely successful campaign for decreasing the population growth. This in turn will ultimately render its economic policies ineffective. Thus it appears that China needs some new joint policy that will bring the economic planning and the population planning policies into agreement.

Half of China's people are under twenty-one years old and will soon be entering their reproductive years. China must check their child-producing potential; otherwise, the new population growth would swamp all development gains, and China would have to give up her hope of attaining a comfortable middle-class living standard for its people.

In 1979, the new population policy was drafted, and by 1981 the entire nation, including many of the minority nationalities, was subject to the one child policy. This policy aims to encourage one child per family, restrict the possibility of a second child, and absolutely stop the birth of a third. The prevailing motto, "late, sparse, and few," (*wan, hsi, shao*) urges the practice of late marriage, deferred childbearing, and the birth of fewer but healthy children. In most provinces, the minimum marriage ages for men and women living in cities are twenty-seven and twenty-five, respectively. In rural areas, the minimum marriage age for men is twenty-five, and for women, twenty-three. The policy also advocates an interval of at least four or more years between the birth of the first and the second child. Finally, it strives to persuade each couple to agree to raise only one child.

To encourage the Chinese people to apply for a "one child certificate," the government offers direct incentives in the form of money, work points, housing, food, medical care, and day-care services. For example, in the cities of Sichuan Province, workers, teachers, and government employees who have only one child and who guarantee not to have a second one are given five yuan a month (the equivalent of ten percent of their monthly pay) for child care, until the child is fourteen years old. In receiving housing, the child counts as two persons instead of one. Also, the only child is given priority, either in admission to school or in allocating jobs.

In Sichuan's villages, families with only one child receive each month a sum of money equal to three workdays for child care until the child is fourteen years old. Also, the single child gets an adult's share of grain from the day of birth. In the distribution of plots for private use, the only child receives 1.5 shares instead of the normal 1.0 share. In addition, the single child receives free nursery care, free primary and secondary schooling, and free medical care. In 1980, Sichuan issued one child certificates to 78.8 percent of its total married couples. China considers Sichuan her national model for family planning.

To make its one child certificate more attractive, the government grants a woman who has consented to having only one child a maternity leave of four to six months. In Shanxi Province, urban couples are paid as usual during their marriage and maternity leave. Their absence will not affect their attendance records, performance evaluations, bonuses, wage adjustments, or promotions. Rural couples are rewarded work points or equivalent amounts of money or grain as usual by their production team. Thus, the government devotes much effort to make the one child policy appealing.

In the same way the government can make the one child policy attractive to the people, it can also make the possibility of having a second child impossible. Should a couple who once agreed to the one-child norm later decide to have a second baby despite the brigade or production team's protests, the couple must not only pay back the rewards received under the one child certificate within a limited period of time, but also pay heavy fines for the second. In Shanxi Province, the urban couple would have fifteen percent of their monthly pay deducted. They would also be deprived of the medical, material, and other benefits granted to first birth. Maternity leave would be granted without pay. Furthermore, they would be deprived of one chance for future wage adjustment. In rural areas, couples would not only have ten percent of their total annual workpoints deducted, but also ten percent of their total annual income deducted in the two years following the child's birth. In addition, they would be allotted less productive plots or assigned higher output quotas. Thus the purpose of these restrictions is to make the second child expensive for the couple.

To gain the people's support for the one child policy, the government conducts educational campaigns, making full use of the mass media to emphasize the importance for the people to restrict the number of births per family to achieve the Four Modernizations for their country. Birth-control propaganda can be found in newspapers, magazines, or television, on billboards and in skits and performances. In the national paper, *Renmin Ribao* (People's Daily), the editors state the necessity for family planning:

> If we do not implement planned population control and let the population increase uncontrollably, rapid population growth is bound to put a heavy burden on the state and the people, cripple the national economy, adversely affect the state's construc-

tion, the people's living standards and their health, and slow down the progress of the Four Modernizations.

As parents have been giving birth according to their own preferences without regard to the nation as a whole, editorials such as this one aim to gradually shift the people's traditional loyalty to the family to that of the nation and the Communist Party.

Although mass media advertise and communicate the importance of the one-child norm, thereby establishing a fertile groundwork for implementation, China realizes that the most effective method to persuade couples to adopt the one child policy is by personal contact. Thus, the government has established a nationwide network of comprehensive services to help implement the policy. Each factory or rural production team has a family planning committee with full-time workers checking up on the married individuals at work. These committees often consist of barefoot doctors, midwives, and health workers, who come from the people with three to six months' training. To persuade each couple to accept the one-child norm, the committee visits the family, making them aware of the need for planned fertility. It also offers assistance and advice concerning contraceptives. Often, the committee presents people who have consented to have no more than one child to share their experiences and explain why their decisions were the best ones. During the persuasion, not only would the woman be approached, but also her husband, her mother-in-law, and close relations, until all resistance wears down. Once the couple accepts the one-child norm, the committee then publicly and immediately announces the couple's decision, notifying employers, friends, and neighbors. Then the committee would hold a celebration, thus making it difficult for the couple to retract the decision.

The family planning committee also decides and announces how many and which couples are to have babies that year under the unit's birth quota. It then monitors the menstrual cycles of the female employees to check compliance. In addition, it reveals each couple's method of birth control. In the Peking No. 2 Woolen Mill, a list contains intimate information about the workers' marriage plans, their plans to have children, the kinds of contraceptives they use, and even the timing of the women workers' menstrual cycles. In the Xihung production brigade near Wuxi, a

117

large pink chart on the wall of the clinic advertises each local official's method of birth control:

> Twenty-seven of the brigade's twenty-nine officials are men and the chart names ten who have had vasectomies. Fourteen other officials or their wives are using the pill or the intrauterine loop.
>
> Two of the remaining five men are married but are not practicing family planning, and the three others are too young to marry under China's strict policy of delaying wedlock until the late twenties. The chart gives the year in which they may get married.

Thus, public posting of birth-control charts is one of a variety of approaches used by the family planning committee to curb China's birth rate.

Should a woman not due to have a baby under her work unit's quota for that particular year get pregnant, the family planning committee would strongly educate, persuade, and plead with her to abort it until her turn comes. The committee would require her and other pregnant women in similar situations to attend study group meetings with counselors until they consent to have an abortion. For each day that the women miss work to attend these meetings, they would be deprived of that day's pay. Thus, the committee makes it in the woman's best economic interest to give up her baby and return to work to avoid any further penalties. Worn down by the countless number of arguments and the endless hounding, the woman often gives in. As Guo Zhenzhen, a thirty-five year-old teacher in Gulangyu Island who became pregnant for the second time, recalled:

> When I was on holiday, they [members of the family planning committee] came four, five, six times a day. When I was at work, the leader of the family planning committee would go to my house and do education work with my family . . . It made me very unhappy.

Finally, after two months of these visits, she gave in. Thus, the family planning committee does its utmost to keep the births down to the required quota. If the woman refused to consent to an abortion, she would be subject to the severe penalties for having a second child, and perhaps be ostracized from her friends. Hence, peer pressure from members of the local family planning committee helps keep the population problem under control.

To aid the implementation of the single child family, the government has set up strong family planning offices with trained medical personnel and health stations offering a wide range of free contraceptives and planned birth-related operations. The government tends to encourage long-term, effective contraceptive measures, such as the IUD, vasectomies, tubal ligations, and induced abortions to keep the fertility rate down. For example, Guangdong Province advocates that those women "who have already given birth to one child must be fitted with IUDs, and couples who already have two children must undergo sterilization of either the husband or the wife . . . Under no circumstances may a third child be born." Moreover, under the marriage law passed in 1980, all couples must practice some form of contraception.

In 1981, more than ten million couples in China obtained certificates for having only one child. The policy fared well in urban areas, such as Beijing, Hebei, Shanghai, and Sichuan, where about eighty percent of the couples adopted the one-child norm. This movement has been successful because most urban couples live in cramped quarters, where housing is limited and where educational, medical, and other services are difficult to come by. Also, most urban couples are educated and more interested in improving their own lives than raising many children. In addition, a large number of party workers, interpreters, and intellectuals reside in the cities, and the demanding work of their careers, plus the four-year spacing rule, usually dissuade them from having a second child.

An increasing number of women in the cities are in the workforce, pursuing careers rather than staying home and raising babies. In 1949, the government upheld the principle of equal pay to men and women alike for equal work. Thus, women, in developing their own careers and interests, are willing to accept the one-child norm. Also, they fear that if they do not conform to the policy, they would be discriminated against at work, and chances for raises and promotions would be damaged.

However, it is not enough that eighty percent of urban couples have adopted the one child policy, for these urbanites make up only twenty percent of the entire country. The other eighty percent reside in the rural areas, and it is here where the one-child-per-family movement has met the most resistance. The rigid one child family policy undermines the current economic policy in the countryside, where peasants now farm their own private plots of land. Thus, an increased number of laborers would mean increased earnings. Also, rural couples still cling to the traditional, feudal concept that the greatest filial impiety is the failure to produce offspring. They hold that "no sons" means "no descendants." The preference for large families and sons to care for them in their old age still exists.

The introduction of the liberal economic policy of private cultivation undermines the government's efforts to control fertility. To increase agricultural production of goods such as oil-bearing seeds, grain, and cotton, the government has implemented the responsibility system, which allows households to farm their own land, select their own crops, and sell any surplus after meeting the official output quota. This new development policy allows many peasant households to become rich through hard work and dedication.

To aid the growth of domestic production and improve peasant incomes, the government has encouraged households to engage in domestic sideline production. Domestic sideline production refers to the production undertaken by the household on an individual basis either for its own subsistence or exchange. The production may be based on the cultivation of the private plot, the raising of domestic livestock, the cultivation of wild plants, or the production of handicrafts—all of which rely exclusively on family labor. Many peasant households have come to depend on the production of domestic sidelines to generate both a major portion of their food supplies (meats and vegetables), and about twenty percent of their cash income.

The expansion of private plots of land, the assignment of output quotas, and the domestic sideline occupations have boosted tremendously the peasants' enthusiasm and productivity. The success of these policies has enabled peasants to increase their incomes, build themselves larger homes, pool their money together to buy tractors, and improve their standard of living. Thus, the more workers a family has, the greater its earnings will be. As a result, many households shun the one child policy, preferring to pay the financial penalties rather than give up a second or third child. For example, in *Renmin Ribao* some peasants have argued:

> We cultivate our own land, eat our own grain, and bring up all our children on our own.

Another peasant in Sichuan Province said:

> We now work on our own. We don't ask for grain, money, or cloth from the Government. If we produce some more children, that's our own problem and nobody can interfere.

Some peasants believe that the benefits of a second child will outweigh the financial costs of evading the one child policy. As a woman in Kiangsi Province who would be fined 1,000 yuan for an additional child reports:

> Between playing with my baby and playing with 1,000 yuan, I'd prefer my baby. Besides, the additional labor power will surely mean more than 1,000 yuan in the long run.

Thus, many peasants are willing to pay the fines for having an additional child.

Furthermore, in Guangdong Province, where in 1980 only 12.7 percent of all couples had adopted the one-child norm, many couples have relatives in Hong Kong or overseas who would provide them with additional financial support should they decide to have more than one child. Since many couples regard the financial costs not worth the many benefits and joys of having a second child, the government must find some way of combining these two contradictory policies concerning economic development and population control.

The economic sanctions which have been successful in restricting fertility in urban areas are less applicable to peasant households. Each peasant household is self-sufficient: it has its own private plot of land, domestic livestock, and sideline productions to counter the effects of food and cash penalties. Moreover, the cost of raising children in rural areas is much less than in urban areas, and a child of a peasant household can begin to contribute to the family budget from an early age. In addition, many of the rewards and penalties dealing with admission to institutions and allocation of housing and job privileges are less relevant in the countryside, where housing is privately owned and where health and education facilities are not as well developed as those in the cities. As a result, many of these penalties for having an additional child are not important to the rural couple, and thus they are ignored.

Perhaps the government should link the peasants' earnings, not only to their agricultural production, but also to their compliance with the new limits on family size. Those who comply with the one child policy could be given a lower production quota. With a smaller family size, each member would then have a greater responsibility in cultivating the land. To help farm the land, the peasant may employ hired help instead of producing his own helpers. Thus, he will be able to enjoy prosperity with only one child. If some peasants do not comply, the government should increase their output quota and give them a smaller plot of land, as well as enforce the provincial penalties for having a second child. In this way, the government may persuade the peasants to accept the one child policy without the need to sacrifice their potential earnings.

Because of the traditional preference for a son to carry on the family name and to care for his parents in their old age, many peasants have resisted the one child family policy. These rural families believe that a daughter would bring nothing but eventual poverty, as she would have to move in with her husband's family at marriage with a dowry, and take his name. Also, as Chinese elders often depend on their children to care for them in their old age, they believe a daughter would be useless since she would be serving her in-laws. Pressured to have only one child, it has been reported that many couples have resorted to female infanticide to ensure themselves of a male descendant. Moreover, reports speak of violence against women who bear daughters.

For example, in Peking, Christopher Wren of *The New York Times* reports the case of Ms. Gao Lihau, who suffered serious abuse for not giving birth to a son:

> When the baby was born, Mr. Chen came home on furlough and beat his wife, leaving her with numerous facial injuries and a brain concussion. Her father-in-law, who sat watching television during one beating, told Miss Gao later: "Don't come to me for help. Our family simply doesn't want you."

The question has often been raised of how applicable the Chinese population-control model is for other developing nations. If we temporarily disregard its negative side effects and look only at the positive aspects of the program, how likely is it to be copied by other countries facing a population overflow? Much of the enforcement behind the government's policies must be carried out on the local level. This requires a high degree of organization on the farms and in the villages. Such a degree of organization would be hard to find in a non-communist developing country. Most of the African and South American countries which face an overpopulation problem are highly decentralized, and the bottom economic layer consists of peasant farmers who have little or no contact with the national government. China's ability to reward and punish is also dependent on the government's control of the national economy and of the individual salaries of the people. This is not the case in a more free-market system, and the rewards and punishments would be significantly less effective.

China's task was made easier by the lack of a religious ideology mandating large families and banning birth control. This is not true in the Catholic countries of South America or the Moslem ones of Africa. The ability of the government to bring women into the work force is also something that would prove nearly impossible in many of the Arab countries. Strong cultural barriers stand in the way of late marriages as well. Female infanticide would probably flourish in much of Africa if a one child policy were attempted.

Other aspects of China's population policy could be used by other developing nations. Easily available, free birth control and abortions would help to reduce overpopulation. A strong educational program, such as the one undertaken by China, is necessary to explain the benefits of using birth control to the general population. A system of community clinics would not only improve health care in general, but would also make contraceptive counseling and abortions more accessible. These are all programs which have proven very effective in China and which could work as well in other countries.

In evaluating the programs adopted by the Chinese government in order to reach zero population growth by the year 2000, we must weigh the positive effects of a population small enough to feed itself, with the negative effects of loss of personal choice, dangerous late abortions, and increased female infanticide. The Chinese model is far from an ideal one, but the commitment the government is making to a secure economic future through population control should be emulated by developing and developed nations alike.

Part V

The Future of Technology and Societies

10.

Biomedical Sciences and Social Patterns in the Twenty-First Century

Claude A. Villee, Jr.

Harvard University Medical School, Boston, Massachusetts, U.S.A.

In considering the social and family patterns that will exist in the mid-twenty-first century and how they may have been affected by developments in medicine and medical sciences, we can dissect the problem into three parts. First, what are some of the present major problems in social and family patterns? Secondly, what are some of the major developments in medical sciences that we can expect over the next fifty to seventy years? Thirdly, will these developments contribute to the solution of our present problems, or might they raise other problems?

High on any list of current social problems is the rapid rate in the growth of populations, especially in some of the lesser developed countries. A separate but related concern is the high and increasing rate of teenage pregnancies seen in the United States and several other countries around the world. A third problem is the reaction of the parents and family to the birth of an unwanted child, and the high probability that this will lead to abuse of that child. Further questions are: (1) What will be the total size of the human population in 2050? Is there reason to believe that the size of the world population will have been stabilized by the mid-twenty-first century? Several of the developed countries of the world have achieved zero population growth and others are nearly at that point. Many of the lesser developed countries have very high rates of population growth at present, and the size of the world's population in the mid-twenty-first century will be determined to a very large extent by what population policies are adopted by the governments of the lesser developed countries and how effectively these policies are carried out by those governments. Until recently efforts to limit population size were directed towards "family planning." Operationally, this meant that efforts were made to enable each family to decide how many children they want and how they should be spaced, and then assisting the couple in having that many children and no more. Now people are beginning to realize that the truly overriding concern is with the total ecology of the planet earth, and that the size of the human population must be kept below the level at which irreparable damage to the earth's ecology occurs. This may mean that couples will have to have fewer children than they might want and would have been counseled to have under the family planning system. Thus, we may inquire what effects might such efforts to restrict population size have on society in general and on the structure of the family in particular? One could even ask whether the institution of marriage and the family will continue to exist. What will be the nature of parent-child relationships in the future?

Let us turn now to the question of what developments in medical sciences can we expect over the next fifty to seventy years. In the past century or so, our improved knowledge of infectious diseases, how to prevent and treat them, the development of antibiotics, anti-tumor agents, and a variety of other drugs have been responsible for the decline in death rates, particularly in the developed countries. In the developed countries, although there is still some room for improvement in decreasing the mortality rates in the perinatal period, there is very little room for any further decline in death rates among children, young adults, and middle adults. If there is to be any further decrease in the death rates in the developed countries, it would have to be due to improving longevity or decreasing the death rates of people over fifty. At the present time, a substantial amount of research effort is devoted to reaching an understanding of the nature of the aging process. What chemical and molecular changes are involved in aging?

What steps might be taken to slow the aging process so that the human life span could be increased? If these research efforts should be successful, that is, if means are developed to retard the aging process, this would markedly decrease death rates and would have a corresponding effect on the size of the population. Such a development would obviously have striking effects on family life and on social patterns. If people not only survived but were effective human beings until the age of 150 or 200, this would drastically change our ideas about retirement. This, combined with the continued spiraling costs and scarcity of housing, may encourage several generations of a family to live under the same roof. This would represent a marked change from the family patterns of today.

In the past, decreases in mortality in the developed countries tended to increase the fraction of the population under age fifteen, for the decreased mortality affected primarily the young. A greater percentage of children survived the perilous years from birth to age fifteen, thus the average age of the population tended to fall and not rise. If future medical advances enable us to minimize or eliminate the effects of aging and greatly increase longevity, this would increase both the absolute number of people more than sixty years of age, as well as the fraction of the population over sixty. Any future decline in mortality rates in the developed countries would have only a minor role in raising the rate of natural increase in the population. The decisive determinant in population growth rates in the developed countries will be fertility. Fertility rates in many developed countries have now declined to replacement levels or below, and many, but not all, demographers believe that these lowered fertility rates will continue well into the next century.

Since World War II there has been a remarkable increase in the life expectancy of people in the lesser developed countries, who make up seventy-five percent of the total world population. The magnitude of the increases in population growth rate registered in the lesser developed countries in the post-war period has had no parallel anywhere in the past. Dozens of impoverished populations have managed to compress generations or centuries of changes in developed countries to within a decade or two. For these populations the traditional link between poverty and decreased longevity has been changed.

In the past quarter century there have been substantial decreases in fertility rates in forty or fifty of the lesser developed countries in many parts of the world. Major exceptions to this are the countries of Africa and the Middle East. However, the present fertility rates in the lesser developed countries are still two or three times greater than the fertility rates found in most developed nations today. The fertility rates of nearly all of the lesser developed countries continue to be much too high from the viewpoints of their own social well-being and their quality of life.

These lesser developed countries have also shown record rates of urbanization over the last thirty years. The number of people living in cities in the lesser developed countries has more than doubled in the past two decades. In the developed countries, urbanization has also proceeded rapidly, nearly reaching the saturation level, and causing profound changes in social patterns. There seems to be nothing to suggest that this trend towards urbanization will be reversed in the next century.

Our ethical judgments of these population trends in both developed and lesser developed countries in all parts of the world will confront new kinds of challenges—ones which are as unprecedented as the trends in populations themselves. Should developed countries extend massive developmental aid to the lesser developed countries when their own poverty problems are far from being solved? What ethical rationale may guide aid from the developed countries to lesser developed countries to enhance their systems of decreasing mortality? If these will simply lead to increases in population and increasing economic misery among the living, such economic aid from the developed countries is bound to be ineffective and even counter-productive. If the populations of the lesser developed countries continue to grow rapidly, should abortion be permitted or encouraged? What sort of social action—permissive or compulsory—should be taken towards reducing fertility? Several difficult issues and dilemmas have been raised by the extraordinary demographic events in recent history. How they are answered will play a major role in determining the kind of world we will be living in in the next century. The decisions reached will affect not only the size of the population, but the very fabric of society which results from such demographic processes.

It is reassuring that a detectable decrease in the rate of population growth has occurred in many parts of the world beginning in the 1960s. The acceleration of world population growth that is unprecedented historically, and that has increased the earth's population by 167 percent during this century, appears to have passed the turning point. What has decreased is the rate of population growth. The total number of the world's population continues to increase, of course, because of the larger base population. The total world population increased by sixty-six million in 1967 and by eighty million in 1977. This decrease in the world's growth rate, which has occurred earlier than expected, will have only a limited impact on the size of the world's population in the year 2000, but if it continues it will have a substantial impact on the size of the world's population during the twenty-first century. The momentum of population growth implies that even after replacement level of fertility (net reproductive rate of 1.0) has been achieved, the populations of countries that have a young age distribution will continue to increase in numbers for another fifty or sixty years. At that time the population may be more than fifty percent larger than it was when it achieved a net reproductive rate of 1.0.

In addition to changes in the total population of the world by the mid-twenty-first century, we can expect a substantial change in the age composition of the population of most, if not all, countries. In Japan, for example, the portion of the population more than sixty-five years old had made up about five percent of the total before World War II. However, it began to increase and in 1975 the over-sixty-five population reached eight percent of the whole. Projections made at Nehon University in 1978 suggest that this will increase further to fifteen percent by the year 2000, to more than twenty percent in 2015, and to as much as thirty percent by the middle of the twenty-first century. There will, of course, be a corresponding decrease in the number of younger people in the population and in Japan, as in the United States and Europe, the "youth culture" of the sixties and early seventies will shift to "aging culture" in the next century.

The People's Republic of China is making a determined effort to reduce the rate of population growth by using social and economic pressures, such as raising the age of marriage, exerting peer and group pressures to limit the number of children to one per family, decreasing economic assistance to families that have more than two children, etc. A comparable program in Singapore has been successful in reducing its growth rate substantially.

Anthropologists have noted increasing tendencies towards violence, dehumanization, and persecution as the size of the population increases. With the increases in population size that will inevitably occur between now and 2050, even with the best efforts to minimize the population growth rate, we can expect the social patterns to reflect this in further increases in the level of violence in society.

At the present time there is a feeling of dissatisfaction in many countries, both developed and undeveloped, about both the quantity and quality of the delivery of health care. There is a general feeling that there has been a failure to meet the expectations of the populations; that is, an inability of the health services to deliver a level of national health care adequate to meet the stated demands and the changing needs of society. The cost of medical care has been rising rapidly without any evident and meaningful improvement in health care services. Many consumers of health care feel, rightly or wrongly, that health services and the personnel within them are progressing out of control along a path which may be satisfying to the health professionals, but which is not what is most wanted by consumers of health care. Efforts are now being made in many parts of the world to devise systems of health care delivery that will address these problems and, hopefully, find solutions for them.

Most of us have the expectation that the advances in molecular biology in recent years will be reflected in the not-too-distant future in advances in medicine. One of the first results of these advances has been the preparation of human protein hormones, such as insulin and growth hormone. These have been synthesized under the direction of human genes that have been introduced into an appropriate plasmid and then placed inside a bacterium such as *Escherichia coli.* These bacteria can be grown in large amounts and will produce large amounts of the human hormone. The human gene produces a human messenger RNA for the hormone, which is then read out by the bacterial protein synthesizing system to produce the desired protein. Several commercial companies are currently preparing not only hormones but other medically important proteins, such as interferon, by similar means.

A somewhat more difficult operation, but one which in theory is perfectly feasible, is to isolate the specific human gene which has the code for a specific enzyme, and then use this gene in the treatment of individuals who have an inherited deficiency of that gene; that is, a specific inborn error of metabolism. This involves half a dozen or more steps, beginning with the isolation of the enzyme itself, preparing an antibody to the enzyme which can be used in isolating the messenger RNA, and then using reverse transcriptase to synthesize from the RNA template the copy DNA which codes for the enzyme. The gene has to be attached by way of a plasmid, and introduced into a bacterium which will multiply and provide many copies of the gene. The specific gene then has to be removed from the plasma in the bacterial cell, purified, and introduced into the cells of the patient to provide a replacement for the missing gene. This set of operations could provide a replacement for the missing gene and provide an effective cure for diseases such as phenylketonuria and glycogen storage disease.

The term cloning refers to the production of exact duplicates of an individual, ones that are genetically identical to it, like identical twins. There has been much discussion in the news media as to whether it would be possible to clone human beings, and, if so, whether it would be ethically and morally permissible. Cloning has been achieved in bacteria, in plants, such as carrots, and in some lower animals, such as the frog. For example, a ripe, unfertilized frog egg is obtained and the nucleus is carefully removed with a micropipet. The egg nucleus is then replaced with a nucleus from a cell from a later developmental stage, a blastula or gastrula. The reconstituted egg then undergoes cleavage and develops into a normal tadpole. If the nuclei of several eggs are all replaced with nuclei from the same blastula, all of the resulting individuals are genetically identical.

A human egg can be obtained by flushing it from the oviduct or by removing it surgically from the ovary. This method was used by Steptoe and Edwards to obtain an egg that was then fertilized with sperm from the father outside of the mother's body. The fertilized egg was replaced in her uterus and developed into a normal, full-term baby girl. In theory at least, the nucleus of a human egg could be removed and replaced with the nucleus from an adult human somatic cell. If the developing egg were placed in the uterus of a woman who had been properly hormonally conditioned, it would implant and become an individual genetically identical to the individual from whom the nucleus was derived. It would be an exact phenotypic copy of the donor of the nucleus. Similar attempts have been successful in frogs and mice if the nucleus is obtained from a cell from the blastula or gastrula stage of early development. However, when the nucleus from a normal adult cell was transplanted into an enucleated egg, development did not proceed normally. The chromosomes from adult cells appear to be unable to divide rapidly enough to keep up with the very rapid rate of cytoplasmic division which occurs during early embryonic development. Chromosomal duplication occurs too slowly. The daughter cells receive an incomplete set of chromosomes, and development is defective. In addition, most of the genes in the nucleus of an adult cell have been turned off during the process of differentiation. For a successful cloning experiment some means would have to be developed to turn on these genes so that they could be expressed during development and differentiation. If these difficulties could be overcome, it would in theory be possible to make many copies of one individual. The number would be limited solely by the number of ripe human eggs that could be obtained and by the number of women who would agree to have such an egg remain in their uterus during its development.

A number of questions immediately come to mind. Who should be cloned and why? What could the benefits to society be? Would cloning dehumanize society? What would we do with mistakes in the cloning process? Would human society be any better if it were possible to clone the most famous and talented men and women from various sections of society? Would modern mathematics and physics be advanced much further if we had one hundred Einsteins instead of one?

Some of the more enthusiastic proponents of human cloning make the naive assumption that the cloned individuals would duplicate the donor in every way. It must be remembered that the members of a clone are identical only in their genetic constituents. Environment and experience play important roles in the development of an individual's personality and behavior. It has been argued that by cloning only those genotypes that are desired, and by prohibiting the reproduction of everyone else, we could greatly improve the quality of the human race. Cloning would permit the preservation and perpetuation of the finest genotypes present in our species. However, since we are currently suffering from an overproduction of human beings, cloning would be distinctly undesirable if it simply led to the production of more humans.

Another aspect of biomedical science, much in the news recently, is that of *in vitro* fertilization. A human egg can be recovered from a woman either by flushing it from her oviduct at a specific time after ovulation, or by surgically removing a ripe ovum from her ovary. This can be fertilized with sperm obtained from the husband, and then the fertilized egg can be returned to the mother's uterus. If she has the proper amounts of the gonadal hormones, estrogens, and progestins, implantation will occur and development can proceed normally. Advances in the future may well increase the probability of success of the operation in any given individual, but it is unlikely that this will become very widely used.

Is it possible that medical sciences will develop the sort of artificial uterus envisaged by Aldous Huxley in his novel *Brave New World*? In that account of the future, human eggs were fertilized outside the body and implanted in an artificial perfusion system which provided them with all of the nutrients so that they could grow to birth size *in vitro*. In the novel, by selectively altering the conditions in this system during development, off-spring were obtained with a range of intelligence, talents, and physical strength to fit them to the specific tasks required in this society. Rejecting, of course, that part of the plan, such a system would finally free women of the problems associated with pregnancy and childbirth, and at long last give them a truly equal opportunity to develop their career potentials.

Although a variety of contraceptive measures have been developed and used, ranging from the steroid oral contraceptive and intrauterine device to condoms, diaphragms, and spermicidal jellies, no completely satisfactory method is available that can be applied worldwide. If we can intensify our research efforts in this field and develop a method which is universally accepted, completely effective, and completely safe, so that all unwanted children can be prevented, this would certainly have a most important effect on population problems and on the organization of the society and family in the next century. Some fifty million births each year are neither planned nor wanted at the time of conception. If contraceptive measures could be developed and utilized to prevent all unwanted births, much of the problem of child abuse would be eliminated, for a major cause of child abuse is the parents' reactions to an unwanted child.

The large and increasing number of pregnancies among teen-age women is a major medical concern at present. Bearing children at too young an age has marked adverse effects on the outcome of pregnancy for both mother and child, with increased maternal morbidity and mortality, fetal malformations, and congenital defects. The adverse socioeconomic effects on the parents, especially on the mother, are marked, and may change their life and career plans, with extensive efforts on their family life patterns. A truly effective and universally utilized contraceptive program, by preventing this, would have very positive effects on social patterns and family life in the future.

11.

A Perspective of Populations In Transition

Edward O. Pratt

The World Bank
Washington, D.C., U.S.A./Sierra Leone

Introduction

The phenomenon of population growth has become an obsessive factor in the overall prognostications regarding the catastrophic consequences from unrestrained growth and the quality of life of future generations. The growth of the world's population over the past four decades to its present 4.4 billion has been enormous, and although there appears to be a downward trend in world fertility, the latest projection (based on the United Nations medium variant) of 10.5 billion by the year 2110 is alarming enough.

Population size, growth, structure, and distribution respond to the forces of change, and population dynamics involve the study of their principal determinants—fertility, mortality, migration, and their interaction with biological, economic, and social variables in a cause and effect relationship.

Over the past two decades there has been intensification of efforts by sundry workers through local and international forums to heighten the awareness of the world at large, policy planners, and decision makers to the adverse economic, social, and political consequences of unrestrained population growth. Various scenarios have been drawn from on-going experiences, and scientifically based projections have been made of the effects of population growth on public health, education, welfare, and environmental quality.

While the consequences of unrestrained population growth and their magnitude are undergoing continuous exploration, some may draw an inference from the historical analysis of the dynamics and behavioristic performance of human populations that economic and social engineering will ultimately lead to spontaneous fertility limitation. The indeterminacy of such a time span is frightening when a sober and deliberate assessment is made of the calamitous consequences to unborn millions during the presumed hiatus. It took a span of about 150 years for high fertility levels in what are known now as the developed countries to respond to the processes of industrialization which occurred in the nineteenth century through the mid-twentieth century.

Within the perspective of a time frame to the end of this century, continuous improvement in technology will contribute to significant enhancement of the quality of life of the peoples in the world and of food production and nutrition status. This will only happen, if it is allowed to, by the policy and decision makers and all those involved in the determination of our social and economic institutions—in the more equitable distribution of benefits. A very good example is the erroneous inference drawn from interpreting per capita GNP which, in truth, does not adequately reflect the disproportionate distribution of a country's income—being skewed away from the poor and needy. However, it is difficult to maintain any sort of equilibrium between resources and population with present rates of population growth; further exacerbations of growth would impose overwhelming constraints on survival at acceptable standards.

Current assessment of population trends by the United Nations indicate that a worldwide demographic transition is on the way and that this is mainly due to the combination of developmental programs and the conscious efforts of developing population strategies to inhibit excessive growth. The World Population Conference, occurring as it did in 1974 at Bucharest, and the Conference on Human Settlements in Vancouver, 1976, awakened the consciousness of nations to their responsibilities to ensure that the machinery is firmly set for laying down a sound foundation for a better quality life and enhanced chances for survival of future generations. These conferences also crystallized developmental and demographic strategies consistent with the quality of life ethic, and as the majority of the world population lives in the developing countries, the issue assumes a higher relevancy for them. The objective is towards eventual stabilization of the world's population. This means appreciable decline in current birth rates, a trend which is dependent on social, economic, and cultural factors involving the processes of change.

The Critical Path of Transition

As the demographic transition gradually develops, world population continues to increase by progression, which gradually assumes exponential proportions to a peak by the year 2000. Thus, additions to the world population are, or will be, of the following order of magnitude: by the end of 1925, 360 million; 1950, 600 million; 1975, 1,520 million; 2000, 2,170 million. Thereafter, decrements occur cyclically in the same time slices and at almost identical rates as in the pre-peak periods, with estimated additions of only 600 million, 100 million by the end of years 2075 and 2100 respectively, due to deceleration of fertility rates, when practically all the regions' populations would have been stabilized.

The year 2000 is thus perceived as being critical, as the turning point when it is expected that the impact of the demographic transition would begin to gather momentum. The various regions would achieve stable populations at different periods in the time scale after year 2000. The earliest would be (using medium variant) Europe (year 2030, population 0.5 billion), followed by North America (year 2060, 0.32), East Asia, including China and Japan (year 2090, 1.7), South Asia and Latin America (year 2100, 4.1, 1.2 respectively), and lastly Africa (year 2110, 2.2). The greatest growth would come from South Asia and Africa, and together both would comprise over sixty percent of the world's stable population in year 2110.

Between 1900 and 1975, world population grew from 1.5 billion to four billion, and the rate of growth speeded up in thirty-five years, between 1940 and 1975, when population rose from two billion to four billion. With the present trend in population growth, albeit the onset of demographic transition, it is estimated that the present population of four billion would double itself in the next twenty-five years. Latest review by informal sources

TABLE 1: *Net Additions to World Population 1925-2100*[1]

1. Journal of the United Nations Fund for Population Activities, Vol 8 No. 2, 1981.

indicates that progress in development is a critical factor in the determination of population growth, and the point of time in which the world's populations will be stabilized would depend on developmental achievements, increased inputs in population related programs, and maintenance of momentum acquired in these activities by the respective governments.

The present scenario suggests that it is less likely for developing countries, where the total fertility rate now averages 4.4 child-

Table 2

	1980 Population (billion)	Year of Stabilization	Stable Population (billion)	
South Asia	1.4	2100	4.1	
East Asia (including China and Japan)	1.2	2090	1.7	China has achieved one of the lowest recorded growth rates (1.2%) and is rapidly approaching replacement level (NRR = 1)[1]
Africa	0.5	2110	2.2	
Latin America	0.4	2100	1.2	
Europe	0.45	2030	0.5	
North America	0.25	2060	0.32	

[1] *Replacement level fertility.* Replacement level fertility is the level of fertility at which a cohort of women, on the average, have only enough daughters to re-place themselves in the population. When net reproduction rate (NRR) reaches 1.0, replacement level is reached. *Net Reproduction Rate.* The average number of daughters that would be born to a woman (or group of women) if she (they) passed through her (their) lifetime from birth conforming to the age-specific fertility and mortality rates of a given year. It is the measure of the extent to which a cohort of newly born girls will replace themselves under a given schedule of age-specific fertility and mortality.

ren, to achieve replacement level (with an average of one to two children per couple) in twenty years. The situation is predicated by such factors as, declining mortality rates, continuing high fertility rates, low age of marriage. It should be noted that attainment of replacement level (that is, NRR of one or a one to two-child family) sets the pace towards eventual population stabilization. The time taken for a country's population to become stationary after reaching replacement level fertility will depend on its age structure and previous fertility patterns.

Population growth in the predominant developing countries had accelerated so much in the last twenty-five years that there is a younger age distribution which will keep crude birth rates at a high level even though fertility trends show some decline; compounding this would be appreciable lowering of crude death rates due to advances and application of medical technology. This, of course, would mean, that while concern is being expressed and strategies are being developed for controlling fertility, more attention should be paid to the recognition of problems associated with accommodating the continuing massive growth of populations, and finding solutions for them. At year 2000, as had been observed earlier, the net additions to population growth may have been reached, and thereafter declines may occur consistently through the year 2100. But at year 2000 the world population may have doubled itself, and the magnitude of the problem is in estimating what state the countries of the world would be in and what designs for living would evolve. Among changes, both structural and qualitative that would occur at this point in time, are: explosive urban growth and transformation by an estimated factor of four to eight, with critical constraints on health and basic standards of living; ecological transformation of the environment as demonstrated during the Conference on Human Settlements, in which considerable pressure would be exerted on food, housing, and shelter, etc., through deforestation, reduction of agricultural production, lowered water tables, and shortages of potable water; considerable transportation bottlenecks; stringent energy supplies and the dearth of non-renewable fossils; transformation of industry and commerce because of increasing interdependency between countries; and socio-political instability through absolute increases in the unemployed.

Poverty Correlation

In quite a few of the developing countries the poverty level is a prime concern and is inter-related with rapid population growth. The concomitants of poverty are poor health, lack of education, low status of women, low educational levels, particularly in women, and lack of job opportunities for women. A cycle develops whereby attacking and setting right these anomalies raises the salience of fertility control to people, which eventually should lead to less population pressure which will in turn establish a more ambient environment for positive encroachments on poverty, resulting in the enhancement of a social well-being or status of the individual, and possibly the community and country as a whole. By more people getting into this cycle, the more a positive trend will be developed towards raising the level of fertility consciousness. Relieving poverty implies socio-economic enhancement of the family which then moves from a family of orientation; that is, one which propagates additional children as service utilities and insurance. The family which is the integral part of the community is responsible for the decisions about fertility which cumulatively, *inter-alia*, determine a country's population profile. The family, because of its size and structure, is thus the important focus for examining the dynamics of social change relating to the population factor.

The Family and Modernization

Social and demographic factors are irretrievably linked to family size and structure. Family relationships shape the course of human behavior, individual and interpersonal experiences. The family, determined by size and structure, plays an important role in the development of social and cultural institutions and the choices which go with them in the evolution of social change and fertility. Inputs, and the processes and outputs which follow to achieve desired fertility outcomes, are therefore initiated by policies dependent on a certain measure of understanding of intra-family relationships within the micro-environment the family exists, and which involve decisions and practices relating to life, death, and survival.

Some population experts have generally agreed that there is a strong correlation between increased infant and child survival

143

and the desirability for fewer children. There is less investment in children primarily because of the uncertainty of their survival, while at the same time the desirability or orientation of the family is to have as many children to meet its functional and insurance needs. As survival improves, there are increasing investments or expenditures on children, with a gradual change in the attitude of the family from perceiving the child as a service utility to one on whom benefits should be bestowed. It is considered that, at this stage, reproductive habits change resulting in reduced family size, the extent of which varies as investments or expenditures on the child increase. Thus occurs a child-centered orientation.

John and Pat Caldwell[1] state that "it appears that the intimacy of the family preceded the decision to restrict size: more money was spent on children, less help was demanded or received from the outside, and the burden of rearing and educating a large family was discovered. The small families experienced a low level of child mortality that is not explained by their socio-economic conditions. Both family size and child survival appear to be products of the new child-centered family."

Along with the process of modernization and the moving from a traditional agrarian-based economic system to an industrialized and urbanized one, there occurs a dramatic change in death and birth rates and in reproductive habits. Thus, a contributory factor to the modernization of the family is the change to a child-centered orientation in which there is a shift to lower fertility rates, and the whole is induced by the processes of social change.

Efforts at developing strategies for regulating population growth would only become appropriate and have a reasonable probability for success if modernization processes are pursued concurrently with vigor.

Assumptions

There are three variants of world population projection in a) year 2000, and b) years of probable stabilization—2070, 2110, 2130.[2]. If present tempo is sustained, stabilization should be achieved in 130 years by year 2110, with a population of 10.5 billion, using the medium variant. The achievement of stabilization is sensitive to the speed and extent of fertility decline.

According to demographic analysis by the United Nations

Year	Population (millions)			Annual Rate of Growth in percent			Gross Reproduction Rate		
	High (H)	(M)	Low (L)	H (a)	M	L	H	M	L
1980	4.4	4.4	4.4	1.91	1.81	1.72	2.01	1.83	1.90
2000	6.5	6.2	5.9	1.82	1.56	1.23	1.71	1.52	1.28
2050	10.1	9.8	9.5						

(b)

Variants	Year of Stabilization	Population (billion)	From 1980
High	2130	14.2	150 years
Medium	2110	10.5	130 years
Low	2070	8.0	90 years

International Economic and Social Affairs Department, the following assumptions (quoted in full) index the course of population projections:

Fertility Assumptions

1) fertility level will generally decline as a country progresses in economic and social development;

2) existing or anticipated government policies and programs, as well as non-government activities, if any, designed to foster development, will expedite the process of fertility decline;

3) the fertility decline will be slow at the beginning, gain momentum, and then will be slow again as it nears replacement level. On the basis of observations of several countries that have gone through the (demographic) transition, the decline is assumed to be most rapid between a gross reproduction rate of 2.5 and that of 1.5;

4) cultural factors and value systems, which are widely diverse among the different geographical regions, must be taken into consideration as important conditioning

145

factors in either facilitating or delaying the fertility decline.

Migration Assumption

Because of the complexity of its causes and the difficulty of anticipating future trends of international migration, it is assumed that the volume of net migration—if there is any at present—will, in the present projections, diminish progressively with the passage of time unless there are strong indications that the present level of migration will be sustained for a considerable period.

Differences between geographical regions present variations in growth and distribution of population within the global context. Already the more developed countries in Europe, Soviet Union, North America, Japan, Australia, and New Zealand have averaged below the replacement fertility level, and it is estimated that in year 2000, they will recover to the replacement level. If the high variant assumption is followed, this recovery will occur in 1990; with the low variant assumption it will not take place until after year 2000. The current gross reproduction rate averages 2.5 for Africa, Asia (excluding Japan), Latin America (including the Caribbean), and Oceania (excluding Australia and New Zealand), and because current fertility declines are expected to be sustained through year 2000, it is estimated that gross reproduction rates for these regions by then would decrease to 1.8, 1.6, and 1.6, in terms of the high, medium, and low variants respectively. As earlier noted, South Asia and Latin America would be just ahead of Africa in being the last to achieve significant fertility reduction towards population stabilization. This would certainly have a dragging effect on the rest of the world and create pressures that will affect developed and developing countries (globally) alike, involving the demand for food, finite resources, clean air, clean water, unpolluted seas, etc. The population syndrome is, therefore, a concern for all peoples of the world. Industrial or developed countries cannot isolate or immunize themselves, by any kind of strategy, from the problems facing the developing countries. It is a case of sink or swim, together. The decision is collective and should be consensual.

As an added note, East Asia including China is experiencing a rapid fertility decline and is projected to reach replacement level by the year 1990, if the medium variant is applied.

Assumptions Altering Estimate of World Population

A brief scenario can be depicted thus. Improvement of literacy levels for all would, among other things, raise the salience for health and family planning interventions and practices, would contribute towards improvement of status for women and entry into the labor force; improvement on health generally and specifically for mothers and children will result significantly in lowered infant and maternal mortality rates; sustained efforts in social engineering would improve social ambience—all these compounded together would lead to decisions of the individual which would affect the gross reproduction rate, which in turn would, given mortality conditions, determine the family size; the crude birth rate will fall in consequence. Because of improved health, the crude death rate also falls. To a greater extent the age structure of the population, along with the changes in fertility and mortality levels, and, to a lesser extent, the net reproduction rate determine the speed with which the crude birth rate approximates the crude death rate. Time, therefore, is of the utmost essence, and an optimum speed achievable over time would produce, *in the target year*, the low population variant; with a moderate boost of current pace, a medium population variant; and, at current or less pace, a high population variant.

Effects of High and Low Population Levels on Social and Family Patterns

There are illimitable possibilities regarding the characteristics of the global population. This is due to the volatility of the demographic situation which allows the possibility for high, medium, and low variant population projections that are based on certain fertility and mortality assumptions. At this point in time there is uncertainty regarding future trends in fertility and mortality.

As the birth and growth rates are so volatile, it would be difficult to predict population projections with any reasonable accuracy. The speed of decline in mortality will outstrip that of fertility for some time and will only be equated when such factors that depress fertility become intensified; such as, use of contraceptives, the process of modernization, and social improvements.

As already noted, the effects of excessive population-growth rate have deleterious consequences on social and economic aspects of a country's development, as well as on its political decisions. The impact is seen on the education of the public, the health and welfare benefits, and the quality of the environment.

The effects of such a growth rate on socio-economic development are indeed complex. To sum up, high growth rates place enormous burden on a country's resources to allow it to keep up with at least the basic needs of its population, by providing increasing amounts of water and food supplies, more housing, and social services. The scenario depicts, to quote a few examples, ever increasing encroachments on resources for education in terms of accommodating ever increasing enrollment rates, on health in the provision of expanded basic health services, on resource distribution to various critical public sectors, etc. And, of course, meeting these demands does not presuppose a dilution in quality standards. However, standards may suffer from the economic and social burden a country is forced to carry by the overwhelming demands of its increasing population, especially at this crisis phase in the world's history of sluggish economic growth. As noted in Planning for Growing Populations[3]: "When the costs of setting (high) standards cannot be met, the consequence is not a uniform provision of sub-standard services, but a high degree of concentration of available resources in favor of privileged areas and groups reflecting a general dualism in the distribution of incomes and assets and also consolidating it." Therein lies the paradox of the population syndrome. The outcome of generating and utilizing a country's resources is dependent on the volume of consumers—how high or low a level of population a country has to contend with and the effects of differing dimensions on each social and family variable.

We would expend a lot of hours computing the effects of high and low levels of population on social and family patterns. The exercise can be matched against a set of variables which would be affected, in varying degrees of application. The main variables are noted as follows:

Social Indicators

1. Education enrollment—literacy levels

2. Health Services Coverage—urban/rural complex and lev-

els of morbidity and mortality (infant and adult)

3. Agriculture — food/nutrition complex — percentage of labor force in agriculture

4. Labor—employment/unemployment syndrome

5. Potable Water—urbanization and population density

6. Public Utilities

7. Housing—environmental factors

8. Income Distribution—savings and investments increases in per capita income

Family Indicators

1. Life Expectancy

2. Nutrition Values

3. Change to nuclear family—influence on total fertility rate (TFR)

4. Dependency Ratio—population structure

5. Net Reproduction Ratio

6. Median Age of population

7. Mean Age of marriage

8. Proportion ever marrying

Notes

1. Caldwell, John C. and Pat. "The Achieved Small Family: Early Fertility Transition in an African City," Studies in Family Planning 9, No. 1 (Jan. 1978), :2-18.

2. United Nations Department of International Economic and Social Affairs.

3. Development Centre of the Organization for Economic Cooperation and Development: "Planning for Growing Population"; ed. Robert Cassen and Margaret Wolfson, Paris 1978.

12.

World Population Problem: Its Impact on the Family and Community

Ruhuna University,
Galle, Sri Lanka

Gervin P. Samarawickrama

Introduction

The continuous increase in population all over the world has remained one of the major phenomena during the second half of the twentieth century. In many developing countries, the problem has indeed become serious. Population growth and changes have an impact on economic and social conditions and therefore on health and well-being. Conversely, evolutions in health also exert significant influences on quantitative changes in the population. Population and its rate of change rank among the primary determinants of health care needs.

Numbering about two billion fifty years ago, global population is now well over four billion and growing by some seventy-four million a year, or a million every five days. Over the past few years the global population growth rate failed to decline appreciably, and still stands at 1.7 percent annually. According to the latest United Nations' assessments, the world growth rate is projected to decline to about 1.5 percent by the year 2000. However, despite this projected drop, the absolute number of people added each year is continuing to rise—to an estimated ninety-five million per year two decades from now, bringing the population over the six billion mark.

Current projections for the world's ultimate peak population range from eight billion, reached about the middle of the next century, to eleven billion in 2125. The difference hinges on when the world as a whole reaches replacement-level fertility, i.e., an average of about two children per couple. Because young people in or about to enter their reproductive years now far outnumber people at older ages, it would take another sixty to seventy years after reaching this goal before births and deaths come into balance and the world population stops growing. For every decade of delay in achieving replacement-level fertility, the world's ultimate stabilized population will be about eleven percent greater.

Progress towards the two-child family is mixed. Childbearing is close to or below this level in most developed countries. This includes the United States where the rate is now at 1.8 children per woman, although births still outstrip deaths by well over a million a year. A handful of European countries are at zero growth or actually losing population.

Among many developing countries which make up the other three-quarters of the world's population, birth rates have now started downward. At the same time, mortality declines are leveling off as the easiest-to-control diseases are conquered. As a result, the huge Third World gap between births and deaths is now narrowing. But not by much, so far. And the pressures of human numbers are mounting. Food production in developing countries barely keeps pace with population growth, already hard-pressed Third World cities likely to gain over a billion more inhabitants by the year 2000, their labor forces growing by 780 million over the same period with some 300 million already out of work or under-employed, and seas, land resources and the atmosphere under assault everywhere.

Consequences

In the world as a whole there appears to be enough land and water to meet food demands during the next half century. But this land and water—plus the know-how, capital, and institutions required for their efficient use—are not distributed in the same way as population. International movements of food will have to grow if per capita consumption is not to fall in regions such as South Asia, where food production is already barely keeping pace with population growth.

The world's energy problems are the most serious, difficult, and dangerous of all the resource problems the world faces despite declining population growth rates, and that the world's per capita Gross National Product might then be as high as $2,600 compared to $1,000 now. Given these projections, the rate of increase in consumption of nonfuel minerals and energy will decline during the period to 2025, although absolute consumption levels will be vastly greater at the end of the period. When these projections are compared with projections of potential supplies, and when the nature of the difficulties in realizing these supplies is considered, it becomes clear that the problems we face in the next half century are associated less with physical exhaustion than they are with unequal distribution of resources, the security of supply lines and trade, environmental problems associated with high levels of use, and, above all, with the transition problems in moving from one resource regime to another in an orderly way.

The situation with respect to nonfuel minerals is similar. We must find substitutes for less abundant resources, such as tin, tungsten, and lead, and more ways to use abundant resources like aluminum, cement, and glass.

We already face balance of payment and security problems so far as petroleum and nuclear power are concerned. During the next fifty years these problems will be compounded by the fact that reasonably priced sources of both petroleum and natural gas will be exhausted. This does not mean that the world must learn to live without liquid and gaseous fuels, but it does mean that ways must be found to acquire these fuels from other sources. Adequate alternatives do exist. Liquids and gases can be produced from coal, shale, tar, and vegetation, to mention only the most likely sources to be used. And nuclear and solar energy can be substituted for liquids and gases in many uses. The problem is to bring these alternatives into use in an orderly, equitable, and safe way—safe both environmentally and militarily.

In all this, a decline in future population growth would be of considerable help, for it would provide the world with more time and resources with which to solve these problems. But whatever future population growth rates may be, the world will still be faced with unsolved problems resulting from past growth. There are no simple explanations or unidimensional solutions for our problems.

153

The Past—Winning or Losing?

For practical reasons all projections take off from past trends. Therefore, it is useful to start with what has happened so far, even though the future will not replicate the past. Have population and economic growth rates been outstripping supply? To answer this question, we can look at several kinds of evidence:

(i) Socio-economic indicators of levels of material well-being, to tell us whether life has been getting better or worse for most people;

(ii) Changes in relative price levels, which reflect changes in resource scarcity; and

(iii) indications of improvement or deterioration in the quantity or quality of material or environmental resources.

Socioeconomic indicators show improvement

If we judge by the goals of economic growth, surely the world as a whole has been winning the race. By practically whatever measure of basic necessities or material well-being one judges—per capita incomes, calories consumed, shelter and clothing, hours of leisure, protection against physical dangers and major famines, medical care, infant mortality, or life expectancy—the average person in the world today is at least somewhat better off than his parents, and substantially better off than his grandparents. As can be seen, even in the poorest of countries there was some progress in practically every indicator between about 1960 to date. In Pakistan, for example, per capita Gross National Product (GNP) increased annually by 3.1 percent compared to 2.3 percent in the United States; energy production per capita increased by 6.0 percent per year, compared to 1.9 percent in the United States; and life expectancy at birth rose from forty-two to fifty-one years, compared to a rise from seventy to seventy-one in the United States (Table 1).

But there are problems with this relatively positive assessment. Most important, these improvements are averages; they say nothing about what is happening to the distribution of material well-being. While there is no evidence that the poor have become absolutely worse off as the averages have increased (Ahluwalia 1976), there is evidence that they are not advancing as fast as the figures suggest, that their numbers are increasing, and that the gap between the rich and the poor has grown. This may be related to the process of economic growth itself. Income distribution appears to be worse in countries that have progressed to middle levels of per capita income, and best in rich countries.

While developing countries are in general materially better off today than they were two decades ago, the gap between rich and poor countries has undoubtedly widened. For example, in 1960 per capita income in Pakistan was $104 while that of the United States was $5,484. In 1976, even though Pakistan's per capita income had grown more rapidly than that of the United States in the interim (3.1 versus 2.3 percent per year), the levels were $170 and $7,890 (Ridker and Cecelski 1979).

This growing gap between developed and developing countries is due largely to the much more rapid population growth in developing countries, which has greatly reduced the benefits of economic development. From 1961 to 1975, the annual rate of increase in food production in developing countries was greater than that in developed countries (Ridker and Cecelski 1979), but because of more rapid population growth, per capita production grew much more slowly. Per capita food production in 1971 −1975 actually declined in Africa and Latin America, the regions with the highest annual population growth rates in this period (2.7 percent). Another illustration is provided by the case of the Aswan Dam in Egypt. When completed in 1970, the dam increased the country's arable land by a third (800,000 hectares). But because of population growth during the decade it took to build the dam, from twenty-six to thirty-three million, food output per capita has hardly improved at all. The gains made in literacy provide a final example. More people are literate than ever before in human history. The proportion of illiterate adults dropped from forty-four to thirty-two percent between 1950 and 1975. Nonetheless, the absolute numbers of illiterate adults have also increased during this quarter century from 700 to 800 million (UNESCO 1976).

The world may be achieving these gains in average well-being at

155

the expense of future generations. This would be the case if this generation is using up the world's resource base or environmental carrying capacity faster than new discoveries and technology can expand them. Thus, while it is useful to know that life has been improving for the majority of humanity, this fact tells us nothing about the future.

Past trends in market prices

A better, though far from perfect, way to judge whether resources have become more scarce is to observe what has happened to resource prices. If resources have become more scarce, their prices, relative to those of other goods, should have risen.

The average price of most raw materials fell or remained stable in real terms between 1870 and 1970 (Barnett and Morse 1963) despite the fact that ores with steadily lower concentrations of minerals were being mined (Cook 1976). This was the result primarily of technological advances in mining and processing, and sharp declines in the costs per unit of output of labor, capital, and energy.

While prices are better than any other signals of scarcity, they are far from perfect. It is tricky to obtain good measurements of the most appropriate prices and to separate out the effects of inflation, short-run fluctuations, and changes in market regulations and controls. Prices of raw materials often do not include the costs of cleaning up the pollution incurred in their production. Also, the market prices may not give adequate weight to the interests of future generations. We leave a heritage of slowly or never degrading pollutants to our descendants. Problems such as the removal of topsoil through erosion and the buildup of carbon dioxide in the atmosphere might not have economic consequences that affect prices until it is very difficult, expensive, or impossible to deal with them. The health costs that future generations will have to bear because of today's pollution emissions are similarly not reflected in today's market prices.

Specific evidence of depletion

If measures of well-being and market prices are not adequate to reveal if we have been winning or losing the race between demand and resources, the only alternative is to look at what is happening to specific material or environmental resources, to see if there is widespread evidence of depletion in stocks or deterioration in quality.

Examples of deterioration can be found, but it is difficult to say whether they are omens or approaching global overload or manifestations of transitional, localized, or manageable problems. There are several important areas where this confusing situation may be studied.

Renewable biological resources

Recent trends in per capita production of various biological resources have been cited as evidence that human numbers have arrived at the limits of the earth's carrying capacity.

Worldwide per capita production of beef did indeed decline for two years in a row in 1977 and 1978. Will the trend be downward from this point onwards? Similar fluctuations have occurred since 1960. Per capita production has also declined for mutton since 1972 and for wool since 1960. But these two trends are related to changes in taste and the development of synthetic fibers, which have made it less profitable to raise sheep and supply mutton.

For wood, the trend in per capita production is clearly downward. Twenty-five years ago forests covered a quarter of the world's land surface. Today they cover only one-fifth, and, if the present trend continues, the fraction could fall to one-sixth in 2000 and one-seventh in 2020 (Ridker and Ceceleski 1979). Most of this deforestation is occurring in developing countries where energy price rises and population growth are intensifying pressures on fuelwood and timber supplies, especially in the delicate ecosystems of tropical forests.

Fisheries, too, are probably overexploited and declining at this time. From 1950 to 1971, the world's total fish catch rose by five to six percent a year from twenty-one million metric tons to a peak of just over seventy million metric tons annually. Production then dropped abruptly to less than sixty-six million metric tons in the next two years and has fluctuated generally downward since then. With growing world population, the drop in per capita yields has been even greater.

If ocean pollution grows over time, consumption will have to be

157

reduced even further to protect the fish population. Inadequate international co-operation has hampered management of ocean fisheries and control of ocean pollution, although the on-going United Nations Law of the Sea Conference offers some hope of correcting this situation.

Indications that the rate of growth in per capita production of cereals has declined since 1971 is sometimes taken as another piece of evidence that population growth is pushing against the earth's sustainable biological limits. If true, the situation is serious, for these cereals—wheat, rice, corn, and other grains —directly supply over half the food energy of the world's population and much of the remainder indirectly when consumed as livestock products and alcoholic beverages.

The food shortages that existed in the mid 1960s and early 1970s were probably the result not of global shortages of land or water but of regional droughts, questionable policies, and the absence of global contingency plans to cover lean periods. Many people have advocated the development of a global reserve of food grains to see the world through such periods, but to this day such a reserve has not been established. The crux of the current problem is unequal distribution of productive capacity and purchasing power. Even with the potential for surplus production elsewhere in the world, the poor countries simply cannot afford to buy adequate quantities of food grains in international markets when their own supplies fall short.

Petroleum

The steep climb in world oil production per capita appeared to break dramatically in 1974, and without further evidence one might be inclined to predict a downward trend from now on. The quadrupling of oil prices by the Organization of Petroleum Exporting Countries (OPEC) from $2.59 in January 1973 to $10.95 in January 1974 (plus the further increase to approximately $20 a barrel in 1979) can also be taken as signals of coming shortages. There are indeed very serious dangers in the current world energy situation, but they stem from the fact that importing countries have become increasingly dependent on supplies from politically unstable areas of the world, not from the growing likelihood of imminent exhaustion.

Environment

Environmental quality might appear to be one area where deterioration on a global scale is indisputable. Pressure on the environment has indeed increased with economic and population growth.

In any country where pollution regulations are taken seriously, there has been measurable improvement in levels of such mass pollutants as carbon monoxide, particulates, hydrocarbons, sulfates, and suspended solids in water. In most developing countries, safeguarding the environment has so far generally taken second place in the struggle to upgrade living standards. In the short run, food and jobs are more important than wilderness protection or even some health losses due to air and water pollution.

There are other growing environmental problems that no country is yet controlling, in part because methods of economic control are not always known. These include cancer-causing substances released by the burning of fossil fuels, highly toxic trace substances with long half-lives, such as arsenic, lead, cadmium, certain pesticides and herbicides, and radioactive pollutants, all of which can concentrate into lethal doses as they move through food chains. Environmental problems like these may be our family's and the community's most threatening legacy from past economic and population growth.

Frequently mentioned examples of concerns regarding the environment are ozone depletion, ocean pollution, and nuclear proliferation. In addition there are a variety of potentially serious problems which could affect the community. Among these are the loss and deterioration of soils, loss of genetic variability due to the spread of monoculture, release of long-lived radiation from uranium mill tailings, nuclear reactor accidents and problems of storage, and the proliferation and buildup of toxic chemicals in food chains.

For a variety of reasons, virtually all the problems in this category are unlikely to be effectively controlled in the near future. In some cases, control is technically and institutionally difficult. Ultimately, for example, the spread of nuclear weapons depends only on the diffusion of relevant knowledge, and this is almost impossible to control. What level of risks are we really subjecting ourselves to when we allow more nuclear plants to be built; and

159

how do they compare with those we accept in other areas, such as coal mining, and with those we could face in the absence of nuclear power, such as a drop in living standards? Even with the same facts, countries with little coal and no oil are likely to view the risks and benefits of nuclear energy quite differently from, for example, the United States. As a consequence, these environmental pressures can also be expected to increase with population and economic growth.

Future demands

What is likely to happen to the rate of growth of demand for resources? To answer this question it is important to distinguish between rates of growth in population and rates of growth in per capita demand for various resources.

Population projections

In more developed, rich countries, rates of natural increase (births minus deaths) have already declined to within striking distance of zero. By 1977, they were actually at or below zero in five countries—the United Kingdom, Austria, East and West Germany, and Luxembourg (PRB 1979). The rates could rise again, but considering that the decline is associated with increased female labor force participation and other changes in sexual roles which tend to reduce fertility and which are not likely to be reversed, whatever rise occurs will probably be small and temporary.

Population growth rates appear to have leveled off in the poor, less developed countries as a whole. They have fallen significantly in many Asian countries and in a few Latin American countries, although almost nowhere in Africa. If the material and social progress of recent years is not reversed and if family planning programs are pursued with no less vigor than they now are in many developing countries, the world's population growth rate is likely to fall, slowly and grudgingly, from this point on. This decline in the rate of increase is not sufficient to reduce the absolute size of the additions, however. Even the reduced rate of 2000 will translate into some ninety-seven million additional people annually (UN 1979).

The United Nations medium variant projection of 1978 puts the total global population at 6.2 billion in 2000 (compared to 4.3 billion in 1979) and about 11.5 billion when births and deaths ultimately come into balance and human numbers stop increasing, somewhere about 2075 (PRB 1979). Thus, even though the rate of growth in demands for the earth's resources, represented by numbers of people, will ease, the sheer size of those numbers will still place increasing pressures on material and environmental resources for a long time to come.

Growth in per capita demand

Per capita demands for material goods in poor countries are likely to expand as fast as growth in their incomes permit—which is likely to be faster than growth rates in rich countries, especially since most of the developing countries are just beginning to industrialize, mechanize agriculture, and so on—the most resource-intensive phase of modernization. But their incomes are so low that their demands for resources will not weigh heavily in total world consumption for some time to come. While less developed countries contain seventy-four percent of the world's 4.5 billion population and will comprise seventy-eight percent of the 6.2 billion now projected for 2000, they currently account for only twenty percent of the world's output of goods and services, and that percentage is not likely to rise to more than twenty-three percent by 2000 (Ridker and Ceceleski 1979).

Of more importance for resource requirements is what happens in rich countries. The best conjecture here is that growth in demands for (and consumption of) material goods will slow down significantly. This is because the rate of growth in per capita income is likely to fall and become a declining fraction of income is typically spent on material goods as incomes rise. The slowdown in the rate of labor productivity, and hence income, in developed countries is already under way. It is likely to continue for a variety of reasons, including increasing investments for new forms of energy, environmental controls, additional health and safety requirements, and more of what is sometimes called on-the-job leisure—a willingness to work, but only at a more relaxed pace as incomes rise.

Then, too, the quantities of material goods which people demand are likely to rise at a deceleration rate as incomes continue

161

to rise in developed countries. This deceleration is partly related to the quantities of goods already possessed. There are just so many cars, refrigerators, and houses that one individual can conveniently own: at some point in the accumulation process he will find that he does not have the time to use and enjoy them.

Implications

Consideration of this array of both shorter and longer terms of problems should lead one to question the usefulness of both the limits and Cornucopian views of the future man. During the next quarter to half century, the world will be faced with a series of transition problems requiring the substitution of one resource regime for another—in particular from reliance on petroleum and natural gas to other fuels. In the process, some countries and groups within countries will be hurt while others are benefited. This could cause tensions which, like shifts in the earth's plates that cause earthquakes, eventually burst to the surface. As a consequence the earth could become an increasingly dangerous place to live. Is it not so now?

Population and economic growth play important roles in exacerbating these problems in most cases where other means of resolving them are not present or are not adequately implemented. More generally, the greater a country's scientific and institutional capacity to resolve problems, the higher the sustainable rate of growth can be without overloading the system. As a consequence, the linkage between population and economic growth on the one hand and resource and environmental problems on the other tends to be looser in developed countries and tighter and more unforgiving in developing countries. But rapid rates of population and economic growth cause at least some problems everywhere. What can be done about them?

Should population growth be restricted? Certainly, for this would slow the speed with which all the problems I have discussed must be solved, and reduce the ultimate size of the global population which will have to be sustained, once zero population growth is reached. An equilibrium population of 10 billion, in place of the 11.5 billion now projected by the United Nations, would present that many fewer problems for the long term. A small one would be still better. But even a cessation of population growth cannot resolve all these problems or keep them from mounting over time. Each new birth brings with it an additional packet of resource and environmental problems. The shape of the future can and must be controlled if problems are to be avoided.

All these problems will remain until they are directly confronted and attacked. Uncertainties about the effects of more carbon dioxide in the atmosphere can only be reduced through fundamental research into climatology and related fields. Risks associated with nuclear fission can only be contained through improved security measures and efforts to find and adopt acceptable alternatives. Poverty-stricken countries and improverished groups within countries can only be helped by lifting the barriers to the flow of the resources, knowledge, and technical and managerial skills into, and/or people out of, these regions, and so on.

There is no simple explanation for these problems; equally there are no simple solutions. We have no choice but to work on both the causes and the symptoms simultaneously. Understanding, the true nature of the world's resource and environmental limitations is a first step in that direction.

In this time of social change, unprecedented in its extent, scope, and pace, there are many forces at work that have a crucial bearing on the future. One of the most important factors to emerge over the past few years is the search for a new interpretation of "development" involving a critical reassessment of ideals, goals, and conceptions about the future. A determined effort to achieve a higher degree of individual and national dignity is anticipated.

A United Nations study that prepared a set of alternative projections on the economic and environmental states of the world makes it clear that development cannot be interpreted in terms of economic growth only, even though economic growth is an indispensable component of a strategy aimed at improving living conditions throughout the world. Indeed, economic and social equity should not be viewed separately or in isolation but as mutually reinforcing goals. Greater emphasis must be put on social concerns, such as the elimination of mass poverty, the promotion of employment, and the satisfaction of basic needs of all people.

In many developed countries social welfare systems help to alleviate some of the direct effects of poverty by providing mini-

163

mum incomes or services. However, very large numbers of people in the developing world live in absolute poverty. They subsist at levels shared by very few people in developed countries, and, since they are residents of poor countries, there is no money for an adequate social welfare system.

The World Bank estimates that nearly 800 million people (about forty percent of the population of the developing countries) are living in absolute poverty. In addition to those in absolute poverty, many other people had inadequate access to public services. In 1975, about 1,200 million people, i.e., more than a quarter of mankind, lived in low-income countries in Asia and Africa where the median per capita income was U.S. $150.

The new perception of people's health needs and the new goal of "Health for all by the year 2000" will constitute an integral part of this changing process; the aim is to enable all people of the world to attain an acceptable level of health and to lead a socially and economically productive life. As was emphasized in the Declaration of Alma Ata, "Economic and social development, based on a New International Economic Order, is of basic importance to the fullest attainment of health for all and to the reduction of the gap between the health status of the developing and developed countries. The promotion and protection of the health of the people is essential to sustained economic and social development, and contributes to a better quality of life and to world peace."

References

1. Anonymous, "World Population Growth 1979," Intercom 1979, 7 (4) 1-5.
2. Anonymous, "A New Look at our Population Predicament," Intercom 1979, 7 (11, 12), 1-4.
3. Ahluwalia M.S., "Inequality, Poverty and Development," Journal of Development Economics, 1976, 3 (4); 307-341.
4. Barnett H.J. and C. Morse, "Scarcity and Growth" in "The Economics of Natural Resource Availability," (Johns Hopkins Press for Resources for the Future) 1963.
5. Cook E., "Limits to Exploitation of Nonrenewable Resources," Science 1976, 191, 678.
6. Ridker R.C. and E.W. Cecelski "Resources, Environment and Population," Population Bulletin 1979, 34 3-41.

7. UNESCO, Address of Director-General on 11th International Literacy Day. Sept. 8, 1976.

8. World Bank, World Development Report, 1978 New York, Oxford University Press, 1978, P.26.

Commentary

Stewart E. Fraser

La Trobe University
Bundoora, Australia

T o project our thinking about social and moral issues well into the middle of the next century takes courage, vision, and wisdom. However, some would perhaps say rather that it is principally an exercise in *conjecture, wishful thinking, and crystal ball gazing* at a highly imaginative level.

Realistically, rather than hopefully, our authors fall into the former category, and their anticipation of a world population stabilizing at about eight to ten billion between the years 2050/2100 is currently being supported by a host of researchers concerned with developing demographically sound projections rather than offering merely sociologically inspired predictions. The United Nations Fund for Population Activities (UNFPA), as noted by its director, Raphael M. Salas in his report "State of World Population 1981," suggests that global population could be stabilized at about 10.5 billion by the year 2100. Dr. Edward Pratt, carefully provides for us statistical evidence to suggest that the decades around 2000 are critical as the turning point in demographic transition. But what might the world's population be by 2050—will it have reached and stabilized at about the 10 billion mark, or will it have in reality reached the 15 billion mark?

In regard to Professor Claude Villee's remarks on aging and its contribution to population growth, it is particularly difficult for any of us to visualize human beings living to 150 years and still continuing to be effective persons as we would perhaps see them defined today. Perhaps in Western Europe one is becoming used to seeing and experiencing a significant number of people in the eighty-year old plus bracket. This is still not necessarily the case in a country such as Australia. It will be another two decades

167

perhaps before this phenomenon has to be seriously considered. The more rapid aging of Europe's population is a phenomenon perhaps only more clearly recognized during the past decade or so. But the suggestion that there is a likelihood of age doubling or life expectancy extended to 120, 140, or 150 years during the next century is still most difficult for most of us to either comprehend or appreciate.

It is now of even greater importance to focus on changes in fertility patterns. The so-called lesser developed countries (LDCs) have evolved their own pattern of decreasing fertility, but there are still enormous variations especially so in Asia.

The total fertility rate (TFR), or the average number of live births per woman over her lifetime, has fallen dramatically in some countries, such as China, Korea, and Singapore, to name just three in Asia during the past fifteen years. These are certainly disparate examples worth noting, with China now about 2.5 TFR, South Korea about 2.7 TFR, and Singapore at about 2.2 TFR (hardly at a replacement rate). I believe demographers use a statistical yardstick of 2.26 TFR as a general borderline for replacement rate.

My own research, based on a number of visits to Vietnam in recent years, would suggest only a modest dampening down of fertility patterns. There are some cautious but discernible developments in Vietnamese family planning programs—still heralded with greater success in northern provinces rather than in southern provinces, for a variety of perhaps obvious or apparent reasons. The Vietnamese TFR was about 4.8 in 1980, which is certainly down from an estimated 6.1 TFR in 1965. On a more despondent note, Pakistan has moved only modestly from an estimated 6.9 TFR in 1965 to about 6.6 in 1980.

Attitudes towards abortion—or pregnancy termination—if one prefers that phrase, have changed throughout much of the Asian world especially during the past decade. It might be relevant here to mention a cross-national study I am currently conducting with my wife, Dr. Barbara J. Fraser, of State College of Victoria, Coburg, Victoria; Professor Kim, Sun Ho of Kyung Hee University, Seoul; and Professor Robert Bjork of Vanderbilt University, United States of America, on social-sexual attitudes of teachers in various countries. We have incorporated a number of questions in an attitudinal survey concerning abortion. We would like to share some of the preliminary results with colleagues as they may be indicative of the attitudes of future teachers working in the related fields of population education, family-life education, and sex education.

Korean teacher trainees numbering over 4000 at two prominent universities in Seoul were asked to provide responses to various attitudinal statements on abortion. The same questions were asked of two similar groups of teacher trainees in the United States and in Australia. It is interesting to see the very great similarity of attitudes of women in all three countries, and likewise it is just as interesting to see the significant differences in the responses of males and females in the Korean sample.

As a tentative generalization we believe that it is apparent that women certainly educated at the tertiary level, and going into the teaching profession in all three countries, had somewhat similar attitudes towards abortion. This is especially so regarding the necessity of abortion where cases of rape, incest, children's defects, and maternal health are concerned. But much more cautious, undecided, or uncertain responses are recorded as to whether pregnancies should be terminated merely because a child is unwanted or because of other social, economic, or psychological reasons during early pregnancy; that is, during the first trimester.

While these are just some random examples of fertility changes put forward for consideration, they do suggest enormous differences in both the direction and in the kind of countries coming to grips with attempts to regulate fertility.

Perhaps there is also need to mention here in passing that there are three countries in Asia, all of them subscribing to communist-Marxist philosophy, which firmly believe that population growth needs to be vigorously nurtured and carefully cultivated. Reference of course is made to North Korea, (19 million) Kampuchea (4.5 million), and Laos (1.7 million). These three areas believe, for a variety of differing socioeconomic, political, and psychological reasons, that planned vigorous population growth should be a cornerstone of public policy. In perhaps somewhat simplistic terms, the so-called imbalance (or inequality) of gross population size manifested by the two entities in the Korean peninsula has led to greatly varying population policies in two coadjacent areas. Likewise, the relatively underpopulated regions of Indo-China, principally Laos, suggest to some government planners in the capital, Vientiane, that family planning activities should be directed towards increasing the size of the general population as well as increasing health levels of all sectors, especially in the infant categories. The two aims are not considered incompatible by the government. The obvious geopolitical fear of Laos' current government leaders is based on holding politically a theoretically and demographically underpopulated area, which lies in the potential path of possible migration and resettlement from two countries, one lying to the north and one to the east, namely, China and Vietnam. The current situation in Kampuchea probably speaks for itself—with the horrendous loss of about half a million people in a short period of time, barely four years ago—has produced a mentality which readily underwrites a government policy to rapidly "replenish and catch up." A U.S. government agency demographic report on Kampuchea (1980) points out great and detailed studies to the unhappy facts concerning the enormous population losses due to death by murder and starvation, and to continuing malnutrition and maintenance of only subsistence levels of living during much of 1980 and 1981.

Thus, we have the apparent paradox, but one perhaps fairly easily explained, of various Asian communist countries, for a variety of enormously disparate reasons, emphasizing somewhat differing population policies. Each country has to face a set of socioeconomic and demographic circumstances greatly differing to one another, and each is tackling the tasks with varying levels of skill and competence. Vietnam, with a population of fifty-five plus million in 1981, has a current annual natural growth rate of about 2.8 percent per annum. It cannot foresee anything less than a population of seventy-five million by the year 2000; in fact, Hanoi demographers have alerted governmental planners to the unpalatable fact that a population of 100 million by 2000 is a very definite possibility if the current TFR of about 4.7 cannot be reduced.

The Chinese, on the other hand, are reported to have reduced the annual natural population growth rate to about 1.2 percent per annum. The mammoth census conducted in August, 1982 (and employing 6 million census takers!) should provide data as to the accuracy of the plethora of population statistics we have been provided from China. The census might also indicate if and when China's population has (had) reached the billion mark. In May 1981, while in China, I was able to visit a number of the new population research institutes established at ten major Chinese universities during 1980 and 1981. Regular visits over some years to China, and extended discussion with Chinese colleagues both in the education and population fields, have convinced me of the difficulty in first obtaining accurate and reliable statistics, and secondly, caution in the extrapolation of regional statistics and interrelating them with national statistics emanating from Beijing.

Statistics provided to me by Chinese colleagues working in demography at the People's University and Beijing University both in Beijing, and Fu Tan University in Shanghai, Chengdu University in Sichuan clearly show the statistical likelihood of China's population increasing over the 400 million mark in a hundred years—if three children per family can be envisaged as the norm for the next century! However, the chart shows less dramatically the greater likelihood of there being two billion Chinese by 2080 if the average family size, currently estimated to be 2.3, is "allowed" to continue for a century. This is China's present situation, and one to which all the authors make important and pertinent references. Certainly the People's Republic of China is not ignoring the opportunity of "exercising peer group pressures to limit the number of children to one or two per family." This family size limitation, in fact, is one of the cornerstones of China's recently announced population policy on small families. But it is part of an overall program of delaying marriages, delaying births, and "restricting" the number of births to one per family, utilizing a cleverly designed package of incentives and disincentives. A program of population education for both primary and secondary schools is now being instituted, but not as yet necessarily including topics which would be listed as sex education issues, as taught in schools in some other Asian countries, viz., Japan.

On the topic of family planning Dr. Villee notes that some "fifty million births each year globally are neither planned or wanted." He rightly focuses on the need to advance the techniques of preventive medicine especially in regard to improved contraceptive measures. While he does not mention abortion—it has been, for a variety of varying social, medical, and psychological reasons —not universally accepted as a satisfactory technique available to be used in family planning programs. There is obviously discussion, dissension, and disagreement on this topic—it is an issue

171

of no small concern. For a variety of medical as well as social reasons, some governments are still reluctant to list it as a major technique for "fertility regulation," or perhaps more accurately we should say for "use in family planning." Yet its acceptance in many Asian countries is evidenced by the growing enormity of the literature and research reports provided on the subject each year.

Part VI

Human Population of the Future: The Food-Supply Crisis

13.

Feeding the World's Increasing Population

Kenneth Mellanby

Director Emeritus
Monk's Wood Experimental Station
Huntingdon, England

How Many to Feed?

Today the world has a human population of more than four thousand million, and this is increasing. Previous estimates of population increase have generally been badly wrong. Thus, in 1945 many Western countries feared an imminent fall in numbers; in the event, their population increased substantially in the next twenty years. Then in the nineteen sixties, when diseases were being better controlled and the birthrate had not started to fall in most countries in the Third World, numbers were seen to be increasing exponentially, and overpopulation, with mass starvation and catastrophic increases in death were confidently predicted in the not very distant future. Fifteen years ago—the days of the doomsters—some scientists stated that the world was already overpopulated, and that whatever the birthrate, numbers would soon start to decrease as more deaths occurred when resources were exhausted and food supplies became inadequate. The world situation looked very bleak.

Today we are not generally so alarmist. The birthrate is dropping in almost all countries, so we now have "zero population growth" (ZPG), or something near to it, in many developed countries. In a few the population is actually decreasing. The birthrate has so far fallen least in the poorest countries, and here, with half the population under twenty years of age, the potential for growth is immense. Birthrates even here are indeed falling, but even if the birthrate falls so that each couple has only two children, in some countries numbers will almost double, as there are few old individuals who will die off as the next generation is being born. So, unless controlled by some calamity, human numbers are certain to increase.

As previous forecasts were so erroneous, we are now more reluctant to foretell future numbers, but the most generally accepted figures are that by the year 2000 there will be at least six thousand million humans in the world, and that this number will go on increasing before it levels off at anything between twelve and twenty thousand million somewhere towards the middle or end of the twenty-first century. Some writers think ZPG will be reached sooner, with a smaller total; others take the opposite point of view. There is always the possibility (some say the probability) that man will exterminate his species with global nuclear war, or that plagues or famines will drastically reduce the number of survivors.

There are many factors which will affect population growth (or decrease). In this paper I am concerned only with one—food. Obviously, unless a human is adequately fed he will be unable to live a healthy life. If food supplies fall below a certain level, widespread deaths from starvation are inevitable. As today, throughout the world there are some millions of deaths each year from starvation, and hundreds of millions of people who are seriously underfed, the prospects of an increasing population do not look good. However, I believe that I can show that the world is capable of providing a nutritionally adequate diet for many more than the present population. I do not think that food need be the limiting factor which will control human numbers.

World Food Production in 1982

This optimistic view is based on an examination of the present world production. First, let us consider cereals, which, while not themselves a complete diet, are the major source of energy and protein for many peoples. In China it has been advocated that it should be government policy to allocate a ration of one pound of rice per head per day, as this is sufficient to act as a basis to which various supplements, often in small quantities, can be added, and with this starvation and malnutrition would cease to be a problem. The world's production of cereals is approximately as follows:

Wheat	450,000,000 tons
Rice	400,000,000
Maize ("corn")	400,000,000
Other (barley, oats, rye etc.)	350,000,000
Total	1,600,000,000 tons

All this is suitable for human consumption. If it were divided equally among the whole population of the world, every man, woman, and child would receive over a pound and a half of grain, equivalent to 3000 calories and over 60 grams of protein. This is substantially more energy and protein than most people actually require.

However, though important, cereals probably constitute only about a half of the total world food production. Over 300 million tons of potatoes, and 200 million tons of legumes (beans etc.) are grown. Yams, cassava, and plantains form the staple food in parts of Africa. Nuts, particularly coconuts, yield considerable crops. Vegetables produce millions of tons, and may be very important food sources to villagers in all continents. Fruit, though generally low in calories, is widely consumed. Finally, some 200 million tons of meat and 60 million tons of fish are consumed.

It is clear that if the abundance of the earth's bounty were equally distributed, there would be enough for something like twice the present world population. Without increased production, if population forecasts are even approximately fulfilled, it will be well into the next century before food shortages need be considered to be problems.

Why Then Do People Starve Today?

If the world is producing so much food, why is starvation so prevalent? The answer is that our economic, social, and political systems prevent those who need the food from receiving it. People go hungry because they are poor and cannot afford to buy the food they need.

Waste and greed are also root causes of maldistribution. We in the richer countries consume far more than our share. We do this by over-eating, to our own detriment, for obesity, contributing to heart and other diseases, is a common symptom of our form of malnutrition. Nearly a quarter of the food bought by housewives in Britain, and an even larger fraction in the USA, ends up in the dustbins ("trash cans"). However, the main reason why there is not an enormous glut of cereals is that about half the world's production is fed to livestock, to pigs, poultry, and to cattle. Now it is generally believed that this is done to produce much-needed protein, an essential part of a civilized diet. What is not generally realized is that all our food, all its energy and all its protein, is derived from plants. When grain is fed to livestock it is very wastefully used. At least half the protein and up to ninety percent of the energy is lost in the process of conversion. A product—meat—which is economically valuable and which gives pleasure to the consumer is the result, but at a great cost.

On the other hand, there is no need for complete vegetarianism to ensure that everyone is properly fed. More than half the cattle and pigs throughout the world graze on plants which are unsuitable for human consumption, and these also produce manure which fertilizes arable crops. Hens and pigs often scratch about living on scraps. Although large amounts of meat may actually harm the greedy consumer, it is much easier to ensure that a diet is dietetically complete if it contains at least a garnish of animal protein. There should be plenty for this purpose without wasting foodstuffs which are needed, and will be needed even more, by the growing human population.

Although the produce of the whole world could easily feed the whole world's population, it is not at present possible for every individual country to be self-sufficient. The greatest increases in agricultural productivity have, in recent years, occurred in the developed countries with the lowest rate of population increase. It is obviously most efficient to live mainly on locally produced food. It is to be hoped that increasing agricultural research will be related to the problems of the poorer countries which today cannot feed their existing, let alone their projected, numbers.

Can Food Production be Increased?

Although present production, properly distributed, could feed the projected world population until well into the twenty-first century, it is likely that more food will then be needed. It is also unlikely that there will, in the near future, be sufficient changes in our economic and political systems to ensure that distribution is radically improved. So increased food production is evidently desirable.

First, I think that we should consider the potentiality of the present agricultural system, using the land and other resources already available. It would be rash to rely on the results of research which has not been shown to be successful, though some of the possibilities should be mentioned as they may affect future planning.

Clearly an increase in cereal production would have the greatest immediate impact. Grain can be stored and easily transported to distant countries. If in surplus, it can be used to feed livestock. The most thorough study of this problem has been made by scientists at the Agricultural University of Wageningen in the Netherlands. This university is renowned for its practical research relating to both tropical and temperate farming. This study concluded that, using present methods and on the land known to be available, grain production throughout the world could be increased by no less than twenty-five fold. Even greater yields were thought to be likely as a result of promising research in the pipeline.

Not everyone agrees with the Wageningen figures. They may be overoptimistic. However, I believe that they were sufficient to make it likely that we can feed more than the population which the earth can support without many other problems becoming intolerable.

Energy and Food Production

Modern farming techniques, particularly as practiced in developed countries, may be productive, but they use a great deal of energy. Manpower has been replaced by machinery, crop yields increased by chemical fertilizers which require much energy to synthesize. The yields suggested by the Wageningen scientists would require an energy input greater than the present total fuel use of the whole globe. This might seem, therefore, to be a target impossible to reach.

However, it should be realized that the most intensive arable farming techniques are those which provide the greatest increase

179

in the energy available to man. It has been shown that for most cereal crops, for every unit of energy (joule, megajoule, calorie, whatever unit you prefer) used to grow a crop, and this included the energy to drive the tractor, to make the tractor, to plant the seed, to make and spray insecticides, to harvest the grain, there will be at least three units of energy in the cereal harvested, and a further one or two units in the straw. Intensive arable farming is the most effective method of trapping solar energy. So, though to grow heavy arable crops uses so much energy, it also provides a substantial surplus for man's use. It would thus be possible, at least theoretically, to use the straw and some of the grain as fuel to power the whole system. At present this is not done because other fuels are available and cheaper, but if there is a serious energy crisis, intensive farming should help to solve rather than to increase the problem.

Arable farming, producing our staple food, is thus energy-effective. It is wasteful livestock rearing, and the production of luxury glasshouse crops, which uses so much more energy than it produces. Also our food processing industry, with its over-packaging of sophisticated junk foods, is the real villain.

Although there may be an energy crisis in the next thirty or so years, there seems the likelihood that eventually mankind will have unlimited energy supplies made available for use. This could arise from fusion power, or from the effective trapping of solar energy, possibly in some process of non-living photosynthesis. If unlimited energy is available, food production will be potentially unlimited also. Water may be a limiting factor, but could be efficiently recycled inside glasshouses covering the Sahara, growing many successive crops during the year by some system of hydroponics. Artificial heat and light could produce tropical crops at the poles. The possibilities are limitless.

Can Increased Production Be Maintained?

Hydroponics can, in theory, be practiced anywhere, but it is probably wise today to rely mainly on crops grown on natural soils. Here two processes are affecting the situation. New land is brought into cultivation, often as a result of irrigation. Crops are also grown on land cleared of forest. It is likely that more land will be available in the future than is cropped today, particularly if the soil is properly managed. On the other hand, much farmland throughout the world is going out of production for various reasons.

In Britain we may be losing as much as 100,000 acres of productive farmland each year to housing, industry, reservoirs, roads, and airfields. The same process goes on in many other countries. It is easier to build on farmland than on rocky, unproductive areas. In Britain the increased production on the remaining farmland has much more than compensated for this loss, but the process cannot go on indefinitely. Mankind will have to safeguard its farmland if food production is to continue to increase.

Agricultural land is also lost for other reasons. Bad farming, which was practiced by our prehistoric ancestors in Britain, and which still continues in many countries, makes fertile soil unproductive. In temperate countries farmers have now learned how to retain and enhance fertility; the field in England which gives four tons of wheat to the acre in 1982 is the one most likely to give a similar, or greater, crop in 1983. We still do not know how best to manage many soils, particularly lateritic soils in the tropics, but in general we are beginning to learn how to manage the land, and I am confident that this is something at which we will get better. Even soils ruined by bad farming can, in many cases, be restored to fertility in a comparatively short time, and areas destroyed by industry and waste disposal can often be turned into good farmland again. With adequate water, suitable crops and rotations, natural and synthetic fertilizers carefully applied, the present trends to greater productivity should continue. However, if we are careless (or ignorant), erosion, salination, and the spread of deserts could reverse the process, often in the very areas where more food is most urgently required.

Perhaps the greatest worry concerns possible changes in climate, and of the weather pattern in countries where the most efficient agriculture is practiced. In the past there have been many changes: in geological time deserts have been below the sea; temperate regions have been tropical. Even within the last two hundred years there have been cool spells and periods of warmth. This can greatly affect crop growth; if Britain were a few degrees cooler, it would be difficult to maintain the present level of yield in wheat, and the developing wine industry would again disappear. However, one country's loss would probably be another's gain, and world supplies would be maintained. Distribution might, however, become more difficult.

Man himself may now be changing the world's climate. The burning of fossil fuels, the cutting down of forests, and the draining of organic soils in marshes all release carbon dioxide, much of which remains in the atmosphere. Atmospheric levels have risen by some fifteen percent in the twentieth century. This may have had some beneficial effect, and may have increased crop growth—it is established practice to raise carbon dioxide levels in glasshouses with this result. However, it is possible that if the process continues, which it will if we continue our present lifestyle, the carbon dioxide will cause the world's temperature to rise, perhaps by several degrees. The reason for this is the "greenhouse effect," when carbon dioxide allows the sun's radiation to reach the earth, but then it traps an increasing amount of the heat re-radiation from this planet. At first sight the rise in temperature might be welcome, at least to those living in cold countries. However, it could have catastrophic effects. First, it might melt more of the Antarctic ice, and raise ocean levels, possibly by many feet, which could flood London, much of the Netherlands, and other low-lying regions. Secondly, the rise in temperature would not be equal at the equator and the poles, and the whole weather pattern of much of the world could change. The grain-growing areas of North America might become too dry, the Sahara could have a plentiful rainfall. Although, here again, gains and losses might, in time, be equal, the immediate upset to food supplies could be catastrophic.

Pests and diseases already take a substantial toll on crops. Research has produced many efficient pesticides, which have boosted yields. However, we also find that immunity to these chemicals is developing, and is making some pests very difficult to control. It is possible that this process will increase more rapidly than our scientists can produce new pesticides. Some hope may be derived from the ways in which we are beginning to learn to use chemical pesticides more sparingly and with greater effect, and with less risk of inducing resistance. I do not myself think that the inability to control pests and diseases is likely to jeopardize our food supplies, though some serious losses are likely to continue.

Are There Important New Foods of the Future?

I have indicated that I think that, with existing knowledge properly applied, and common sense, the world should be able to produce enough food for any likely increase in population. However, current and future research may make this task even easier.

Heavy cropping relies today on the use of fertilizers, particularly nitrogenous compounds, produced using much energy. Even though this energy may be easily available, it would simplify things if less chemical could be used. Legumes need little additional nitrogen, as they (or their bacteria) fix atmospheric nitrogen and even enhance soil fertility for succeeding crops. More use could be made of this process, but even more promising is the possibility that cereals with their own nitrogen fixers may be on the way.

There are considerable possibilities for new types of food derived from algae or fungi, living perhaps on the nutrients in sewage effluent. These foods have been used as animal feeding stuffs, and there is no reason why they should not become part of the human diet. At present they are not really needed.

People tend to think of spun proteins derived from soya and other beans as novel foods. These are, of course, only a method of eating beans with the unnecessary expenditure of much energy in processing. However, a substantial addition to protein supplies for man or his livestock may be obtained by extracting the protein from otherwise inedible plants. If protein supplies were short, I have no doubt that these techniques will be more widely exploited.

People tend to look upon the sea as a source of boundless wealth. In fact, in proportion to its area, it is very unproductive. Only about sixty million tons of fish, with overfishing in many waters, is harvested. Although species now neglected could be caught, and marine organisms like the Antarctic krill could be harvested, the total productivity is limited. Fish farming, particuarly in sea lochs and fjords, could become an important industry, but in global terms the yield would be small.

At present we can synthesize many foods from their elements, but to do so uses far more energy than does ordinary farming. If, as has been suggested, mankind has unlimited energy at its disposal, then it may be possible to produce unlimited amounts of most foods in the laboratory. Whether we will be clever enough to produce substances which will appeal to the gourmet, I very much doubt.

Conclusions

The world already produces twice as much food as is needed to nourish the present world population. The reasons why many starve are economic, social, and political. I also believe that food supplies could be increased to feed a far larger population than that for which the world could provide civilized facilities. I do not therefore feel that food is a major limiting factor for mankind on earth.

14.
National Policies for Population Control
Gervin P. Samarawickrama

Ruhuna University College
Galle, Sri Lanka

Introduction

Population growth and changes have an impact on economic and social conditions and therefore on health and well-being. Conversely, evolutions in health also exert significant influences on quantitative changes in the population. Population and its rate of change rank among the primary determinants of health care needs.

World population is expected to increase by almost sixty percent, exceeding 6 billion by the year 2000. By the turn of the century almost eighty percent of the world's population will be living in what are now considered as developing countries (U.N. 1979).

Rapid population growth stretches family and national budgets thin with increasing numbers of children to be fed and educated, and workers to be provided with jobs. Owing to high fertility, developing countries typically have about twenty-five percent of their populations in the primary school ages (five to fourteen) compared with fifteen percent in developed countries, and far lower income resources to invest in education. They have also been faced with a doubling of their population of working ages (fifteen to sixty-four years) in the past twenty-five years.

Besides high unemployment, this has meant disproportionately youthful, inexperienced labor forces and consequently lower average productivity and slower per capital income gains.

Conversely, the low income, high infant mortality, and lack of education of the poor contribute to continued high fertility and all its disadvantages. Poor parents who see little chance of educating their children, and expect to lose some through death, are unlikely to reduce family size in order to "invest" more in each child. They also view children as sources of desperately needed family income, both in childhood and later in the parents' old age.

The most widely cited population expert in the world today is Thomas R. Malthus, an English clergyman, who wrote his major treatise on population nearly two centuries ago. In his classic work, *An Essay on the Principle of Population*, he focused on the relationship between population growth and food supplies. Malthus believed that population tends to increase geometrically, while food supply increases arithmetically. Though this has proved only partly true, he was quite right in his broad contention that population growth often presses against the limit of food supplies.

During the two centuries since he wrote, famines have claimed countless millions of lives. Famine and the threat of famine are still common place. Hundreds of thousands have starved to death during the seventies and eighties in Ethiopia, Somalia, Haiti, Honduras, and Bangladesh. Worse, hundreds of millions still suffer from energy and protein malnutrition.

In general, the priority health problems of mothers and children and high levels of mortality and morbidity derive, to a large extent, from the synergistic effects of malnutrition, infection, and uncontrolled fertility, themselves consequences of poor environmental and socioeconomic conditions, including unavailability of health care. It has become increasingly clear that activities and programs in all developmental sectors are essential to improve the health of the community.

Development cannot be interpreted in terms of economic growth only, even though economic growth is an indispensable component of a strategy aimed at improving living conditions throughout the world. Indeed, economic growth and social equity should not be viewed separately or in isolation but as mutually reinforcing goals. Greater emphasis must be put on social concerns, such as the elimination of mass poverty, the promotion of employment, and the satisfaction of basic needs for all people.

An Integrated Approach

In recent years, an increasing number of governments of developing countries have become more aware of the serious challenge of rapid population growth to their social and economic development. Yet population factors have been integrated into development planning schemes only to a limited extent, primarily because of inadequate knowledge of various important interactions among population and socio-economic variables. Problems relating to health care also stem from insufficient facilities, inadequate training and health personnel, transportation difficulties, and an existing social gap between health staff and villages resulting in irregular services.

With the limited resources available to national planners, it is quite understandable that any suggestions for the adoption of an innovative measure in development planning require the backing of a convincing and carefully pretested formula. The shared objectives of such programs must also converge to a point at which the desired long-term goals are the eradication of poverty and a lasting improvement in the quality of life.

Figure 1 shows the conceptual framework of a project in Thailand—the Samerng Project.

Population, food, and nutrition, viewed as independent factors in the growth process, have their individual significant role and influence on development. Each again has a mutual bearing on the other in the development process. The critical element in this relationship is the interdependence of these factors. For example, the size of the population determines to a great extent the food requirements, which in turn determine the nutritional status of the population, which again indicates the quality of life of the population.

In solving these problems, attempts are being made to use resources available within the villages, including traditional midwives, school teachers, and volunteers for the delivery of primary health care services to the people. An important concept of primary health care is that health services should be fully integrated with the activities of the other sectors involved in community development. It is therefore necessary to develop a multi-sectoral, integrated approach, involving health, agriculture, community development, and education promotion at all levels.

Objectives of the Integrated Program

An integrated approach should aim at

a. improving the nutritional status of the target population, identified as women of child-bearing age, infants, pre-school, and school-age children, through an integrated, multi-sectoral approach in provision of basic health and development services.

b. increasing the awareness among mothers that improvement of the nutritional status of the family will help reduce the rates of morbidity and mortality of their children, and this will increase acceptability of the family planning services in the medium and long term.

c. increasing public awareness that more appropriate use of foods and increased production of necessary foods within the community will strongly promote the health development and social well-being of the family.

d. studying models of health and development work which use multi-disciplinary approaches, integrated services, and close co-ordination of development-related agencies.

In all cases the basic purpose of integration is the bringing together of specialized and differential units or activities into a single or more co-ordinated set of activities. As such, several types of integration are possible. It can operate at different levels of organizational structure, it can vary in the scope or kind of activities brought together, it can be formally prescribed and observed.

In many countries it is now widely accepted that programmatic efforts to reduce fertility require more effective linkages to specialized services designed to meet other basic human needs, such as health and nutrition, food, clothing and shelter, education and the opportunity for self-fulfilling work, and family life. Hence, the

Figure 1 *The conceptual framework of the Samerng project*

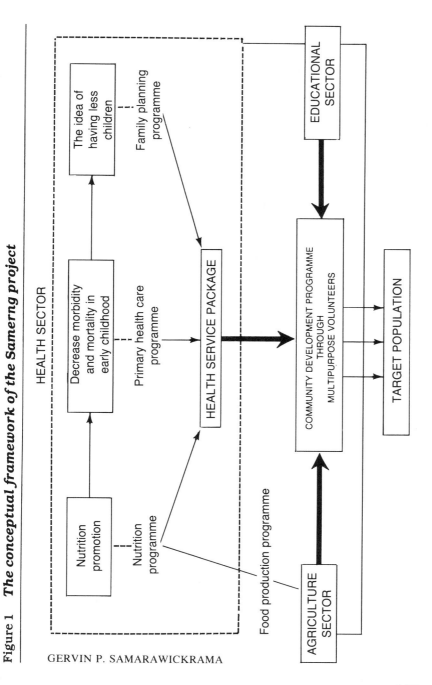

GERVIN P. SAMARAWICKRAMA

population control activities have been made an integral part of the total socio-economic development efforts involving various development ministries, agencies, and voluntary organizations.

In the Southeast Asian countries several pilot projects to integrate family planning, nutrition, and parasite control, co-sponsored by the Japanese Organization for International Co-operation in Family Planning (JOICFP) and the International Planned Parenthood Federation (IPPF) are making good headway.

It seems feasible to progress a step further and to identify six basic reasons for the integration of policy and programs in the three areas, population, food, and nutrition.

a. There is the basic fact that malnutrition and poor health are especially serious manifestations of poverty, and inequality in the availability of health services to a large part of the rural population is particularly extreme in many countries.

b. Improvements in nutrition and health can be expected to yield significant economic benefits along with the increase in well-being of the individuals affected.

c. Strong presumption that integrating nutrition and health services with family planning activities will increase the effectiveness of efforts to slow the rate of population growth.

d. Integrated approach is more cost-effective than single-service programs. Of particular relevance here is the fact that an integrated program provides a number of strategic "entry points" wherein the local health worker can introduce family planning information at a time when clients are relatively receptive and the appeal of adopting family planning practices is likely to be high.

e. Because of the relevance to three major objectives of development, i.e., attaining self-sustaining growth, reduction of poverty, and slowing of population growth —there is a realistic possibility that the launching of integrated programs could muster the political, administrative, and budget support required to achieve wide coverage of the rural population. Some political leaders and officials at both national and local levels will find it easier to support a "family health program" than one focussed exclusively on "family planning".

f. There is sufficient evidence that the integrated programs are feasible and effective. (ESCAP 1980)

The Mode of Integration

Having examined the rationale for the integration of population, food, and nutrition programs, the next step to consider is the approach to implement such integrated programs. Here, two factors come into play. One factor is based on the mode or manner of integration, i.e., logistical, vertical, and horizontal links, etc. The other is based on the perceived beneficial interactive effects, such as cost-effectiveness and the enhanced acceptability of such integrated efforts.

Seen in a broader context, integration implies the existence of identified linkage points between the selected areas which can be utilized in the process of integration. These may be administrative linkages, such as contacts between officials at the same or different levels, or direct service linkages in which a number of specialized activities are brought together at the point of providing services to clients. From the implementor's point of view, it is imperative that the application of the principle of integration be backed by clear-cut policies emanating from the top-echelons, at ministerial and senior administrative levels.

Implementation of Integrated Programs

In formulating integrated programs, the aim should be to achieve a balance between what people want and what administrators and subject-matter specialists think is good for the people. In this manner, it may be possible to ensure that the programs formulated will be acceptable to the people and at the same time will achieve their basic objectives. At this stage too, it is necessary to make a clear assessment of natural needs and available resources.

Either prior to or following an assessment of the situation, it is advisable to set up a high-level national unit to formulate policy and negotiate with the three sectors concerned in the implementation of such policies. This high level unit should ideally

a. review existing needs,

b. examine resources and allocations, and

c. establish priorities.

At the implementation level there should be co-ordinating committees at three levels; namely

a. Policy, or the national planning office;

b. Program, or ministerial planning level;

c. Operational, or local level.

Role of the Government

Such a varied problem has to be settled at the top level representing legislators, scientists, humanists, and media personnel. It will be the politicians who will have to advocate change and press for solutions to be adopted. It will be up to the politicians to formulate policies and ensure that they are put into practice. The politicians will need to spell out what the continuing population explosion means to the man in the street, how it will affect his future and that of his children, and what it will mean for his expectations and aspirations.

Discussions involving politicians, planners, etc., must be held regularly in various parts of the world to meet the following objectives—

To promote co-operation and collaboration amongst parliamentarians of the different countries through greater and continuing interchange of experience and knowledge in population and development.

To further improve and enrich the quality of life of the people through a more effective utilization and management of resources by the integration of population, resources, and environment in the development process.

To attain social justice and economic progress through a more effective mechanism to hasten the process of an integrated and balanced approach to population, resources, and development at national, regional, and international levels.

To consolidate the efforts and strengthen the co-operation between and amongst countries of various regions to achieve the early realization and establishment of the New International Economic Order.

All parliaments and governments must undertake to—

- increase the awareness and promote greater understanding of the interrelationships between population and development amongst parliamentarians;

- formulate strategies and programs for the socio-economic development of their peoples, not to ignore the wealth of intellectual, philosophical, and cultural traditions, but to draw upon the richness of this knowledge and its scientific basis for direct application to planning and implementation efforts;

- establish a national co-ordinating body, where it does not exist, for the formulation and effective implication of population policies and programs;

- increase financial allocation for family planning and population programs within their country according to their needs;

- review the existing targets and goals in the implementation of population and development programs so as to contribute to the attainment of the one percent population growth by the year 2000;

- strengthen and expand socio-economic development programs and ensure that development is directed towards reducing and narrowing social and economic disparities, thus hastening the creation of a just society;

- plan an effective strategy for the conservation of their natural resources and their effective utilization, while being mindful of the need to safeguard the environment;

- enact and implement laws on family rights, where necessary, to ensure full and equal rights for men and women and to raise the level of education of women to make possible an increase in their social responsibilities and rights, particularly in their role as mothers;

● initiate and promote and utilize studies and research for better understanding of the problems of youth, so as to introduce programs to harness these vast human resources in the best interest of future development;

● strive for early achievement of the goals and objectives of the New International Economic Order by intensifying co-operative and collaborative efforts in areas of mutual interest;

● increase meaningful dialogue between the developed and the developing countries in order to improve trade relations and effect a more equitable share of resources, technology, and expertise.

In order to achieve these goals and objectives there should be an increase in the over-all allocation of international assistance to population programs. The contributing governments designate a meaningful proportion of their development aid for population programs.

Current Trends—

A step in the right direction was taken in 1979 with the holding of the International Conference on Population and Development in Colombo, Sri Lanka. Parliamentarians from sixty-two countries returned home from this conference armed with the Colombo Declaration and a strong commitment to call for the implementation of population policies as an integral part of socio-economic development plans. This five-day meeting was the first ever funded by the United Nations' system specifically for legislators.

Parliamentarians from nineteen Asian countries have called on governments in the region to support stronger population programs and to "review existing targets and goals in the implementation of population and development programs so as to contribute to the attainment of the one percent population growth rate for the Asian region by the year 2000." The "Beijing Declaration," adopted unanimously at the close of the Asian Conference of Parliamentarians on Population and Development,

held in the Chinese Capital in October 1981, says that governments should demonstrate their political will:

- to give greater impetus and support to existing population
  programs;

- to allocate adequate resources to meet the needs of the
  programs, in addition to adopting comprehensive population policies as an integral part of national development
  plans.

- The conference called on parliaments to encourage the
  formation of national groups of parliamentarians concerned
  with issues of population and development, in order to
  promote awareness and understanding.

The Beijing Declaration reiterates and reaffirms the initiatives
and objectives of two earlier declarations on population and
development by parliamentarians meeting at Asian venues,
namely, the Colombo Declaration on Population and Development
and the Kuala Lumpur Declaration on Resources, Population, and
Development. The major thrust of all these three declarations is
the recognition of the inextricable relationships between people,
resources, and the environment in the challenge of alleviating the
effects of continuing poverty by promoting development and
creating employment towards this end. The conference delineated
a few areas where action could be taken.

These meetings were preceded by the first Asian Population
Conference held at New Delhi in December 1963. In inaugurating
this conference Shri Jawaharlal Nehru, prime minister of India,
said that population growth was a world problem with social and
political as well as economic implications. This was followed by
the second Asian Population Conference in 1972, held at Tokyo,
which aimed at providing a better understanding of the central
role of population trends, studies, and action in the achievement
of development goals. The Third Asian Pacific Population Conference was held in September 1982 at Colombo, Sri Lanka.

Thus, step by step, the parliamentarians of Asia are moving
towards creating an institutional mechanism by which this
commitment can be sustained. They pledged themselves to "promote the formation of groups of parliamentarians concerned with
population and development at national, regional, and interna-

tional levels." Such programs could be adopted by countries of the other regions, especially the developing world. In many instances, while the interrelationships between population variables and policies in other vital sectors of development are being acknowledged as a pivotal consideration in all societies, our understanding of the relationship falls just short of ignorance. As a result of this shortcoming, satisfactory progress has not been made in implementing integrated programs giving adequate treatment to population elements. There are several explanations for this slow progress; in some countries it is the inadequacy of data or inadequate use of existing data; in others it is the lack of properly trained personnel to deal with integration; in some it is the lack of an integrated perspective and methodology of national development, and in still others it may be due to inadequate commitment and direction from the top.

To execute these integrated programs parliamentarians, policy makers, and senior administrators must meet regularly and funds for such deliberations be made available by the donor agencies.

References

Economic and Social Commission for Asia and the Pacific Population Research Leads No. 7, 1980, p. 5.

United Nations, "The World Population Situation," Population Studies No. 63, 1979, p. 7.

World Bank, World Development Report, 1978. New York, Oxford University Press, 1978, p. 26.

World Health Organization, "World Health Forum," Vol. 2, No. 2. 1981, p. 264.

15.

Resources Versus Population

University of Oklahoma
Oklahoma City, U.S.A.

B. Connor Johnson

It seems to me that there are two questions involved:

1. Is it not the desire of the great majority that resources and population in any country (or any cultural group within a country) so balance that all individuals are able to enjoy a standard of living at least roughly approaching that of the fifteen to twenty-four countries that have of the order of $3,000 to $7,000 average GNP per capita per year?

2. Is it not the desire of most also that this be accomplished at some level of population which permits considerably more space than standing room only? Is not the varied ecology, biology, life of the world worth preserving, particularly if the only reason for not doing so is the paltry wish of reproducing freely with no thought for the world or its future?

It also appears that all such decisions are only up to us. Just as man made man's history, man will make man's future.

Food Production

Thus, while I have no disagreement whatever with Prof. Mellanby's statement that there is enough food produced to feed the world's population and probably to feed double it, I would observe that first it is not being done and probably won't be, and if it were, would we like the crowded world we eventually produced?

If you agree with some forty plus organizations in the United States and many more in the rest of the world, as I do, such a crowded world is not necessarily a desirable goal even *if* reachable.

The Zero Population Growth Society works to achieve zero population growth as soon as possible. Perhaps even better, the Negative Population Growth group has worked for only ten years toward promoting drastic reduction in world population during the next one hundred years to make possible a world economy sustainable indefinitely. Their aim is to reduce the population of each nation and cultural group to half that of the 1979 level. This certainly holds great appeal to me. In 1975 there were fifteen countries of the free world with a GNP per capita of $3,000 to $7,000 per year; there are another twenty-seven countries at the $1,000 to $3,000 level; while there are 114 plus countries at various levels of between $60 and $1,000 GNP per capita. The numbers in the communist dictatorship world are of the same order one, six, and six; the *one* being lower than any of the fifteen first mentioned.

It seems to me, however, that rather than go totally for the ideas of all negative population growth, that the real goal should be to aim in each individual case at a balance between resources and people so as to provide an acceptable standard of living for all citizens. I have used the word "resources" rather than food because as Prof. Mellanby points out, food is available, it just needs to be bought (traded) by whatever resources are available in the specific cases.

Currently, on a very rough average, for the 114 "underdeveloped" countries to achieve the average yearly per capita income of the fifteen "developed" countries of $4,000 to $7,000 per year per capita GNP, an average population reduction of fifteen-fold would be required; and by the year 2000 this would be about thirty-fold. While this is obviously impossible in twenty years, it is possible in one hundred. The increasing of production fifteen to thirty fold within this time span is at least as difficult to achieve. By working at both, there should be a meeting place between these extremes.

It appears to me obvious that the first concentration of effort, the first priority must be the teaching of responsibility of all individual families to have no more children than they believe they can reasonably expect to be able to feed, clothe, and educate to a level essential for competing in the modern industrialized, computerized, agriculturally efficient world.

In the United States currently one farm family provides food and fiber for sixty families, while in most of the world this figure is closer to two. Providing resources (food or means to purchase food) for an ever-expanding population in any finite world must be difficult, and for some groups very difficult indeed. I also wonder who wants either standing room only or starvation, war, and disease. Surely the human race, which has survived some two to three million years, which has shaped man's past and will shape man's future, can accept the responsibility of assuring that man's future is controlled by man. I believe mankind will survive and evolve; that is one of the top priorities of the nature of life on this planet, i.e., survival and evolution. However, it seems worthwhile for each individual to assume responsibility for the decent survival of his future generations. Let us make *use* of what has been learned in medicine, in agriculture, in history, and science. Give me a fish and I'll eat for a day; *teach* me to fish and I'll eat for a lifetime.

Education for responsibility is the key to freedom. A Soviet commune worker, when asked by an official the question, "Won't it be wonderful when all the world's countries are communist dictatorships," replied "Yes, but then where will we get our wheat." The other side of the same coin, of course, is to ask the North American or European, etc., wheat grower—"Won't it be wonderful when all farmers are as free and as knowledgeable as you?" Currently he would reply, "Yes, but then where would I sell my wheat?"

Certainly, at some cost, food can be provided for the present world's population. One could bring icebergs from the Arctic and Antarctic to Arabia, Australia, North Africa, etc. Pipe water from all lakes and rivers to all deserts. Bring the world's farmers the agricultural knowledge of the American or, even higher, the level of the Western European farmer. But why, who wants to? Do we want to live in a world like Waikiki Beach—standing room only?

I see no valid reason why any country or any group of people, any culture within a nation, wants to bring its own population to the edge of poverty and starvation. With current knowledge of sanitation, water purification, parasite control, infectious disease

199

control, agricultural productivity, one would think that any group of people would want to balance population and productivity so that practically everyone enjoys a reasonably satisfactory standard of living.

The Soviet Union, for example, admits readily that thirty percent of its actual food consumption is raised on the small amount of agricultural land privately permitted to each individual farmer. If this knowledge of food production along with the fertilizers, tools, and income incentives, were all permitted, the Soviet Union would probably be a wheat exporting (rather than importing) nation.

Population control apparently must be wanted, learned, and taught as an individual's responsibility to his future and that of his children. We all know that there is no way in which the fifteen "developed," industrialized countries can support the biological ability of the world's population to reproduce beyond the limit of the resources of the nation involved.

There appears to be only one practical reason why an expansive power should support unbridled reproduction elsewhere, and that is to obtain surrogate manpower to use as "cannon-fodder" in place of its own citizens.

Government Control of Population Expansion

Absolute population control by government must imply either an absolute totalitarian dictatorship or a majority rule that has no protection for minorities, even if they constitute 49.9 percent of the electorate.

Two systems of government are known in various modifications: one is totalitarian dictatorship, the other is representative government. The idea of government of the people, by the people, for the people while the aim of all, is very difficult to realize. Truly representative government can still mean only majority rule unless, by checks and balances, minority rights and all human rights, are protected. This then gives me great difficulty in supporting government control of reproduction, and thus of population. Let us remember that even total extermination of a population group, without anyone being killed, is on paper still very easy. If, purely as an example, every male of such a group were to have a vasectomy, that group or nation would not exist one hundred years later, merely by attrition.

But this and many other methods do provide the possibility for free men and women to decide the kind of world they want for their children, in terms of standard of living, population density, balance between resources and people.

It is thus not knowledge that is lacking; but will, freedom, understanding, which are missing.

16.

Changing National Policies of Population Size

La Trobe University Bundoora,
Victoria, Australia

Stewart E. Fraser

A s a background to the most interesting practical and programatical papers provided by Kenneth Mellanby and Gervin Samarawickrama, we should keep in mind some of the more recent highlights of population development during the past two decades, and how the world's growth rate has peaked and then gradually declined. As a generalization it can be said that barely two generations ago few countries had a "developed population policy," whereas today over eighty percent of the total population of the so-called developing world live in countries which believe that their fertility rates are much too high and want them reduced drastically. These countries would include today in Asia of course, China (1008 million), India (714 million), Indonesia (152 million) and Vietnam (56 million.) Some seventeen percent of the world's population live in countries where their governments are evidently satisfied with their current fertility levels; presumably this would include countries such as Australia (14.9 million) and New Zealand (3.1 million).

However, it should be noted that the remaining three percent of the world's population live in nations in which their governments believe that their fertility rates are too low and would like to have them increased, especially through the use of a series of a pronatalist social-economic-welfare bonus incentive schemes. These countries which wish to see their fertility levels increase would include in Europe, the Union of Soviet Socialist Republics, (especially the western or European segments of the Soviet Union), Bulgaria, German Democratic Republic, and Rumania. In Asia, perhaps the most aggressively pronatalist country is North Korea (DPRK), followed by Laos and Kampuchea—but for somewhat different reasons. Even Malaysia has a pronounced pronatalist view, and her government officials speak optimistically of a two to four fold increase in population in the next twenty to thirty years "to take up some of the abundant space and develop resources with which Malaysia is renowned." Some statistics of relevance . . . The world's birth rate has declined by nearly fourteen percent from the period 1965-70 to the period 1975-80. But the less developed world showed a decline of over sixteen percent during these two periods.

The world's growth rate peaked in 1960-65 when it was almost two percent annually. It has continually declined and was approximately 1.7 percent in 1981-82. The United Nation medium variant projection for the world population in 2000 is now 6.1 billion people, with "reasonable to high" expectation that the world population will stabilize at 10.5 billion about the years 2110-2120.

The International Conference on Population held in 1984 in Mexico City was able to assess the decade-long progress since Bucharest 1974. Instead of fertility the emphasis was on a new set of problems which the demographers have identified for us. The difficulties of uncontrolled urban development and unplanned growth loom large, just as the problems of uncertain migration patterns due to political as well as economic causes. Some countries may have to face more seriously than in the past the issues of a gradually aging population because of rapid declines in fertility patterns.

These are merely some of the evolving critical issues which are important to recognize as we consider such a topic as "feeding the world's increasing population." Kenneth Mellanby perspectively and accurately identifies certain key issues, certain critical paths, and certain innovations which may help us understand the equation cycle of population growth—consumption—resource development —and expansion.

His arguments in a diagramatic way suggest the following schema in a somewhat simplified—input—throughput—output systems analysis.

(A) *Population Projections*		(C) *Supply*
(1) High	Consumption	(1) Increased
(2) Medium		(2) Increased yields per acre
(3) Low		(3) Experimental new crops
Variants		(4) Synthetic-processed foods

(A) *Population Projections*
   (1) High   Consumption
    (2) Medium
     (3) Low
    Variants

(B) *Countered-Offset by:*
   (1) Family Planning Programs-:
      Birth Reduction (+)
   (2) Entropy: Social-Economic Disorder (−)
   (3) Disaster: Malthusian (−)
   (4) War-Disease-Famine (−)

(C) *Supply*
   (1) Increased
   (2) Increased yields per acre
   (3) Experimental new crops
   (4) Synthetic-processed foods

(D) *Distribution*
   (1) Efficiency
   (2) Rationing
   (3) Supplements

(E) *Waste*
   (1) Storage losses
   (2) Vermin losses
   (3) Processing losses
   (4) Recycling losses

Kenneth Mellanby's views are obviously optimistic, and he believes that the causes of starvation, disease, and malnutrition are essentially ones of an economic, social, and political nature. The enormous differentials in either GNP (perhaps not the best of measuring sticks in which case use GDP) and in resource consumption between specific countries and between specific parts of some regions is well documented.

I work on a regular basis in two major Asian socialist countries, namely, China and Vietnam. The East Asian GNP in 198182 approximated 1,330$ U.S. but China had under 300$ U.S. and Vietnam, by my own estimate only, hardly half this or about 150$ U.S. On the other hand, for a variety of special reasons, Hong Kong would record 1,200$ U.S., Singapore 4,480$ U.S., Japan nearly 9,900$ U.S. and Korea 1,520$ U.S.

If you take another, and probably a much more suitable social index for a quality of life comparison, in regard to the above named countries, we would have the following table for *Life Expectancy at Birth* (men and women combined):

This somewhat selective sample from East Asia also shows enormous variations between nations as reflected in either productivity scales or general health scales. If Kampuchea (thirty-seven years) and Laos (forty-four years) were included, their life

East Asia	66 years
China	65 "
Vietnam	53 "
Hong Kong	76 "
Singapore	71 "
Japan	76 "
Korea	66 "

expectancy at birth rates would rank among the lowest in the Asian region.

It is against such an uneven background of diversified, baffling, and differing statistics that we can look more carefully at Gervin Samarawickrama's schema for promoting effective population control policies. He shows, by an interesting diagram, how the Samerng Project for Community Health Development is implemented in Thailand. I am somewhat familiar with the project and have first hand experience with its effectiveness in some parts of north eastern and central Thailand. The core of the problem is threefold, and involves demographic forces (fertility), agricultural productions (food), and health (nutrition). The development process is regarded as an integrative one and all factors are interdependent. Because of a special personal bias, I would be inclined to lay the greatest preventative emphasis on health—nutritional skill development conjointly with fertility control and careful birth planning programs.

Dr. Samarawickrama is optimistic, as many of us are who work in the population, education, health fields, that the Thai Samerng Project has immense possibilities in both reducing poverty levels as well as initially slowing and then ultimately controlling population growth.

The emphasis I believe for countries, with politically diverse systems such as Thailand, China, Vietnam, Laos, Kampuchea, lies in emphasizing a "family life program" involving equally health education and birth planning. The focus nationally on a "family health program" has possibly greater social involvement at grass roots levels than a mere "family planning" program. Unfortunately, political emphasis is all too often being placed primarily on birth control programs as essential and singularly important components of overall national production plans. In China a birth control program has the quaint saying, "Keep up the production by keeping down the production (of babies)." The draconian Chinese One Child Family Program now being implemented in rural China with great vigour is based on birth quota factors as established in all provincial, and commune levels. The more popular and, probably in the long run, more efficient programs are being run on a total health, welfare, maternal, and child basis—rather than merely on "keeping the production down."

It is perhaps a useful axiom to say that all countries face the same demographic analyses, namely, concerning fertility, mortality, moribundity, and longevity issues. But the national and regional situations may differ so drastically, with countries co-adjacent to each other, that comparisons almost become meaningless. Both Dr. Mellanby and Professor Samarawickrama have addressed themselves, respectively, to global food production issues, and population policy issues. The latter focusing on lesser developed countries and the former emphasizing the disparity between the have and have not nations.

In conclusion, I would like to draw our listeners' and readers' attention to the peculiar and unusual demographic situation now occurring in the Soviet Union. This may again illustrate a further dimension of the kinds of problems both authors have raised in their respective papers.

The Soviet Union provides some very clear illustrations of food-distribution problems and population-control problems within the boundaries of one major nation. The Union of Soviet Socialist Republics is faced with a waning population growth, and labor predictions, for the 1980s and 1990s, which indicate that a severe shortage of workers is to be expected in many fields of industry.

The lack of workers, of sufficient training, will have decided effects on economic development, not to mention a severe fall in the quantity and quality of young recruits to maintain the five million military force level which is considered necessary. Intra-Soviet republic ethnic problems are also surfacing where enormous fertility differentials lie, between the Central Asian Muslim minorities of the Union of Soviet Socialist Republics and the currently dominant Russian (Slav) ethnic majority living predominantly in the western part of the Soviet Union. The Soviet government has deliberately favored a pronatalist policy to increase fertility among the currently still dominant Slavic-ethnic groups in the multi-national country which makes up the Union of Soviet Socialist Republics. Lump sum grants of fifty rubles (U.S. $68) for first births, one hundred rubles ($186) for second and third births are paid, and unmarried mothers are paid an extra allowance of five to ten rubles per month per child. Fertility stimulating measures, such as extra leave, child care bonuses, and creche facilities were promised for 1983, and special allowances of nearly thirty percent monthly extra wage bonus made for women in Siberia and the Far East sector of the Russian republic where Slavic populations have been stagnant in recent years. The high fertility non-Slavic populations are to be found in Kazakhstan, Azerbaydzhan, Uzbekistan, Tadzhikstan, Kirgiziya, and Turkmenistan.

The Slavic Republics currently have barely a 0.7 percent annual population increase rate, while the non-Slavic republics have closer to a 2.8 percent annual increase rate. Put another way, the three Slavic republics would take about 120 years to double their populations, while the eight non-Slavic republics in the Transcaucasus Central Asia would take on an average between them barely forty years to achieve a doubling!

Hence, the considerable concern within the Soviet Union, (but primarily between Russian government leaders, party officials, and academic demographers) as to how to develop differential population control policies, which will simultaneously dampen down Central Asian fertility patterns while specifically encouraging the growth of a long term baby boom among Slavic women. The demographic dilemma of Soviet leaders may be summed up in the now discredited expectations that Central Asian peoples in the Soviet Union would be subjected to a withering away—a dismantling—of traditional Islamic cultural patterns based on religious upbringing, the peculiar, i.e., special status of women, and Koranic dominated family formation patterns. These would be replaced entirely with Marxist modes for modernization and industrialization and political emancipation based upon the Communist Party ideological guidelines. These patterns, instead of decaying, have in the last two decades become revitalized and the assertiveness of Pan Islamic forces, based primarily on Pan Turkism formed by the Turkic Muslims, become more pronounced.

17.
Interactions Between Food Supply and Human Populations

Gerald Stanhill

The Volcani Center Ministry of Agriculture Bet-Dagen, Israel

Looking at the developments that have occurred in the 180 years since Thomas Malthus first formulated the quantitative but dismal relationship between food supply and human populations, we can find strong arguments to both refute and support his argument that whereas food supplies can only increase arithmetically, populations do so geometrically[1].

To take the example from the country of both Malthus and Mellanby—Britain, as an example of the developed nations—we find that the yield of the major food crop, wheat, is now three times the national average in Malthus' time, and has been increasing at a supra-exponential rate since the end of the Second World War[2]. By contrast, Britain's population is now in a more or less steady state of zero population growth.

Against this refutation of Malthus' thesis, it can be argued that whereas in his lifetime Britain was self-supporting in food, today only half of the calories consumed by its population are home grown, and that each of these that are, degrades nearly three calories of irreplaceable and polluting fossil fuel energy in its production[3]. Further increases in food production are certainly possible by increased intensification, but this could be expected to require an even greater fossil fuel subsidy with an accompanying pollution that could eventually have negative effects on food production. Such negative feedback effects could include loss of soil fertility and climatic changes.

Despite these cautionary arguments, there is no doubt that Dr. Mellanby's central thesis is correct: that is, the world currently produces sufficient food to adequately feed its population *if a rational, egalitarian and global food distribution and production system was implemented,* and that a considerably larger world population could also be fed given such a system. Dr. Mellanby has shown in some detail how this could be done in the case of Britain[4].

Quite apart from the difficulties in implementing such a food distribution and production system on a global scale, there are a number of important questions that still remain open and that require answers before one can say even in theory that the world's food supply need not pose any problems.

First is the strong and negative interaction that appears to exist between the food production and distribution systems. For example, although the centralized socialist bloc of countries led by the Union of Soviet Socialist Republics has the size, power, and declared intent to impose a rational and egalitarian food distribution system, it is in fact chronically subject to food shortages due to failures in agricultural production. In contrast, the Western world, although very successful in food production, has failed to rationalize its production or distribution system, even within individual national borders.

There are two additional important interactions between food supply and human populations about which too little is known. First is the role that historically population pressure has played as the forcing function for increased food production. Secondly, there is the question of the effect of the level of food supply on the rate of population increase.

Although the developed world appears to have solved its food population problem, it is by no means certain that the developing world has the time, capital, technical skills, or fossil fuel energy supply available to implement the same solutions. Thus, the major question for areas where the food and population problem is acute is—Can food production systems be devised and implemented that will promote a negative correlation between increased food supply and population growth, and yet be attainable and appropriate to the developing world?

Notes

1. Malthus, T. R. (1798) An essay on the principles of population, as it affects the future improvement of society, with remarks on the speculations of Mr. Godwin, M. Conderet, and other writers. J. Johnson, London, 396 pp.

2. Stanhill, G. (1976) Trends and deviations of the yield of the English wheat crop during the last 750 years. Agro-Ecosystems 3: 1-10.

3. Leach, G. (1975) Energy and food production. Int. Inst. Environm. Develop., London, 151 pp.

4. Mellanby, K. (1975) *Can Britain Feed Itself?* The Merlin Press, London, 61 pp.

18.

Full Utilization of Food Resources

P. V. Sukhatme

Maharashtra Association for Cultivation of Science, Pune, India

Ⅎ am sure that we are all satisfied with Professor Mellanby's analysis that the world has enough capacity to meet the food needs over the next one hundred years, possibly longer. I am not, however, sure that the problem of distribution will be solved. The very fact that some of us have spoken of the need to intensify population control and use eugenic measures to limit global population is not a good pointer to develop distributive justice. We need to develop a better understanding of the problem and look inwards in the way suggested by Professor Mellanby, namely, austere living.

Professor Mellanby's calculations of future food needs are based on the yardstick of 3,000 cals. This yardstick errs on the excessive side. I say so because results of intake and expenditure in subjects engaged in fixed tasks, reported by physiologists all over the world, show that one can live on much smaller intakes *without* adversely affecting one's health or level of work output. If these results are taken into account, it means that the world can feed, not twice but thrice the population even with its present food supply. Indeed, I go further. Available data suggests that the body simply works more efficiently at the lower than at the upper end of the homeostatic range of intakes.

My reason for supporting austere living therefore is that those who eat enough and more will be well advised to cut down on their intakes in their own interest and not in the name of helping the poor. Food requirement of man for health and desired level of work output is in part under biological control and in part under behavioral control. Experimental results, such as those reported by the British physiologists, show that the body can tolerate changes in energy balance of several thousand kcals per day, without gaining or losing body weight or adversely affecting one's level of work output. Evidently, the real controlling variable of health and work output is not intake alone but some homeostatic mechanism which works for the good of the whole body. The fact appears to be that the more one eats above the lower threshold limit, the more one dissipates food as heat, showing that energy is used with variable efficiency, decreasing as intake increases, and vice versa. Clearly as man moves in time under sustained environment, he becomes a different individual, with nature and nurture interacting and providing a source of variation to regulate his intake within the ontogenic framework of growth. When therefore I ask you to turn inwards, I do so on the strength of this finding. Man's requirement for food is not genetically fixed as believed in current nutrition literature; it is dynamic and varies as a matter of course from day to day in a manner that allows man to eliminate disruptive forces and to regulate the variation. In other words man has the genetic capacity to speed up or slow down his metabolism under the impact of sustained environment. This capacity with genetic basis is considerably greater than is believed and allows man to vary his needs over a range which is found to stabilize from seventy-five to one hundred twenty-five percent of the average requirement and yet allows him to maintain health and work output. Energy requirement of man is thus a self-regulated process with a genetic basis, and enables us to look upon the entire problem of food needs from a philosophical angle of self-help. The notion that those with intake below the published norm for intake are poor and hungry has no basis to support it; had it been correct it would have meant that those with intake above the published norm would be overnourished and exposed to risk of obesity. Undernutrition and overnutrition are terms which simply do not have any meaning within the homeostatic threshold range for intake. As the intake decreases below the average norm, the BMR also decreases, but a point is reached below which a body is forced to part with its fat; that is the point of undernutrition; exactly the opposite happens at the upper end. There is therefore no basis to believe that because people in the Third World eat less than what those in the rich countries eat, their productivity of work is low, and that because the productivity of work output is low they become even poorer. This vicious circle has no valid basis within the homeostatic range. The incidence of hunger in the poor countries is much smaller than is believed, but this does not mean that the numbers of poor are small. In a sense almost all the people in the rural areas are poor. However, their poverty arises not so much for lack of food as from lack of drinking water, inadequate hygiene and sanitation, crowded living conditions, and, above all, lack of education. The limiting factor in using food is morbidity from poor environment and not food itself, except perhaps with ten to twenty percent in the lowest decile. The finding can be used to great advantage in preparing self-help programs where people not only can be self reliant, but also altruistic at the same time. Community kitchen programs and village uplift programs built around village school and well, using soil as an effective filter to reduce diarrhea and biogas as an effective tool to improve the efficiency of animal and human excreta, are examples of programs now in operation near Pune. I would urge that the poor countries develop such scientific approaches to solve their food problems.

19.
Total Management of Health Care for the Aged

Kikuo Fujiwara, M.D.

University of Tsukuba Japan
Chiba City, Japan

$\mathcal{R}$ecently, the prolongation of human life has been reported all over the world. Since 1975 the average life of women increased to over seventy-five years in many countries, i.e., Sweden, Japan, the United States of America, and others. This trend is regarded as the result of the following events. At first, the change in chemotherapy has decreased the fatality rates of the various infectious diseases by application of many kinds of antibiotics which were discovered after the Second World War. The second factor is the improvement of nutritional conditions in the countries mentioned above. Especially, the prognosis of the patients suffering from tuberculosis can be improved by appropriate nutrition, and by this means even the provocation of the same disease in carriers may be inhibited. Although cancer is the most outstanding disease among adults, recently, it can be treated successfully with surgical removal of the focus tissues and various new types of radiation therapy. As a result of the improvement in living conditions the incidence rate of apoplexy has been decreased by the use of room heaters in traditional houses for winter seasons. The relationship between temperature and the incidence rate of apoplexy has been confirmed by epidemiological investigations.

In spite of these advances, the aged people in our society at present are not always healthy, physically or mentally. Various kinds of infirmities and diseases are observed among them. Though they can continue their lives, if they have any trouble concerning their health, they have to survive in pain. In such cases, pertinent procedures should be devised to maintain their well-being and their social activities. However, the management of health care must be considered from various points of view. Consequently, unity within the variety of sciences, medicine, psychology, biology, philosophy, theology, and sociology is always necessary to develop a comprehensive health management procedure for well-being in old age.

Preventive Measures for the Aged

In order to prevent many troubles caused by aging, various problems exist. The hereditary nature of adult diseases, for example, the trend toward hypertension, must be controlled beginning in early adulthood. According to the statistical studies concerning identical and fraternal twins, it was discovered that the disposition toward hypertension is hereditary (Table 1), and consequently the tendency toward apoplexy is also hereditary. From this evidence early preventive care for such circulatory diseases is regarded as essential in the cases connected with those hereditary factors mentioned above from the adolescent stage. Periodical health examinations and the control of salt consumption are necessary in daily life. Diabetes mellitus can be caused by hereditary factors as an adult disease as well. In this case the preventive care should be begun at a young age, as for hypertension. The periodical quantitative determination of glucose concentration in the blood and the control of sugar consumption as well as calorie adjustment are essential. These preventive measures can compensate for the disadvantages due to the adult diseases to some extent. Usually, these hereditary diseases produce severe difficulties in the process of aging unless they have been given appropriate preliminary care.

Environmental improvements are important to prepare for well-being in old age. The epidemiological investigations suggest that the control of the temperature in the cold seasons can decrease the incidence rate of apoplexy and heart attacks, including myocardial infarction. Various heating systems and apparatus should be employed in dwellings and other buildings.

218

The microbial contaminations of the environment may provoke many kinds of infectious diseases frequently among the aged. Recently, clinical reports suggest that some species of opportunistic pathogens cause new types of infection especially among the aged. Some strains of *Pseudomonas, Serratia,* and *Klebsiella* have been isolated from aged patients of sepsis or other infectious diseases, although the species had been regarded as non-pathogenic formerly. The frequent applications of antibiotics and steroids have decreased the resistance against the microbial strains in human bodies. Furthermore, the distribution of antibiotics in the environment increases the occurrence of strains resistant to the antibiotic agents among the pathogenic micro-organisms. Besides, these pathogens may increase the lethality rate of some infections among the aged people. Consequently, the effective disinfection of the living environment should be practiced frequently to keep microbiological cleanliness and prevent severe infections.

Usually, the incidence rate of food poisoning among the aged is high, because they have little resistance against the pathogenic agents. Sometimes, even lethal cases of food poisoning have been reported among the aged, while no death in the other age groups of the same outbreak appear. Furthermore, diarrhea and related problems of the digestive organs cause malnutrition and systemic infirmity which often result in death in the aged. Consequently, food sanitation is one of the most important health cares for the aged.

Nutritional conditions strongly affect the health status of aged people. The deficiency of any nutritional element may be introduced easily as the result of insufficient digestive activities, including absorption, whereas an excess of food consumption impairs their digestion. The design of nutritional programs for aged people is very difficult. Control of the total calorie intake should be included to prevent obesity, which may cause circulatory diseases and diabetes mellitus, and the amount of salt consumption must be limited to check hypertension. Finally, the balance among the nutritional elements should be checked especially carefully for the aged.

Aged people must be given particular care concerning the amount of labor they do. Some tasks should be given correlating the individual activities. Even if they hesitate to work they ought to do a minimum, unless they have some physical or mental

Table 1

Coincidence Rate of Essential Hypertension in Twins

Reporter	Identical			Fraternal same sex			Fraternal other sex		
	N	coincident	not coincident	N	coincident	not coincident	N	coincident	not coincident
Watanabe (1942)	1	1	0						
Oka (1952)	1	1	0						
Soh, Yanase (1955)	1	1	0	1	0	1		0	1
Awano, Takahashi (1966)	31	20	11	9	3	6	2	0	2
Miyao (1966)	10	9	1	2	2	0	1	0	1
Mimura (1978)	13	8	5	5	1	4	2	0	2
Total	57	40	17	17	6	11	6	0	6
		(70.2%)			(35.3%)			(0%)	

trouble. If they are left alone with no work for a long period of time, they may lose their remaining capacities for labour, and the activities of the muscles will weaken, resulting in atrophic changes in the tissues. Hence the appropriate work should be encouraged to prevent such degeneration of the organs. Even in intellectual work the conditions are the same. In Japan one woman novelist who is 97 years old is still working very energetically as a famous specialist in many fields. Though she is one of the exceptions, human beings do possess such latent capacities naturally. However, if they stop to think about their work after retirement, their occupational ambitions will be lost gradually. On the other hand, over-working must be avoided to prevent various psychosomatic disturbances caused by hard work, often due to nervousness, i.e., circulatory diseases or apoplexy. Generally speaking, an appropriate amount of work is helpful to maintain good health in the aged.

Starting at childhood the main problems of health in old age should be taught as an essential part of the school education program from primary school up to college. Furthermore, social education ought to include specific topics about problems correlating to the progress of aging. Especially, in the various places of work, i.e., business offices, workshops and other occupational institutions, up-to-date information on aging after retirement must be offered to all members of the staff and employees periodically.

Care for the Aged People

At first, mass examinations must be performed to obtain general information on the health status of aged residents in a fixed area. This should reveal the kind of infirmities and problems due to aging as screening data. Usually, this examination consists of two steps. The primary one contains, 1) the inquiry, 2) the physical examination, 3) the hemodynamometry, 4) the qualitative tests of the urine (protein, glucose and urobilinogen), and 5) the quantitative tests of the hemoglobin content. As the secondary step, detailed examinations can be performed as occasion requires. It consists of quantitative tests of the urine (protein and glucose), the detection tests of parasite eggs and occult blood in the feces, the preparation of the hemogram, the red cell sedimentation test, x-ray examinations of the chest and digestive organs, ophthalmological tests (eye-ground and ophthalmodyna-mometry), glucose tolerance tests, liver function tests, total serum cholesterol determination, and the respiratory function tests.

According to the lists of records obtained by the tests above, individual persons are selected for specific care respectively correlating to the physical situations. They are classified into groups. For the members of the first group, special health care is unnecessary except for usual cautions for leading a healthy life. For the second group, some preventive precautions and concrete individual directions should be given to prevent the progress of illnesses or unexpected deaths. This group generally contains cases of hypertensive nature and of recovery periods from apoplexy. Consequently, they have to be examined periodically, but admission to the hospital is not necessary for them except for specific examinations. Serious cases should be treated in the hospitals and other suitable institutions. However, the staying period in such institutions must be limited to as short as possible, since a long period of hospitalization renders the aged patients debilitated and finally causes the loss of their vitality.

Most of the aged people live in their homes with families or alone at present, because the numbers of the beds in the institutions receiving the aged are not sufficient. However, even if the aged patients can be admitted to suitable institutions, they are not always completely happy, since the human relationship does not satisfy their emotional demands in such places. Modern civilization has changed the nature of human society to a mechanical one with the development of the materialistic culture. True spiritual happiness cannot be found in such environments. Even the usual institutions for aged patients suffer from the same conditions at least partially, since they constitute a part of the present social system which is managed by the prevailing economic principles. The recent abrupt increase in the number of the aged people all over the world has brought various problems in present society; therefore, some counterplans should be devised especially for this situation.

The day care system has two advantages to solve these problems mentioned above. According to this system, the old patients live with their families, usually receiving the periodical care at day hospitals or other institutions, and in the case of emergency they can be transported to the hospital. Besides this, public health nurses and physical therapists visit their homes as specialists. Since the aged with infirmities or diseases can continue their family lives according to this system, they do not feel so much loneliness. Furthermore, the beds not occupied by the aged can accommodate emergency patients as occasion demands.

One of the most important problems in the aging is the solution of emotional troubles. In the process of aging, human beings are considerably weakened and impaired psychiatrically, with the exception of very few. In the final state, various degrees of senile dementia can be observed frequently. Consequently, mental care is essential for the aged. Generally, the emotional status can be kept in good condition when they are living with their own families, even though some troubles may occur at their homes. If their lives are worth living they can maintain good spirits. In order to achieve such a condition, religion is necessary. Their daily life will be appreciated when they are able to control their desires and feel gratitude toward everybody. Statistical results reveal that aged people can be at their best when they are among happy home circles. (Table 2).

Sciences Concerning Aging

Comprehensive and interdisciplinary sciences are necessary to solve the problems related to aging. The cooperation of specialists in the fields of these sciences is also essential to establish

Table 2

The Life Worth Living (Percent)

	Total	Above 60 years old	50 to 59 years old
Total	100.0	100.0	100.0
Keen work	32.4	22.7	36.4
Scientific or cultural study	5.5	2.5	3.3
Hobby or sports	12.9	6.6	5.9
Relaxation	16.0	19.6	17.7
Happy home circles	41.1	33.1	41.8
Social acitvities or services	3.9	4.8	3.9
Others	2.1	5.0	1.8
Unknown	11.1	23.4	13.2

appropriate procedures to care for the aged. The items to be investigated in the various kinds of sciences are as follows:

Medicine: Etiological and preventive studies on aging should be performed as the first step. Furthermore, appropriate procedures for therapy concerning infirmities and various diseases of the aged must be established. Vocational aptitude tests should be given also.

Psychology: The special problems concerning human relationships of the aged at home and at their working places should be investigated to find out the best living conditions for them.

The science of rehabilitation: Improvements in physical and mental troubles of the aged are essential to recover their own capacities. On the basis of results obtained by appropriate rehabilitations they can restore their health.

Sociology: The labour policies for the employment of the aged must be investigated sociologically. Senior citizens should try by themselves to be as independent as possible, even if they are ill or impaired, assisted and supported by the surrounding communities. The promotion of work among the aged must be carried out with social cooperation. The actual application of the wisdom and capacities of the aged people, who are rich in social experiences, must be considered once more within the community. Although care in the institutions is not a social problem concerning aging, the social efforts to arrange such institutions, including such special hospitals for the aged, are naturally essential.

Theology: Since ancient times many religions have taught the living principles, and man has been spiritually supported by such doctrine. The aged especially need to confirm the purpose of their lives, and therefore spiritual guidance must be provided for them from the area of religion.

General Philosophy

Modern industrialization in the world brought about the abrupt increase of the aged population and the nuclear family system. Furthermore, the recent tendency of housing encourages nuclear families. On the other hand the joint family system is necessary to care for the aged at their own homes. However, the joint living of the aged and the young generations in such a residence creates troubles frequently. Nevertheless, if the best living places for the aged people are their own homes, all members of families have to make efforts to establish happy joint families. Actually, even the best institutional care in welfare countries in Europe has been gradually replaced by home care, and the tendency is conspicuous. Many people have a chance to live longer, but this does not necessarily mean the elongation of a happy life. It may only mean the postponement of death in the state of weakness or suffering from some diseases. In order to provide for happy lives the exaltation of the significance of humanity is essential. The social security system has reached its limit at the present time, since the population of the aged has increased abruptly and the economical responsibilities of the community are out of balance.

The effectiveness of the mutual help system has reached its limit also. For the future, the spirit of mutual self-sacrifice is essential instead. The philosophy of mutual help is offering help to other people while still preserving one's own life safe, while the principle of self-sacrifice means to give all and deny the self to support other people. From now, we have to sacrifice ourselves more in order to save our old parents. We have a Sanskrit word *Śūnyatā*, which means the transience of everything, and according to this conception four phenomena, i.e., birth, disease, aging, and death, are essential in all living things. Therefore, we have to face all the difficulties concerning aging with a benevolent heart. When we decide to adopt the spirit of self-sacrifice to work for the aged at our homes, they will be able to continue their lives in the future more happily. We have a famous proverb in Japan, "People can not be refloated unless they throw themselves into the water."

20.

Geriatric Care in Western Countries

Zedena Harant

Toronto General Hospital
Toronto, Ontario, Canada

T he total management of health care for the aged could be approached from two points of view:

> Firstly—what we think should be done for geriatric patients, the best possible approach and organization of health care;
> Secondly—what can be done in present circumstances?—that means limitations compared to ideal expectations.

Professor Fujiwara has summarized his opinion on several topics in practical geriatric care in the eastern part of the world, and on what he thinks should be included in a good and satisfactory management. I would like to complement his comprehensive view with a few more basic, conceptual specific points, which are being ignored or misinterpreted in the present medical approach in Western countries.

The increasing problem with geriatric health care represents a response to the realities dictated by demographic changes. Because of the technological progress of modern medicine and control of major infectious diseases, people are living longer than ever. Increase in both the number of older people throughout the world, and in their proportion relative to the population as a whole, requires broad new cultural trends of adaptation, including changes in work and retirement patterns, and the development in our social, cultural, economic, and political institutions. But perhaps nowhere will the impact be greater than in the health field. This accumulation of old people presents one of our greatest social and health care problems. Unfortunately, our society was unprepared for this "demographic revolution." We did not have the social institutions, the medicare system, the employment policies, and the nursing homes to properly respond to the change. The situation is quite advanced now and will be even worse in a few more years. It will increasingly influence biomedical research and teaching as well as the organization and financing of health care. Elderly people are proportionately the biggest consumers of health care.

Based on current projections the present population of old people, those of sixty-five years and over, for instance in the United States, will have more than doubled by the year 2030. We can expect to have here more than fifty-million people in this age group, at which time they will constitute about seventeen percent of the total population. That would mean that by the year 2030, as many as one out of every five Americans will be sixty-five years or over. This situation will require a much better understanding of the aging process itself.

1. The problem closely associated with the quality of health care in gerontology is understanding of the process of aging and pathologic conditions during aging. In order to deal with deficiencies in geriatric medical care, an entirely different level of physiologic and pathologic thinking must be used. There occurs a set of quantitative and qualitative deteriorative changes of organs, tissues, cellular, and molecular components. The man's biological capacities and adaptation processes estimate the quality of life and the character and the rate of aging. A barrier to progress and understanding of the aging process is in the traditional pattern of the concept and approach in geriatric research and medical care. The tendency to isolate parameters and biologic processes and factors, the isolation of each involved field, purely static observations, simplified causality, and classical statistical methodology are some of the typical characteristics of the present system. As a result much of the information on aging is still superficial and inadequate. Besides, there has not been any evaluation or clarifi-

cation of the special quality of pathology in geriatrics, or of its complexity and dynamics.

2. The second problem involves directly clinical medicine. The characteristic pattern of geriatric clinical medicine is well-known. It is associated with an increasing incidence of diseases of all types and an increasing mortality rate. It involves the occurrence of multiple diseases that are usually chronic, becoming progressively worse over time. The manifestations of diseases are often different from other age groups and different from those described in medical textbooks as typical. The eventual outcome is a final disintegration of the whole biological system.

Medical science, education, and practice are chiefly concerned with acute, isolated, easily reversible conditions. The underlying chronic process, both preceding and following the acute condition, has neither adequate conceptualization nor management. The significance of the duration of pathology is usually overlooked. Unless there is an immediate life-threatening situation, no attention is paid to this progressively damaging development. Many pathologies of minor degrees are not even treated, and when they are, the therapy is most commonly done in a routine, simplistic way. The conservative level of the present medical model, developing strictly from a pathologic-anatomical substrate and dealing only with a single static abnormal state, does not take into consideration any of the functional, physiological, comprehensive, or dynamic qualities that seem so appropriate in understanding and defining geriatric pathology. Different disease processes first manifest themselves at different times; the clinical manifestations usually have been present for years in an elderly patient. Before that, there is another period of time which cannot be recognized by our available means in clinical medicine, in which the clinical symptoms or dysfunctions are not yet apparent. The significance lies in diagnosing and acknowledging the appearance of new regulatory or dysregulatory phenomena in a situation that to all appearances remains normal in the traditional clinical sense.

Findings on the health habits and unattended symptoms of adults in their middle years may be indications of the chronic health deviations that they will develop later in life. A new level of assessment of the aging process and its pathology might bring attention to a different concept for prevention and clinical management in geriatric medicine. The present medical practice, relatively satisfactory in the past, is inadequate for medical problems emerging now as a result of changes in the environment. The changing pattern of diseases, chronic diseases of aging, and the lifestyle diseases, areas in which medical research has traditionally been less interested and medical services less successful, dominate the picture. There is an urgent need for a new medical concept, which concentrates on functions and supersedes the old, strictly pathological-anatomic medical model that is presently obscuring the fundamental causes of ill-health. Prevention of deterioration of chronic problems, or development of acute clinical manifestations (e.g., acute myocardial infarction or heart failure), and of development of the initial pathologic process, recognition, and control of risk factors are of primary importance.

It has been observed that although elderly patients present more problems and take longer to give and receive information, the average length of encounters between physician and patient declines with the patient's age. This trend holds true for both generalists and specialists, regardless of the severity of the patient's primary problem or the complexity of the encounter. Careful assessment in one geriatric evaluation unit uncovered an average of 3.4 treatable problems per patient, in patients who had been discharged from acute care teaching wards. This report is in agreement with our experience. Both of these observations clearly draw attention to critical shortcomings in geriatric medicine, developing from a basically misunderstood medical philosophy.

3. Another important quality, missing in geriatric health care, is the functional approach to the disease process. An evaluation of available homeostatic mechanisms and available reserves should be attempted so that an optimal level of individual functioning could be reached, in close cooperation with the patient. This may be the best way to keep him independent and comfortable in his environment for many years despite his disturbed and diminished functions. The appropriate health care is different in many ways for completely or partially independent patients as compared to dependent patients. We have to consider the independent living in the community as an optimal desirable goal. The functional aspect as the criterion of patient's condition should be more important than lists of diagnoses. The impact of diseases should be measured by specific dysfunctions that compromise efficient participation in daily living.

4. There is an urgent need for a multidisciplinary approach to geriatric medical problems. There is often a complex influence of other negative factors—social, family, work—that contribute to health deviations and interfere with treatment and healing. To perform medicine on the level of specialties and sub-specialties only, especially in geriatrics, contributes considerably to oversimplification of the health problem. Comprehensive geriatric care, with a special attention to factors contributing to deterioration of the health state, should be involved in the clinical program. Hinkle and Wolff carried out ecological studies of the relationship between illness, life experience, and social environment. Over 3,000 cases have yielded evidence suggesting that the reaction of a man to his life situation has influence upon all forms of illness, and plays a role of significance in at least one third of all episodes of disease regardless of their nature, location, cause, or severity. An old person's health may be compromised by a variety of factors. According to many of the experts, care of the elderly is a problem requiring a coordinated system of community and home health services to reach a modern, effective, and full scale geriatric care.

Research in the field of aging must be multi- as well as interdisciplinary in nature. Humans have tremendous genetic, environmental, nutritional, sociologic, and psychologic diversity. All these factors exert a profound effect on the life and its course, pathology, and, in this way, on the aging process. A sophisticated understanding of the interactions among diseases, environment, psycho-social factors, age, and time might be made possible by more productive collaborations between members of various disciplines. We have to look at medical care not in isolation. Our environmental problem has developed to its present dimensions, and the attention paid to biological life and physiological processes is minimal. A further critical difference and risk factor, as compared with other societies in history, is the rapid progress of industrial growth, technological progress, and innovations of enormous dimensions. In our modern society, this technological growth, economic progress, and the present-day philosophy appear to develop without any concern and understanding for the biological system. Regulatory efforts aimed at this development by authorities from the various fields of science, health professionals, sociologists, environmentalists, philosophers, and politicians are lacking. Inevitably, research in the field of aging should emphasize the unity of science rather than the compartmentalization of knowledge.

Geriatrics has entered a stage in which there exists a wealth of descriptive material. The complexity and difficulty of the subject matter is the reason that widely different approaches and methodologies have been proposed. However, the nature of the process of senescence has proved to be elusive and intractable. Even if one grants that semantic problems should not be overemphasized, it has to be admitted that their appearance is a sure indication of profound conceptional difficulties. Modern medicine in the Western world is currently known to be facing a crisis, despite the great advances being made in science and technology. Even the medical profession is becoming increasingly aware of the problem of a growing dissatisfaction with modern medicine and its institutions, and of the fact that the quality of life is not improving. The view that is most widely held by non physicians invariably focuses on the compassionate, humanistic ideology of society as a whole. Our present technological society thrives on the "material wealth" concept, thus allowing the economic balance between producer and consumer to influence all other thought processes. In this way, moral values and issues are strongly affected by this pervading economic outlook. As a result, it is easy to understand why the attention being paid to biologic life and physiologic processes is at a minimum, and why the humanistic approach in all the life disciplines, including medicine, has been so neglected. These humanistic inadequacies in medicine appear much more striking in geriatrics, where there is an exceptional accumulation of negative and destabilizing factors.

Our society too often sees old age as a period of disablement for which little can be done. Certain specific difficulties seem to result from the fact that the health care system tries to solve problems caused by changing disease patterns, while not changing their own structure. In fact, care of the elderly is often disorganized, dependent upon ultra-high cost institutional care, and often insensitive to the most acute needs of growing masses of old people. Medicare reimbursements in the United States and Canada continue to cover only non-preventive expenses—those that are generally hospital-based. This forces into hospitals people who should not be there, and who could be managed better and more humanely in their homes. If the elderly are to be adequately treated, existing health care institutions and programs must undergo some radical and significant changes in organization, scope, and autonomy, with knowledge of the human aging process. Institutionalization is the last resort, and such steps are taken only after all other alternatives have been exhausted. The World Health Organization definition "to keep elderly in good health and happiness in their own houses for as long as this is possible" is an important point. Disease is not eradicated; rather death is postponed by costly supportive therapies. The modern-lifestyle-associated disease pattern further complicates this state of affairs. Health can no longer be considered in terms of medical intervention alone, no matter how important the latter might be. The health care system will be expected to play an important role in preserving the integrity of society confronted with health and disease problems, not only the integrity of the individual.

There are many questions not yet answered: the effectiveness of medical care as related to patients' acceptance, the dependency of sick people on public support, lack of active attitude, and personal responsibility for one's own health. There is a possibility that all these difficulties and the pressing need to understand both the manifestations and the mechanisms of human change over the life course stimulate a search for entirely new qualitative approaches and new biological and medical models.

At the top of the list of important health-research subjects must be the ability to postpone chronic illness, to maintain vigor, and to slow social and psychological involution. We must know whether change is possible, and how to accomplish it best, so that it could lead to a decent, dignified, financially affordable old age.

21.
Learning and Aging

Giselher Guttmann

University of Vienna
Vienna, Austria

One of the oldest, most persistent, and least critical views of psychology has been the assumption that performance in general wanes with increasing age—with learning capability and memory supposed to be considerably reduced.

More recent studies have shown that this viewpoint will have to be revised entirely. Whereas, for instance, a decrement in some dimensions of intelligence has in fact been demonstrated to be age-dependent, others remain completely unchanged or are even marked by substantial improvement. One can observe a decrease in performance of older persons regarding learning functions, when they are tested under the same experimental conditions as are groups of youths. However, it is false to draw conclusions about "learning capability" per se from such data.

An essential which must be included in any such study is the time variable. With advancing age, our "internal clock" runs successively slower. We can easily recognize this by considering functional changes as registered physiologically. Metabolic processes decelerate markedly in old-age, or, as another example, wounds take longer to heal.

Now, if we ask young and old to take on tasks of performance or, in particular, learning under the same time conditions, we are automatically putting the elder group at a disadvantage, and these persons will exhibit poorer performance. If we, by contrast, take the age-dependent slackening of tempo into account and present the same material under adjusted time conditions, the supposed performance discrepancies between the young and the elderly often disappear completely. We therefore propose that modern psychology distance itself from the usual prejudices regarding performance deficits by the aged. We even dare to maintain, albeit with conscious optimism, that every "senior citizen" has far more potential for accomplishments, with the sole reservation that certain functional characteristics be taken into consideration. The disadvantages become quite apparent when we examine the situation of the elderly—that they are forced to come to grips with an environment that is a *world for the young* in most countries. Give thought to the tempo with which our traffic signals change phases, or the speed with which an announcer reads the news over radio or TV. This is all synchronized to the "internal clock" of youth.

In our society, learning has become increasingly independent of the completion of formal schooling. Professional demands in later stages of life necessitate learning anew. Some must adapt to a new situation within their profession; others are faced with learning a completely different profession. For this reason, special techniques and strategies for the facilitation of learning processes take on particular significance, especially those related to committing new information to memory.

On the basis of our brain research we have been able to construct a self-contained model for learning, which is represented below.

Our ability to perform, whether expressed as the assimilation of new information, the perception of critical signals in cognitive and decisional processes, etc., is incessantly subjected to perpetual fluctuations. If a brief, critical event happens to occur during a favorable phase, we master it; however, if it chances into a phase in which performance is at a low, errors and mistakes are the result.

This psychological phenomenon was already known at the turn of the century. Up until recently, however, charting it systematically was thwarted by the fact that it is next to impossible to pinpoint objective indicators for these minimal fluctuations going on in our organism. Of late, we have succeeded in using the cortical spontaneous shifts as reliable and sensitive indicators for the actual level of cortical activation. With the aid of a very unique registration method, we are now able to record the fluctuations of electrical potentials of as little as one millionth of a volt, and then over and above this, to observe whether the baseline of the total process has shifted by a whole volt (Guttmann, G. & Bauer, H.: The Brain Trigger Design—6. Internal Conference on Event-Related Potentials of the Brain, Illinois, 1981). These registration techniques were prerequisite to observations of cortical brain-waves during presentation of quite varied tasks over a longer time-span.

Right at the outset of our studies we were confronted with surprising results. Presenting a simple decisional task at regular intervals over a longer period of time results in a specific pattern of activation: Our brain obviously adjusts to this repetitive de-mand for performance and shows a brief but marked shift to negativity at the onset of each such demand, only to swing back to a brief phase of positivity (equal relaxation) immediately following execution of the task. This simple experiment demonstrates one of the most basic facts of the physiology of performance. No one can maintain a uniform state of high activation over a longer period of time. All the more decisive is the continuous interplay of activation and relaxation, of their waxing and waning. Being able to perform at high levels basically means that one is capable of repose.

An analysis of the misguided reactions led us to the discovery of just how decisive the state of cortical negativity is for successful performance. All false reactions were registered when briefly preceding the demand for performance, this "getting into step" of the brain to a rhythmic increment of negativization was dis-turbed, and the presentation of the task did not coincide with a phase of increased negativity. In the quest for a definitive answer to the question of the role played by these minute potential shifts, we have developed an appropriate experimental design. With the aid of a computer, performance can be demanded exactly at that moment when the human brainwave shifts toward either negativ-ity or positivity. A sufficiently fleet computer system registers the on-going slow potentials continuously,thereby allowing an exact regristration of the spontaneous shifts, i.e., those variations in the direction of positivity or negativity that appear without having been provoked by an external stimulus.

As soon as a shift has reached adequate proportions, the computer signals for transmission of the task under study. As an example, in a learning paradigm the computer presents a study-item via TV-monitor. It is thereby possible to examine how the performance of a person is modified by the state of cortical activity—what happens when the person in question learns strictly during states of negativity increments, and how this performance compares with that recorded during learning in phases of reduced negativity. This Brain Trigger Design, developed and verified at our institute, provided straightforward answers. Although the potential shifts are extremely minute, the modification of performance for which they can be made responsible is considerable. After triggering the learning of syllables at shifts of twenty-millionths of a volt, the difference in learning performance was twenty-five percent, no less. In other words, learning during states of increased cortical negativity proceeds one fourth faster; in any given time-span, if one learns during states of increased negativity, about a fourth more information will be retained!

The next and decisive step toward putting these findings to practical use was making it feasible to will these states of increased negativity. This is surprisingly simple by means of suitable biofeedback training. If we couple the actual negativization to a tone whose pitch signals the degree of negativity (rising pitch equals increase in negativity), it becomes possible to enable a person to regulate his/her level of activation at will, after only a short training period.

Our studies have demonstrated that a testperson is capable of responding to a ready signal with a shift in cortical negativity of a magnitude encompassing the entire range of that otherwise observed under neutral conditions.

The decisive step toward practical uses in everyday life is of course that of replacing these techniques that depend upon laboratory facilities and elaborate electronic equipment with others of a more mundane nature.

In this attempt we availed ourselves of a chance discovery during the observation of persons who were especially quick in profiting from the biofeedback training. These persons had purposively and consciously used muscle tension as a tool for controlling activation. Follow-up studies have verified the usefulness of this strategy. A state of increased physiological activation can be induced by appropriate isometric training in muscle-tensing; in-depth relaxation of the skeletal muscles serves as an effective tool in deactivation. These types of training methods based on muscular relaxation can easily be introduced into quite commonplace situations. In fact, we have had a special program going in Austrian schools for many years, and it has met with remarkable success with pupils at all levels of education (primary, secondary, and adult). Critical phases of learning and information processing can be initiated by this type of program for self-control which leads to a striking improvement in retention.

We purposely commenced testing these methods on children at the school level in the hope of conveying to them methods for learning-to-learn at an early stage. We have presently begun work with older persons, with the goal of working out supportive strategies for learning suitable for this group in particular.

No society can or should afford to exclude the elderly from its performance structure simply as a natural consequence of retirement. If it is possible to prepare for this stage of life by means of appropriate re-learning processes, this post-professional phase can take on new and vital significance for the individual as well as society. Our attempt to develop practically-tested learning techniques based on neurophysiology appears to be immeasurably important to the group of the elderly, especially under such conditions as we are faced with today, which increasingly demand learning and re-learning to be considered life-companions.

We should like to thank Susan Etlinger for advice and help.

22.

Health Care Systems and the Elderly

Roberta Spohn

New York City Department for the Aging
New York, New York, USA

I believe that never in human history have we had the tools of analysis, the organizations to identify future problems, and the ability to solve these problems. Today we can predict a plague of wasps and destroy them in twenty-five countries in Africa, if we choose to do it. We have computers which can print out human and agricultural production rates under various assumptions. For the first time in human history, we cannot escape our mutual interdependence and our need for each other for economic survival. We are so aware of the questions of population growth, it is inconceivable to me that we will permit the gloomy population predictions to come true. I therefore conclude that our human intelligence will give us the tools, the will, and the desire to shape our future.

It is also reassuring that the experts who have written the preceding papers were optimistic. They conclude that we can expand our food production to support a larger world population, and that we can produce both energy and food to support a growing population. The question always is: "Do we have the willingness to solve the problems of distribution?"

I am a public administrator primarily concerned with contemporary issues but acutely aware of future trends. In the field of the elderly in the United States, we must have a seventy-five year perspective, as we hammer out public policy on income support and health care for the aged. If you read our newspapers, you know that the future of the social security system is high on our political agenda.

Even with our eye on the census, I must report that the growth of the elderly, particularly the old-old, in the past decade was unanticipated. In the City of New York, we gained a whole generation of older people in less than ten years. In the industrialized countries, ten years have been added to the upper end of the life span. We have had experience with doubling our population of children, but never before in history have we added a decade of life at the upper end. It is so new, I suspect, that most of us don't even know the appropriate questions to ask. Society does not yet know how to cope with an enormous population growth of eighty year olds. This is a major emerging issue.

A second new pattern is the mobility, even within this country, among the elderly. In New York City we lost tremendous numbers of vigorous, young sixty year olds who moved south. Our elderly are increasingly members of minority groups.

Within our bounds, we have to care about the Chinese elderly, the black elderly, the Hispanic elderly, the Italian elderly. I will tell you even the homosexual elderly come to us to ask for special programs to meet their needs. But it is the frail, poor, old-old who in less than ten years have become our primary concern. For this population, the provision of longterm care, both in the home and institution is essential. This society has reached a consensus on certain values, including the sacredness of human life, when there is catastrophic illness. Anyone, at any age, can go into a hospital and any doctor can order $100,000 of care for that person. Hospital care and treatment is provided equally to the ninety year old, the seventy year old and the forty year old. Nobody talks cost containment when an individual is sick. Keep the person alive. Heroic measures are in order. My mother-in-law, at eighty-nine, recently had a hip replacement. My aunt had two hip replacements at eighty-five. The hospital bill was $35,000 for two hip replacements. For the eighty-nine year old, hopefully it will be only $18,000 to $20,000. Medicare and insurance covered the hospital bill, but once they were discharged there was no program to support home care.

Many factors contribute to our willingness to spend any amount to save lives. The high priests of our society—medical doctors—have such prestige and respect that no one will question their decisions. And society concurs in their decisions, namely, that anyone is entitled to any amount of money and resources to keep people alive, and that includes the elderly—as long as the sick are inside a hospital and under the care of doctors. But when the patient moves back to his home to secure care, he is then confronted with bureaucracies which determine: "Does the person need twelve, fifteen, twenty-two hours of help in the home?" Five levels of bureaucracy will second guess the assessor. If the person is poor enough, and lives in New York City, we can get some help for him in the home. But we haven't agreed that when you are going to add a population that lives into their eighties and nineties, with its inevitable disabilities and frailty, you need more than hospital care. It is a myth to talk about the family providing the care. The children of eighty-five and ninety year olds are in their sixties. Inter-generation support means sixty-five year olds taking care of eighty-five year olds. The sixty-five year old is usually a woman, in all likelihood, taking care of a seventy to seventy-five year old husband who is often sick and frail. Now will it be the forty year old grandchildren who will provide the care? The family has not deserted their old. They do provide the greatest amount of care. However, income support is provided through income transfer payments—social security. My husband and I pay $5,000 to $6,000 a year into the social security system in order to give my mother and his mother their income. That is the inter-generational transfer of income which contributes to family solidarity.

Don't romanticize the way the aged were treated in the past. Those few who did survive without property and money were competing within families for the small available resources. They did not have a good life. For some the county poor house was their last home. As a matter of fact, the aged in the society have been treated better and better. Decreasing inter-family competition for money has permitted generous giving of time and care. Adult children do as much as they can, but I believe that society is responding to some energy concerns by building smaller homes, by decreasing use of fuel so that reestablishing a two-generation household is difficult. Further, we have a society which condones independent living. You cannot live independently for forty years from the time the children set up their own households and then say, "Bring them all together." Older people don't want it, and neither will their adult children. Therefore, you are going to have a very large frail population dependent upon the public sector for their survival. The public sector already insures income. The public sector in a limited fashion guarantees selected medical care. The public sector even distributes food. The question is "How much will the public sector do to provide care in the home for the oldest and frailest."

First, society must reach a consensus that this care must be provided. Then it will devise a political solution.

Society may be willing to talk about population control by eliminating the elderly. So we will have to care for those we keep alive. But I suggest that the presence of so many old people is both comforting and terrifying. Comforting in its promise of a long life, but terrifying in its promise of death. Up until this century, death was in the midst of life. It was not shocking for children to die, for women to die in childbirth. We have reached a point in society where it is an outrage for the young to die. The elderly then frighten us by their physical changes and their testimony to our own mortality. I believe we translate our terror into programs to keep the aged alive. If we keep them alive, we keep ourselves alive. The elderly do have a national support system: Social Security, Supplementary Security Income. It is the only group, save the blind and disabled, that we guarantee a national income standard. The elderly were the first group for which we provided some health insurance. We have created national programs, which have resulted in my agency growing from $1 million in 1973 to $40 million in 1982. That growth is proof that this society, while it has cut other benefits and been punitive to poor people, has not yet been punitive to the aging. I believe that our values concerning aging are such that society—whether there are shortages or abundance—has basically determined that it will support the aged. I believe there are acute problems to be faced with a graying population. "How will our institutions change—both public and private? How will our medical services change? How will we pay for the social support systems—particularly of in-home care—to permit these elderly to live a decent and dignified life in the coming centuries?" We will find the way.

Human Populations: Yesterday, Today and Tomorrow

Claude A. Villee, Jr.

Harvard University Medical School
Boston, Massachusetts, U.S.A.

Conclusion

The concern about human overpopulation, which began with Thomas Malthus in 1798, continued in a low key until the 1960s when, as the effects of overpopulation became more acute, it gradually came to be perceived as a problem by the general public. One of the first to revive concern about human overpopulation was Karl Sax, who published in 1960 a book entitled *Standing Room Only*. In this, Sax assumed that the world could support a population of about ten billion. He then calculated that if humans continued to multiply at their 1960 rates the only solution would be large scale emigration—it would be necessary to move 170 million people per year to some other planet. This would require eighty-five million space ships per year, each costing several billion dollars! Sax's book was followed by books by Ehrlich, Asimov, and others, each painting an apocalyptic picture of the results of human overpopulation. Foundations such as the Ford and Rockefeller Foundations began to support research in the field of population planning and contraception, when they found their economic plans to help Third World countries were countered by excessive rates of population growth. The development of the oral and injectable steroid contraceptives provided population programs and the general public with effective means to limit the number of births if a couple wished to do so. The establishment of the National Institute of Health and Human Development in 1963, and the subsequent development of its Population Division, demonstrated the U.S. government's support of research in human reproduction and in the safety and efficacy of the several types of contraceptive measures. These moves by the National Institute of Health stimulated research in human reproduction and gradually removed the fear of many scientists that, if they applied for a grant to support research on human reproduction, they might be placed on some kind of a black list and subsequently be denied support for research in any other field.

There was a general realization that overpopulation was the number one problem facing the human race, and that other problems such as nuclear war, environmental pollution, and the rapidly escalating cost of energy were all consequences of the overpopulation problem. In the 1970s and early 1980s the attention of the general public, and especially of the media, was directed elsewhere, and concerns about nuclear proliferation, energy shortages, unsettled conditions in the Middle East, and worldwide terrorism pushed the overpopulation problem from the front page to the back of the newspaper, among the classified advertisements for used cars. Indeed, it led some national and international figures to deny that there is a problem with human overpopulation.

Recent coverage by both television and still photographers of the famine in Ethiopia has brought the overpopulation problem back to the front page. Unfortunately, the devastating famine that is striking not only Ethiopia, but the entire band of subSaharan francophone nations, is being treated as a sudden disaster due to drought. In the area just south of the Sahara are the countries of Mauritania, Mali, Chad, Niger, Senegal, and Upper Volta. These countries represent some of the poorest in the world, but they have an average growth rate of two to three percent. Years of persistent drought and crop failure have reduced millions of inhabitants who originally were either pastoralists or horticulturists to the status of refugees. These individuals live in disease ridden camps on the outskirts of the urban areas, where they survive as dependents of either the local governments or international agencies that supply relief. Public health measures have succeeded in reducing the death rate in this region of the world considerably. Even though the infant death rate is still very high, the birth rate remains at very high levels and the rate of growth of the population is exceedingly high. It seems unlikely that a demographic transition, that is, the reduction of the birth rate to the level of the death rate, will come to Africa in the near future. Ninety percent of the population gain a very subsistence level of existence, either as pastoralists tending large grazing herds of sheep, goats and cattle, or as horticulturists trying to raise crops in a land with a marked scarcity of water, even under the best of situations. The pastoralists have a lower birth rate than the horticulturists because, (among other reasons) for their style of living, children are not particularly helpful. Horticulturists have a much higher birth rate because of their perception that children, even young children, can be helpful in agricultural pursuits. During an earlier drought, from 1968 to 1973, large segments of the population had abandoned their traditional grazing or agricultural land and moved to urban areas and centered in refugee camps. When the drought eased in the early 1970s most of these people left the refugee camps and returned to their original lands. Overgrazing by their herds then continued the degradation of the grazing land, and the farming practices of the horticulturists, together with the practice of both groups of chopping down all trees and bushes for fire wood, continued the denuding of the land. As a result of the drought in the early 1970s, Lake Chad became reduced to only one-third of its former size, both the Senegal and Niger Rivers shrank to small streams, and the Sahara Desert moved south onto the land denuded by these agricultural and pastoral practices of the vegetation necessary to hold water. Droughts have appeared cyclically in this region of Africa for a great many years. The difference this time was in the much larger number of people present in the area, a number which has essentially exceeded the carrying capacity of the land.

At present, a decade later, a recurring cycle of drought conditions has once again led to widespread suffering and famine in subSaharan Africa and in Ethiopia. Ethiopia had previously been able to produce enough food for its own population and to export some, but its situation has been made chaotic by a succession of civil wars and by incredibly stupid governmental decisions. In all of this time, however, no serious effort has been taken by the government of any African country to initiate an effective population policy. Television commentators interviewing some of the refugees seen in the Sudanese camps—people fleeing from

Ethiopia—were shocked to find a woman speaking about her family of ten children that had made the long trip with her.

The apparent effectiveness of the rather Draconian measures instituted in the People's Republic of China raises the question whether some similar program could be initiated and be effective in this region of Africa. As we saw in earlier chapters, the government of the People's Republic of China has made it feasible, both economically and socially, for a family to reduce the number of offspring to one. They did this by providing measures of security to retiring workers and by providing communal welfare funds for those unable to work. Such systems alleviate the need for children to support their elders. In addition, women were encouraged to join the work force, and were enabled to do so by convenient nurseries and maternal leaves. Raising the age of marriage for both men and women reduced the number of children a family could raise during their reproductive years. These reforms were accomplished by very effective peer pressure, backed up with financial incentives and disincentives in jobs, housing, and school enrollments.

The countries of the subSaharan Africa are among the poorest in the world and have no national family planning policy. There is a general absence of government funding for what contraceptive measures are available. In many countries, family planning programs are operated by a national health service, and the population trusts the advice given by these health service personnel. In these countries contraceptive measures are integrated with maternal and child care. However, in the subSaharan countries there is very little in the way of a basic health network to which a contraceptive program can be appended. The vast distances in these countries, and the tremendous dispersion of the population, renders very difficult the establishing of anything but mobile units for the dispensing of health care and contraceptive information. The people, living as subsistence horticulturists, are convinced that a child, even one who is only eight years old, can bring in a net food or income benefit to the family unit. They can fetch water, firewood and dung, glean fields, and cut stubble. This perceived necessity of children becomes translated into the customs of a culture. In many societies, full development as a complete person is not achieved until one becomes a parent, representing as it does a commitment by the parents to transmit the cultural heritage of the community to the next generation.

Another factor in the difficulty of establishing contraceptive measures in these countries is the fact that women have very little power in making decisions about reproduction; these are made largely by the man of the family. Thus, many women say they would be happy to use contraceptive measures if given a chance, but they are trapped by the cultural mores of their patrilineal society.

In industrial societies women have the option of altering their role as housekeepers and becoming employed outside the family. This transition results in decreased fertility. However, in these African countries there is very little, if any, opportunity for women to have employment outside the family. There is no urban option for women that they can achieve either by education or labor. To change all this, the governments must embark upon an energetic program of education designed to change these customs, and a program to make readily available the necessary medical and family planning that will reach out to all members of their community. Clearly, to achieve these goals, the African governments must have strong support from the international community and from the developed nations.

As we have seen, the techniques of the Green Revolution increased the potential yield of crop plants in many parts of the world. However, this requires the input of large amounts of energy for fertilizer, for the management of soil and water, for establishing and improving roads, for the utilization of pesticides, insecticides and rodenticides, and for research to increase the yield of crops suitable for African soils, and to assure the health and genetic improvement of herds of animals. Africa is the only major region of the world where per capita food production has actually decreased over the past two decades. This is a consequence of stagnant food production and high growth rates of the human population. Even after the present drought-induced crisis ends, these underlying trends will continue to cause shortages of food. The record is replete with instances of misguided efforts by the developed nations to assist these developing nations in the past. For example, the United States funded the drilling of wells during the 1970s' drought. Some wells were drilled in marginal areas adjacent to the desert, which led to the augmentation of herds of livestock without safeguards against overgrazing. These wells probably contributed to the worsening of the drought by lowering the water table and by leading to the stripping of the large areas of their protective vegetation. The report by the U.S. Office of Technology Assessment in 1985 recommended that there be a shift in agricultural policy in the region towards helping small-scale subsistence level farmers and herders to survive. This is much more difficult, of course, than concentrating on raising the productivity of fewer but larger agricultural units. It requires extensive programs to develop the appropriate technology and then to transfer them to the field. The generally underdeveloped state of national agricultural research and extension services in these nations is proving to be a major barrier to the transfer of new technologies from research centers to farmers.

A reasonable goal for these nations is that of achieving modernization at subsistence levels. This means a reduction in infant mortality, a reduction in fertility, and in improvement of the technologies of farming to a level available to all members of the nation. It must be clearly stated that the goal is to create a sustainable society—a society that operates in a manner that will not cause it to exceed the boundaries of its renewable resources. No longer can production and consumption occur at levels which exceed the limits of environmental capacity. These nations are on the brink of an irreversible environmental crisis.

In these countries of subSaharan Africa and in similar areas worldwide, efforts to curb population growth must begin now. The success of the Chinese model provides an outline of the direction needed and evidence that it can succeed. These programs will probably proceed by trial and error, and mistakes undoubtedly will be made, but the greatest mistake of all would be to do nothing.

Each nation must develop as a unit in balance with its available natural resources. Nations cannot continue to rely on the resources of their more richly endowed neighbors, for these resources are also being exhausted. The achieving of these goals will require that the nations of the world work together on a scale not previously attempted, and it remains to be seen if the disparate nationalistic interests of the various nations can be compromised to achieve this goal.

Contributors

C.O. Akerle is coordinator for the World Health Organization in Dar es Salaam, Tanzania.

Samuel Baum is chief of The Center for International Research of the U.S. Bureau of the Census in Washington, D.C.

Paul Demeny is director of The Center for Policy Studies of The Population Council in New York City.

Stewart E. Fraser is professor of education at LaTrobe University, Bundoora, Victoria, Australia.

Kikuo Fujiwara is professor and director, Institute of Community Medicine, University of Tsukuba, Chiba City, Japan.

Giselher Guttmann is head of the Department of Psychology at the University of Vienna, Vienna, Austria.

Zedena Harant is a professor in the Department of Family Practice at the University of Toronto, Toronto General Hospital, Toronto, Ontario, Canada.

B. Connor Johnson is a distinguished career scientist at the Oklahoma Medical Research Foundation of the University of Oklahoma, Oklahoma City, Oklahoma.

Toshio Kuroda is professor of demography at Nihon University, Tokyo, Japan.

Kenneth Mellanby is Director Emeritus of the Monk's Wood Experimental Station, Huntingdon, United Kingdom.

Edward O. Pratt is professor and head of the Department of Medical Services, University of Sierra Leone.

Richard L. Rubenstein is the Robert O. Lawton Distinguished Professor of Religion at Florida State University, Tallahassee, Florida.

Gervin P. Samarawickrama is professor of community medicine at the University of Sri Lanka, Peradeniya, Sri Lanka.

Roberta Spohn is deputy commissioner for the New York City Department for the Aging.

Gerald Stanhill is with The Volcani Center of The Institute of Soils and Water, Agricultural Research Organization, Ministry of Agriculture, Bet-Dagan, Israel.

George Stolnitz is professor of economics at Indiana University, Bloomington, Indiana.

P.V. Sukhatme is honorary professor of biometry at the Maharashtra Association for the Cultivation of Science, Pune, India.

Claude A. Villee, Jr. is Andelot Professor of Biological Chemistry at the Harvard Medical School Laboratory of Human Reproduction and Reproductive Biology, Boston, Massachusetts.

Sources

The primary sources for this volume are the Proceedings of the Eighth, Tenth and Eleventh International Conferences on the Unity of the Sciences. The three exceptions are the following articles, written by Dr. Claude A. Villee Jr. for this work: "Population Policies: Past, Present and Future;" "China's 'One-Child Family' Program;" and "Human Populations: Yesterday, Today and Tomorrow."

Papers included in *The Responsibility of the Academic Community in the Search for Absolute Values - Vols. I & II*, Proceedings of the Eighth ICUS (Los Angeles, November 22-25), International Cultural Foundation Press, copyright 1980, are: "Ethical Dimension of International Population Trends" by George Stolnitz; "World Population Trends in the Second Half of the Twentieth Century" by Samuel Baum; "Japan as a Typical Miniature of World Population Growth" by Toshio Kuroda; "Ethical Dimensions of World Population Growth" by Richard L. Rubenstein; "Health Services and Development: Population Issues" by C.O. Akerle; "Health Systems and Population Growth" by Gervin Samarawickrama; "Consequences of World Population Growth on Natural Resources and Environment" by Claude A. Villee Jr.; "Consequences of World Population Growth: Labor, Migration and International Trade" by Paul Demeny.

Papers originally published in *The Search for Absolute Values and the Creation of the New World - Vols. I & II*, Proceedings of the Tenth ICUS (Seoul, Korea, November 9-13, 1981), International Cultural Foundation Press, copyright 1982, are: "Biomedical Sciences and Social Patterns in the Twenty-First Century" by Claude A. Villee Jr.; "Populations in Transition" by E.O. Pratt; "World Population: Impact on Family and Community" by Gervin Samarawickrama; "Population Problems in Southeast Asia" by Stewart Fraser.

Papers first appearing in *Absolute Values and the Creation of the New World - Vols. I & II*, Proceedings of the Eleventh ICUS (Philadelphia, November 25-28, 1982), International Cultural Foundation Press, copyright 1983, are: "Feeding the World's Increasing Population" by Kenneth Mellanby; "National Population Control Policies" by Gervin Samarawickrama; "Resources Versus Population" by B. Connor Johnson; "Changing National Population Size" by Stewart E. Fraser.

Index

A

abortion xi, xiv, 44, 119, 169
Africa 4, 11, 20-22, 59-70, 123, 130,
    139, 141, 146, 155, 160, 164, 177,
    241, 247-250
  North 98, 199
  Sub-Saharan 98, 246-248
age doubling 168
aged (elderly) 38, 129, 217-225
  day care for 222
  health care of 227-233, 241-242
  home care for 225
  learning and 235-239
  medicine and 224
  mental health of 223
  population growth of 242
  preventive measures for 218
  psychology for 224
  rehabilitation for 224
  sociology for 224
  theology for 224
  work for 219
aging, human
  dual structure of 235
  learning and 235
  researching and 228
Agricultural University 179
agriculture, Chinese 114, 120
Ahlawalia, M. S. 155
Akerle, C.O. 59
alimenta xiii
America. *See* Latin America; North-
    America; South America
Antarctic 199
apoplexy 217
Arabia 63, 123, 199
Arctic, the 199
Aristotle ix-xi, xv-xvi
Armenians 44

Arusha Declaration (1967) 64, 69
Asia 4, 10-11, 20, 63, 73,146, 160, 164,
    168-172, 171,190, 194-195, 203-
    205, 208
  East 139, 141, 205
  South, 98, 139, 141, 146, 152
  Southeast 98, 190
  West 98
Asian Population Conference 195
Asimov, Isaac 245
Aswan Dam 155
Atlantic, North and Western 89
austerity 214
Augustus xi-xv
Auschwitz 46
Australia 4, 21-22, 146, 167, 169, 199,
    203
Austria 160
Azerbaydzhan 208

B

baby boom (1947-1947) 31
Bangladesh 186
Bantu 63
Barbados 28
Barnett (N.J.) and Morse (C.) 156
Baum, Samuel 9, 14
Bauer, H. 237
Beijing 119, 171
Beijing Declaration, The 194-195
Beijing University 171
biogenetics 132-133
biological catastrophies 88
biological resources 157
biomedical sciences 127-172
birth control xiv, 44, 113
  abortion xi, xiv, 44, 169
  mandatory 111
  propaganda 115
  quota 117

255

See also conception control
birth rate 87, 204
 declines 12
 trends 13-14
births
 illegitimate 73
 trends of 12-13
Bjork, Robert 168
"boat people" 46
brainwaves 237
BRALUP (Bureau of Resource Access-
 ment and Land Use Planning) 67
Brave New World (Huxley) 135
Britain. *See* Great Britain
Bucharest 138, 204
Bulgaria 204

C

Caldwell, John and Pat 144
calorie intake, reduction of 213
Cambodia 44-46
Canada 4
cancer 217
Caribbean 146
"Catholic countries" 123
celibacy xvi
Celts 50
Census, U.S. Bureau of the 10, 13,
 16-19, 22-26
cereal production 179
CFSC (Community and Family Study
 Center) 24
Chad 246
Chama Cha Mapinduz (CCM) 64
Chengdu University (Sichuan) 171
Chen 110
child abuse 86
child population 38
child spacing practices 66-69
child survival 143
childbearing, patriotic 7
Chile 13
China, People's Republic of 10-11,24,
 46, 97-98, 107-123,131, 139, 141,
 146, 168, 170-171, 176, 203, 205-
 207, 248
 agriculture in 114, 120
 Culture Revolution of 109
 daughters in 122

demography of 171-172
 national census of 107
 See also Taiwan
Christianity xiii
class stratification 42
climate modification 92, 181
cloning 133-134
Columbia 13, 15
Colombo, Sri Lanka 194-195
Colombo Declaration 194-195
Community and Family Study Center
 24
conception control 74, 135
 See also birth control
Conference on Human Settlements
 138, 142
Constantine xiii
contraception 119, 135
Cook, E. 156
Costa Rica 13
crop diseases 182
 See also insect pests
Cultural Revolution, Chinese 109
Cunning of History (Rubenstein) 42

D

Danforth, John C. 45
danwei organizations 112
Dar es Salaam 68
daughters, Chinese 122
day care system for the aged 222
DCs. *See* developed countries
DDT 91
death camps, 41, 46
death control 44
Declaration of Alma Ata 164
Demeny, Paul 95
demographics
 Chinese 171-172
 programming 7, 29-30, 130, 160
 quotient of 90
 revolution of 228
 Soviet Union 207
 transition of 29, 139
Denmark 35
developed countries (DCs) 4-8
developed population policy 203
development, progress in 141

developmental approach, Tanzanian 63
distribution of wealth 155
divorce xiv
DNA 133
Downs Syndrome 87
DPRK 204
droughts 247
Durkheim, Emile 47

ecology 94, 128
economic and social indicators 155
economic policy in China 108
Ecuador 89
Edwards (and Steptoe) 133
Egypt 155
Ehrlich, Paul 245
elderly. See aged
energy and food production 179-180
environmental factors 65, 159
    See also pollution
equation cycle of population 204
ESCAP (1980) 191
Escherichia colt 132
Essay on the Principle of Population 186
ethics and population 43
Ethiopia 186-248
ethnic problems in Soviet Union 207
Eugenic Protection Law 31-32
Europe 4, 11, 21, 42, 63, 72, 87, 131, 139, 141, 146, 152, 168, 199, 204, 225
Europe, Eastern 21-22, 96-98, 100
Europe, Western 21-22, 44, 96, 98, 100, 167, 199

family
    indicators 149
    one-child 107-123
    pattern, Koranic 208
    relationships 143
    two-child 152

family planning 75-78
    committee 117-118, 128
    See also birth control
famines 186, 246
farmland, losses of 181
Fearey, Robert A. 25
fertility
    assumptions 145-146
    control 75, 85
    decline 31
    downtrends of 6
    pattern, Central Asian 208
    pattern, Slavic 208
    rates 72, 85, 203
    replacement level of 142
    transition 30-33
fertilization, extrauterine 133
"final solution" 46
"fire-horse" years (1965-1967) 31
First World War. See World War I
fish farming 183
Florida State University (U.S.A.) 41
food
    distribution of 210
    maldistribution of 178
    new types 183
    poisoning 219
    production 176-250
    shortage 88, 14, 175-250
    supply and human population 210
    supply increases and population 186
    synthetic 183-184
    waste 178
food-supply crisis 175-250
Fird Foundation 245
Formosa. See Taiwan
Four Modernizations, The (in China) 116
France 34, 38
Fraser, Barbara J. 168
Fraser, Stewart E. 167, 203
Freedman, Ronald 25
Fujiwara, Kikuo 217, 227
Futan University (Shangai) 171

Gao Lihau 122
genocide 44, 47
geriatric care 227-233

See also aged
Germany 38, 42-43, 160, 204
Ghana 13
Glycogen 133
GNP. *See* Gross National Product
government
   control of 200-201
   role of 192-194
Grand Canyon 88
Great Britain 38, 160, 178, 181, 209-210
Great Leap Forward 108
Great Rebellion, The 89
Green, Marshall 25
"Green Revolution" 89, 249
greenhouse effect 182
Greenland 93
Gross National Product 71, 138, 153-154, 198, 205
Guangdong Province 119, 121
Guatemala 13
Gulangyu Island 118
Guo Zhenzhen 118
Guttman, Giselher 235, 237

H

Haiti 186
Hamid, Abdul 44
Han Chinese 113
Hanoi 170
Harant, Zedena 227
Harvard University 85, 107, 127, 245
Hauser, Phillip M. 25
health care delivery 132
health care of the aged 227-233, 241
health education 78-80
health systems 55-81
Hebei 119
Hee University (Seoul) 168
high fertility countries 28
Hitler, Adolf xv
Hobbes, Thomas xv
home care for the aged 225
homeostatic mechanism 214-215
Honduras 13, 186
Hong Kong 28, 121, 205
horticulturists 247
human ecology 94
Hungary 35

hunger, mass 175-177
Huxley, Aldous 135
hypertension 220

I

illegitimate births 73
India 13, 21, 28, 203
Indiana University (Bloomington, Indiana) 3
Indo China 169
Indonesia 13, 21, 28, 45, 203
infant death 66, 246
infanticide xi, xiv, 111, 113, 122-123
insect pests 92, 182
integrated program 187-192
International Conference on Population 194, 204
International Planned Parenthood Federation (IPPF), 68, 190
international *triage* 44

J

Jamaica 13
Japan 4, 21-22, 27-39, 96-98, 100, 131, 139, 141, 146, 171, 205, 217, 225
Japanese Organization for International Cooperation in Family Planning (JOICFP) 190
Jews 50
   of Europe 43-43, 46
   of Southern Asia 46
Johnson, Connor B. 197
Judeo-Christian tradition 41, 44

K

Kaibab
   deer 88
   Plateau 87
Kampuchea 169-170, 204-206
Kazakhstan 208
Kennedy, Edward 45
Khmer people 45-46

Kiangsi Province 121
Kilimanjaro 63
Kim, Sun Ho 168
Kirgiziya 208
Kiswahili 64
Korea, Republic of 13, 15, 168-169, 204-205
Kuala Lumpur Declaration 195
Kuroda Toshio 27
Kurtzman, Joel 49
Kwangtung Province 113

L

Lake Chad 247
Laos 169-170, 204-206
"later, longer, fewer" campaign 109
Latin America 4, 11, 20-22, 96-98, 141, 146, 155, 160
LDCs. See less developed countries
learning and aged 235-239
Lenin, Vladimir 46
less developed countries (LDCs) 4-8, 168
lex Iulia xi
Leyser xv
life expectancy xiv, 5-6, 205-207, 217
Lima 50
Los Angeles 91
Luxembourg 160

M

Mainichi Shimbun 31-32
Malaysia 28, 204
Mali 246
Malthus, Thomas R. 186, 209, 245
manpower shortages 73
Mao Tse-Tung 108-109
marine harvest 89
marriage
    age at 71-72, 111
    early 66
mass starvation, predictions of 175
Maternal and Child Health 59, 68, 75
maternal mortality
Mauldin, Parker 12, 25

Mauritania 246
MCH. See Maternal and Child Health
Medical sciences 128-129
medicine and the aged 224, 229
Mellanby, Kenneth 175, 198, 203-204, 207, 209-211, 213
mental health of the aged 223
Mexico 13
Mexico City 91, 204
Middle East 130, 246
migration assumptions 146
minority group problems 113
miscarriage xi
Missouri 45
Moby Dick (Melville) 43
Montesquieu xv-xvi
"Moslem countries" 123
morality
    poverty and 6
    public and private 43
mortality
    declines 5-6, 205-207, 217
    infant 66, 246
    maternal 66
    rates 72, 85
    reduction 33-35
Muhimbili Medical Center 69
Murdock, George Peter 49
Muslim minorities (Soviet Union)
Mussolini, Benito xv

N

National Academy of Sciences 91
National Institute of Health and Human Development 246
national identity 7
natural resources, waste 90
Negative Population Growth 198
Nehru, Shri Jawaharial 195
Nepal 13
Netherlands 34
New Delhi 195
New York City 14, 242-243
    Department for Aging 241
New York Times 122
New Zealand 4, 21-22, 146, 203
Niger River 246-247
Nihon University 37, 131
North Sea 89

Norway 34
North America 4, 21-22, 89, 96-98, 100, 139, 141, 146, 199
North-South (U.S.A.) differentials 96
Nyerere, Mwalimu Julius 67

O

Oceania 4, 11, 20-22, 96-98, 100, 146
Odum, E. P. 93
Ohio 89
one-child program 107-123
OPEC 158, 102
overpopulation xvi, 245-250

P

Pacific, Northern and Western 89
Pakistan 13, 154-155, 168
Pan Islamic forces 208
Panama 13
Papius xii
Pan Turkism 208
pastoralists 247
Parker, Mauldin 25
Peking 117, 122
  Woolen Mill 117
Pemba 63-64
People's University (Beijing) 171
Peru 50, 89
petroleum 158
Phenylketonuria 133
Philippines 15
Planned Parenthood. See International Planned Parenthood Federation
"Planning for Growing Populations" 148-149
Plato ix-x, xv, xvi
Pliny xii
Polanyi, Karl 47
pollution 90-91, 156
polygamy xv-xvi
Poppaeus xii

population, world 71, 185, 245-250
  child, change of 38
  consequences 99-104
  control ix, 55-81
  cycle 204
  density 93
  differential, control (Soviet Union) 208
  disincentives 102-123
  estimates 147, 160
  explosion 27-39, 62
  forecasts 176
  future of 175-250
  growth 9-26, 71-72, 85-104, 108, 138, 142, 169, 185
  pattern 96-99, 140, 146, 204
  peak 152
  planning 148-149
  program areas 55-56
  projection of 20-26, 36-39
  replenish policy 170
  society and 111, 151-165
  surplus 41
  trends 3-26, 139-149, 176
  violence and 49
Population Council (New York) 95
poverty xvi, 143, 161-164
  mortality and 6
Pratt, Edward 55, 137, 167
pregnancies
  illegal 111
  number of 74
  teenage 86, 127, 135
  unwanted 86-87
prematurely born babies 86
preventive medicine 218
projection of population 20-26, 36-39
prolongation of life 217
pronatalist policy xi, xv
pronatalist views 204
pronatalist policies xi, xv
psychology for the aged 224
Puerto Rico 28
Pune 215

Q

q (demographic quotient) 90

R

rationality 43
rehabilitation for the aged 224
religion 123
Renmin Ribao (People's Daily) 116, 120
reproduction rates 34
research in gerontology 231
resource prices 156
Ridker (R.C.) and Cecelski (E.W.) 155, 157, 161
"right of three children" xii
RNA (nucleic acid) 132-133
Rockefeller Foundation 245
Roman census xiii
Rome, ancient xiii-xiv
Rubenstein, Richard L. 41, 50-51
Ruhuna University (Galle, Sri Lanka) 151, 185
Rumania 204
Russia. *See* Soviet Union

S

Sahara, the 246-248
Salas, Raphael M. 167
Samarawickrama, Gervin 71, 151, 185, 203, 206-207
Samerng Project 187, 189, 206
Sax, Karl 245
Sea Conference 158
Second World War. *See* World War II
Senegal River 246-247
Seoul 169
seraglio xvi
Shanghai 119
Shanxi Province (China) 116
Siberia 208
Sichuan Province (China) 115, 119, 121
Siegel, E. 74
Singapore 28, 93, 102, 131, 168, 205
Slavic population 207-208
Slavic Republic 208

small pox, eradication of 62
social indicators 148-149
social patterns 127-172
Socialist Education Movement 108
socio-economic indicators 154
sociology for the aged 224
soil cultivation 89
Somalia 186
South Africa 15
South America 21, 50, 89, 123
Soviet Union xv, 11, 21-22, 45, 96-98, 100, 146, 200, 204, 207-208, 210
Soviet Union demographic 207
Spohn, Roberta 241
Sri Lanka 13, 15, 28, 151, 194-195
Sri Lanka University 71
Stalin, Josef xv
Stanhill, Gerald 209
starvation, mass 175-177
Steptoe and Edwards 133
Stolnitz, J. George 3
Sudan 247
Suetonius xii
sunyata 225
surplus population 41
Sweden 33-34, 217
synergistic effects 186

T

Tadzhikstan 208
Taiwan 13, 15, 28, 93, 102
Tanganyika African Nation 67
TANU (Tanganyika African National Union) 67
Tanzania 59-70
technology and population 50-51, 127-172
ten-cell leadership systems 64
TFR. *See* Total Fertility Rate
Thaland 13, 15, 28, 45, 186, 206
theology for the aged 224
Third Asian Pacific Population Conference 195
Third World 7, 59, 61, 69, 152, 175, 215, 245
Tokyo 27, 91, 195
Total Fertility Rate 168, 170
Trajan xii-xiv

Tsukuba University (Japan) 217
Turkey 15
Turkic Muslims 208
Turkmenistan 208
Twentieth Century 21-22
two-child family 152

U

Ujamaa 64
UMATI 86
United National Fund for Population
    Activities 167
United Nations Institute for Training
    and Research 49
underdeveloped countries 198-200
underpopulation xvi
UNESCO 155, 165
United Kingdom. See Great Britain
United Nations 9-10, 14, 24-27, 35,
    137-138, 144, 151, 158, 160, 162-
    163, 194, 196, 204, 228, 242
United States of America 4, 34, 42,
    86-94, 96-104, 114, 127, 131, 152-
    155, 160, 169, 178, 198-199, 198-
    199, 205, 217, 228, 241, 249
United States Bureau of the Census 9,
    17, 22
United States Judiciary Committee 45
United States Senate 45
University of Chicago 10, 18, 24
unmarried mothers 74
Upper Volta 246
urban trends 7
USSR. See Soviet Union
uterus, artificial 135
Uzbekistan 208

V

Vancouver 138
Vanderbilt University (U.S.A.) 168
vasectomies 119
venereal disease 73

Victoria State College (Coburg, Victo-
    ria) 168
Vienna University (Austria) 235
Vientiane 169
Vietnam 45-46, 168, 170, 203, 205-206
Vilagization (Ujamaa) 64-65
Villee, Claude xi, 85, 107, 127, 167,
    171
violence and population 49
Volcani Center (Israel) 208

W

Wageningen, Agricultural University
    (Netherlands) 179
Waikiki Beach 199
"wan, hsi, shao" campaign 106-108,
    115
Washington, D.C. 18-19, 22, 26
Weber, Max 47
World Bank 10, 18, 24, 55, 164-165,
    196
World Health Organization (WHO) 59,
    61, 69, 196
world population. See population
World Population Conference 138
World Population Project 27
world resource problems 153
World War I 31, 44
World War II 3, 7, 14, 29, 31, 35, 41,
    129, 131, 209, 217
Wren, Christopher 122
Wuxi 117

X

Xihung 117

Y

youth, world preoccupation with 236

Z

Zero Population Growth Society 198
ZPG. *See* Zero Population Growth

Zanzibar island 63-64
Zachariah, K.C. 18
Zero Population Growth 175, 209